ABOUT THE AUTHOR

Roger Maynard has worked as a journalist for more than 40 years in Britain and Australia.

After nearly 20 years with the BBC, in 1987 he moved to Sydney, where he worked as Australian correspondent for a number of British media outlets, including the London *Daily Express* and Independent Television News.

Since 1993 he has been Sydney correspondent for the London *Times* and CNBC, the global business and finance television channel.

His previous books include *Milat*, based on the serial killer who murdered seven young travellers in New South Wales.

He is married with three children and two grandchildren and lives on Sydney's Northern Beaches.

WHERE'S PETER?

Unravelling the Falconio Mystery

Roger Maynard

HarperCollinsPublishers

HarperCollins*Publishers*

First published in Australia in 2005
by HarperCollins*Publishers* Australia Pty Limited
ACN 36 009 913 517

HarperCollins*Publishers*
25 Ryde Road, Pymble, Sydney NSW 2073, Australia
31 View Road, Glenfield, Auckland 10, New Zealand
77–85 Fulham Palace Road, London W6 8JB, United Kingdom
2 Bloor Street East, 20th floor, Toronto, Ontario M4W 1A8, Canada
10 East 53rd Street, New York NY 10032, USA

National Library of Australia Cataloguing-in-Publication data:

Maynard, Roger
   Where's Peter? : unravelling the Falconio mystery.
   ISBN 0 7322 8167 9
   ISBN 9 7807 3228 1670
   1. Falconio, Peter. 2. Lees, Joanne. 3. Murdoch, Bradley.
   4. Murder – Investigation – Northern Territory. 5. Trials (Murder) –
   Northern Territory – Darwin. I. Title.
364.1523

Cover design by Stuart Horton-Stephens, Geeza,
and Katy Wright, HarperCollins Design Studio
Images courtesy of Newspix (Peter Falconio & Joanne Lees; Peter's graduation;
photofit picture of gunman) and Getty Images (landscape)
Typeset in 11/14 point New Baskerville by Helen Beard, ECJ Australia Pty Limited
Printed in Australia by Griffin Press on 79gsm Bulky Paperback

9 8 7 6 5 4 3 2 1   05 06 07 08 09

'Hear all
See all
Say nowt'
OLD YORKSHIRE SAYING

INTRODUCTION

If this book reads like a work of fiction it is because the storyline, the sub-plots, the characters, the red herrings and the backdrop to the drama could have come straight from the pages of a carefully crafted thriller.

This is not to sensationalise what happened on that lonely desert road in the middle of the Australian outback on 14 July 2001, but because so much of what preceded the crime and followed it appears to have more in common with a novelist's fertile imagination than the cold-blooded reality of murder.

First there was the horror of the killing and the desolate location in which it was carried out. Then the frightening ordeal of the victim's girlfriend as she hid in scrubland for several hours in the dead of night, while the attacker searched the bush for her in vain.

It was the worst of nightmares, the essence of every woman's latent fear. Everybody could relate to the sheer terror she must have endured, not knowing whether she would be raped, tortured, strangled or shot if her assailant found her.

There was the immense relief of her eventual escape, the outback heroes who came to her aid and supported her as she fought to cope with the initial trauma.

And there was the hunt for the killer, whose actions sparked one of the biggest manhunts in modern Australian history.

But there were also the questions. Where was the body of Peter Falconio? How did Joanne Lees manage to evade her boyfriend's murderer who was equipped with a torch as he came within a few feet of her? And why was the lone survivor of this most heinous of crimes so seemingly reluctant to talk about the attack?

Even the media, who at first reflected the massive public sympathy for the young British backpacker and actively supported her in the immediate aftermath to the murder, began to wonder about perceived inconsistencies in her story.

How did she bring her handcuffed wrists from behind her back to the front? How did she manoeuvre her bound body from the cab of the killer's truck to the rear tray, when few, if any, vehicles offered such behind-the-seat access?

Why did she show such little outward sign of physical injury when her attacker had behaved so roughly with her as he threw her to the ground, tied her up and punched her about the head?

And how did the victim leave only a comparatively small pool of blood at the roadside and no sign of spatter when he had been shot at almost point-blank range with a revolver?

While some of these questions were eventually answered, doubts remained over the veracity of other key elements of the case. What was the motive? Were Peter and Joanne on the brink of splitting up after her self-confessed affair with another British backpacker in Sydney? Could drugs have been involved? Had they met the alleged killer earlier in their journey? Had the murderer brushed alongside Joanne at the crowded Alice Springs Camel Cup races on the same day? Could this explain the tiny speck of DNA subsequently found on Joanne's T-shirt? And even more improbably, was Peter Falconio still alive?

While police had dismissed allegations of his involvement in a life insurance scam, how was it that two highly credible witnesses had reported seeing him in the company of two other people a week after his disappearance?

Doubts, inconsistencies and outlandish theories have dominated this case over the past four years and led to much wild speculation about the truth behind Peter Falconio's death.

In the following pages I have pieced together the evidence, the statements and the courtroom cross-examinations of the key players in this most extraordinary of cases in an effort to establish a clear picture of what really happened. I have returned to some of the witnesses to discuss their evidence and sought out those who played mere walk-on roles in the drama, as well as those who had no part in the legal process but were able to shed light on the possible circumstances surrounding the crime.

My objective has been to separate the fact from the fiction, to place a dividing line between the reality and the many lurid and fanciful tales that grew up around the events that culminated in the terrifying attack on two young British travellers on the Stuart Highway north of Alice Springs.

How did they find themselves caught up in this tragedy? What sort of people were they? And why did the young woman who survived such a frightening experience, which attracted the sympathy and understanding of all those who read about her ordeal, behave so oddly in the weeks, months and years that followed?

And what of Bradley John Murdoch, who was accused of the crime? How could a man who had the manners of a perfect gentleman, according to one of the women who knew him, have also acted as a ruthless killer? Or was he himself set up by those who had their own good reasons to remove him from the scene?

The murder of Peter Falconio is a complex web of violence, deceit, love and greed, all of which were fuelled by factors that until now had to remain undisclosed for legal reasons.

And behind the truth there are the tears and the sorrow for a young man whose untimely death destroyed a loving relationship and devastated two families.

This is their story, a factual account of what was to have been the dream journey of a lifetime but which turned into a nightmare.

CHAPTER 1

....

THE TRAP

Even by Australian standards it is a very long road. The Stuart Highway from Port Augusta in South Australia to Darwin in the Northern Territory stretches nearly 3000 kilometres.

In imperial measures it converts to almost 1900 miles or longer than the journey from Land's End, at the far southwestern tip of England, to John o'Groats on the extreme north coast of Scotland and back again.

A flat, straight, two-lane highway that cuts through some of Australia's most inhospitable terrain, it is also a lonely thoroughfare where tourists rarely drive at night for fear of mechanical failure or hitting a kangaroo. (Even most of the rental car companies forbid driving between the hours of dusk and dawn.)

There are few emergency road services in these parts, no friendly mechanic to repair an engine problem or provide a can of petrol, and only the very occasional public telephone from which to summon help. And forget about the mobile. Outside of a few small towns there is no digital-phone reception for most of an area more than 20 times the size of Britain.

Peter Falconio and Joanne Lees were by now familiar with the long distances of Australian travel and were well aware of the demands that their odyssey had placed on their 30-year-old campervan, which was showing signs of fatigue.

It had taken about three weeks to make their way from Sydney to Australia's red centre. On the way they had passed through Canberra, the Snowy Mountains and on to South Australia, turning north to Port Pirie, Port Augusta and Coober Pedy, and detouring to Yulara to visit Uluru, formerly known as Ayers Rock, before finally arriving in Alice Springs on 10 July. They had considered travelling as far as Darwin and possibly Broome and then returning to Tennant Creek to take the Barkly Highway to Queensland via Mount Isa.

Quite why the two young Britons set off from Alice Springs at about 4 p.m. on Saturday, 14 July 2001 is one of many questions that remain unanswered. Why did they want to get away that afternoon? Had they intended to share the driving and motor through the night so they could take advantage of the quiet road and cooler temperatures?

Or were they simply planning to find a peaceful and secluded spot in which to camp along the way? They had a small bed behind the front seat of their VW Kombi so they could sleep in the back if necessary and avoid the inconvenience of pitching a tent.

But why leave so late if they were planning to look for a place to stay the night? Or was there another, more pressing reason that prompted their late-afternoon departure?

Had Peter spotted someone he was anxious to avoid?

Or did he have a secret rendezvous planned elsewhere, a discreet meeting with a person or persons unknown?

Questions, questions, questions. They would eat away at people for years, as those close to the case, and many more who were merely curious, attempted to seek an explanation for what happened on that fateful day.

Whatever the reason, Peter and Joanne were determined to head for the open road. They had enough petrol to get them to Ti Tree, a couple of hundred kilometres further north, so climbed into the orange-painted Kombi with its distinguishing white stripe around the middle and slammed the vehicle into gear.

There are few more exhilarating moods than the sense of freedom and adventure engendered by the beginning of a long journey, and as Peter and Joanne drove off they may have felt that this next stage of their travels would be an opportunity to put past differences behind them.

Joanne knew she had risked endangering her relationship with Peter by having a fling with another backpacker in Sydney before they embarked on their travels. And Peter, who may have had his suspicions, might have sensed the added tension between them.

They had agreed to part company for a week when they reached Queensland so he could make a trip to Papua New Guinea and she could return to Sydney. It would provide a breathing space in their relationship after being in each other's pockets for several weeks. At least that is how it would appear. Or maybe Peter had other plans, which Joanne, who had her own close circle of friends back in Sydney, did not wish to know about?

Right now they were alone. It was an opportunity to share the thrill of the next stage of their Australian jaunt and relish the uncertainty that lay ahead. On that bright outback afternoon they were two young travellers against the world, pitting their wits against an environment which could sometimes be as hostile as it was welcoming.

For now though it was familiar territory. They had grown accustomed to the architectural similarity of the many country towns that dotted the Australian landscape. The banks, the post offices and the shop facades often looked the same though they were still subtly different from the urban environment of their English homeland.

Peter was hot and tired. Dressed in light-coloured cargo pants and a blue, button-up, short-sleeved shirt, he decided to lie down in the back as Joanne took the wheel and drove out of Alice Springs.

They had been to the annual Camel Cup races at Blatherskite Park near Heavitree Gap, an area of open land just across the Ghan railway line. It is not a serious competition but an afternoon of fun in which jockeys cling to their charges for dear life while the camels often seem to gallop in several directions at the same time.

Peter and Joanne had seen enough of Alice and the surrounding area, coincidentally the scene of another infamous Australian criminal case, the prosecution of Lindy Chamberlain, who was wrongly accused of murdering her baby daughter Azaria at Ayers Rock. It would be one of many parallels to evolve as the Falconio case proceeded and unlikely connections emerged.

Before leaving town they had a shower at a caravan park and Joanne went to the library to send some emails. They also called in to the Red Rooster for a bite to eat.

They were on the outskirts of Alice now, back on the Stuart Highway and a few ramshackle wooden homes with their corrugated iron roofs were the only sign of human habitation. Ahead a sign warned of an unfenced road and wandering cattle. Another reminded travellers of the road trains which thundered back and forth between Australia's top end and the south. These three- or four-truck leviathans used to play a crucial role in transporting food and other essential goods from the temperate south to the tropical north of this vast country, but the extension of the railway line from Alice Springs to Darwin in 2004 took away much of their business.

As Peter and Joanne left the suburbs behind and approached the dried-up bed of the Charles River, a panorama of arid, rocky plains and scrubland appeared. The empty road whose tarmac sizzled in the afternoon heat shimmered like a mirage as it vanished into the distance. The speed limit changed to 100 kph and as they passed over Colyer Creek the young Britons would have become vaguely aware of the tiny communities they would pass through on their way north.

A sign told them that Ti Tree, where they planned to refuel, was 180k's away. They could have continued to Barrow Creek, about 90k's further on, where there was a pump in front of the pub, but Peter had already decided on the timing of his early evening recreational puff, which was scheduled for sunset.

He and Joanne could roll a joint from their ample supply of cannabis and in their shared euphoria could listen to music and watch the sky turn crimson.

On they drove, past four-wheel drives returning from their winter sojourn in the north, while a sign identifying the Tropic of Capricorn added an astrological dimension to their travels. (You don't get this on the M6 to Yorkshire.) Wedgetail eagles swooped low over the highway to inspect the roadkill, a feast of kangaroo and goanna mown down by passing traffic. And as if to remind the British travellers that they were guests in a foreign land, groups of Aborigines would occasionally appear along the roadside.

Such everyday scenes epitomised outback Australia, where indigenous people and their Dreamtime folklore seemed a world apart from the Britain the couple had left behind.

And suddenly after mile upon mile of uniform terrain, through Aranjero country and the little hamlet of Aileron, past distant mountain ridges and gently undulating bush, where only the hardiest of vegetation could survive, they came to Ti Tree, proud of its one and only claim to fame — the most central pub in Australia.

It is a community of not much more than a couple of hundred souls with a health centre, police station and a few dozen homes, as well as several shops and an Aboriginal art gallery. There is a camping site next to the roadhouse and a bar where cold beer flows. Next door a playground is set aside for passing families and local children.

Many who live in these parts are indigenous people whose standard of living would shock most western societies. Peter and Joanne did not have the time or the inclination to take it all in. They had their own plans for the early evening that probably did not include a debate on Australia's racial injustices.

Parked on the left-hand side of the road opposite the Ti Tree service station, they drew long and deep on their shared joint and marvelled at the spectacle of the immense outback sky and its changing colours. It was a rare moment of tranquillity before refuelling and continuing the arduous drive north.

Little did they know that they were already close to the end of their journey together; that something so catastrophic would happen in the next hour that would end one life and change another for ever.

Peter grabbed the petrol nozzle and slid it into the Kombi's tank. Then he screwed on the cap and together with Joanne sauntered into the roadhouse, an old-fashioned Australian facility combining cafe, restaurant, shop and garage. They bought some snacks and paid for the petrol with cash. The bill came to $14.

Robert Lake remembers serving them that evening and says they seemed quite happy. He also recalls Peter asking for a receipt on which he could record his odometer display. Peter was meticulous about keeping track of the distance he had travelled. It read 89,272 kilometres. From here to Barrow Creek was another 90 kilometres, followed by a further 11 kilometres to the lonely stretch of the Stuart Highway that would soon become the centre of one of the biggest manhunts in Australian history.

Yet when the empty Kombi van was found the next day there were an additional six kilometres on the odometer, which could not be explained by the official distance between Ti Tree and where the vehicle was abandoned. Where had it been driven in the meantime? And who had been at the wheel? Had there been an off-road detour along the way or a short drive north or south before the VW was finally dumped?

These were important questions which would puzzle detectives for months and years to come.

But first they had to find a killer.

CHAPTER 2

....

THE ATTACK

It was several kilometres out of Ti Tree that Joanne noticed something odd. Small grassfires had broken out beside the road and her boyfriend, who was now at the wheel, had wanted to stop to extinguish the flames.

For some reason Joanne cautioned against it.

'They looked as though they could have been started deliberately. Pete wanted to stop to put the fires out. I said it could be a trap or a trick and asked him to drive on,' she told the pre-trial hearing.

It was a strange conclusion in the circumstances, given that they were miles from anywhere and there was no sign of another person or vehicle nearby. Or was she more alert to the possibility of danger or attack because of a previous encounter or veiled threat?

Peter took her advice and continued driving but the relaxed atmosphere had been shattered. She was clearly worried about something, fearful of an as yet unspoken risk. Was it a premonition, a foreboding of something far more sinister? Or perhaps just a snap decision based on human instinct, a better-safe-than-sorry attitude which was easily understandable on an isolated road.

Night falls quickly in the outback. The further north you drive, the closer to the tropics and the shorter the dusk. By now it was pitch black outside and no moon to help make out the landscape. The young couple in their Kombi did not even notice Barrow Creek as they drove through the roadside hamlet with its hotel and historic telegraph station, a reminder of a distant past when the only communication between Australia and the rest of the world was transmitted up the Stuart Highway and across the Arafura Sea by underwater cable to Java and beyond.

It was between 7.30 and 8 p.m. when Peter became conscious of another vehicle closing in behind him. It was going faster than the Kombi and appeared to want to overtake. But as the vehicle drew out on to the right-hand side of the road as if to pass, the driver throttled back alongside the VW.

Peter wanted him to accelerate, but the man at the wheel remained parallel with the campervan and started gesticulating towards the back of the Kombi. He could clearly see the driver, who was illuminated by an interior light in the cab.

Joanne also got a detailed view of the man at the wheel, as well as his dog which was sitting obediently beside him in the passenger seat.

'The man was looking across into our vehicle. The dog was sitting straight ahead sitting up,' she said.

Given the low light it was surprising how much she saw.

'He was wearing a blue baseball cap and a dark T-shirt with a check shirt over the top with long sleeves.'

13

What did he want? He was pointing and mouthing something. He was telling them to pull over, to stop. It looked as if he was saying there was something wrong with their van.

Once again she felt uneasy about stopping.

'I asked Peter not to,' she recalled.

But her boyfriend took his foot off the accelerator and braked. The other vehicle, which appeared to be a four-wheel-drive truck, drew up behind him and Peter got out, leaving the door slightly ajar.

The engine still running, he sauntered to the back of the Kombi to investigate. Joanne moved across to the driver's seat, looked over her shoulder and out of the window and saw Peter in conversation with the other driver at the rear.

'I heard the man say there were sparks coming out of the back and Pete asked if it had been happening all the time. Pete said, "Cheers mate," and then came back to the driver's side and asked me to rev the engine.'

Their vehicle had occasionally backfired before, so it did not surprise her that the exhaust was playing up.

Peter seemed relaxed enough and reached inside to get his cigarettes.

Joanne gave her boyfriend a few seconds to return to the back of the vehicle and then pushed her right foot hard on the accelerator pedal. All the time she was listening out for Peter, in case he had further instructions.

As the engine raced there was a noise 'like the sound of a vehicle backfiring'.

It could have been a gunshot but she was not sure, though it was certainly a distinct bang.

Joanne had little time to ponder the alternatives. Suddenly the driver of the other vehicle was staring menacingly at her through the window, a long-barrelled silver revolver in his right hand aimed precisely at her head.

Instantly she realised that something so terrible, so tragic, so appalling in its ramifications had taken place behind the campervan.

Joanne Lees never saw Peter Marco Falconio again. Was he dead? Was he lying mortally wounded on the ground? Was it a random act of violence, a fit of rage or a carefully calculated attack?

Only the gunman knew the answer and Joanne was in no fit state to enquire further. Gripped by panic, she looked into his piercing eyes.

The face! She would never forget that 'evil, oval head' with the droopy moustache which went down the side of his mouth, or the deeply etched circles under his eyes. He was aged between 40 and 45 with straight, grey-brown, collar-length hair hanging beneath a black baseball cap which had a motif with a yellow border.

Like his cowboy-style gun with its scroll-like markings, he had the hint of a callous character from a Hollywood western about him. Here was a hard man who went about his sordid business with not so much as a flicker of emotion, a cruel giant of a figure with a slightly hunched back and stooped appearance.

Although committed to overpowering his next victim, the gunman's final intent remained unclear. Joanne was equally determined not to find out.

He ordered her to turn the ignition off but Joanne was trembling so much that she couldn't find the key. Frozen with fear, she was pushed across the bench seat into the passenger side of the campervan.

Shaking uncontrollably, she sat there as he fumbled with her body, forcing her head down on to her knees and wrenching her hands behind her back.

What did he want with her? He hadn't shot her so was he saving her for later? Did he plan to rape and kill her before dumping her body alongside Peter's in some remote makeshift grave, where they would never be found?

Joanne began to struggle but she was no match for the strength of her attacker. He clasped her wrists together and bound them with home-made handcuffs fashioned from black cable ties and cloth tape.

Although she was powerless to fight back with her hands, which were now tethered tightly behind her back, she was still able to use her feet and legs.

She does not remember how it happened, but somehow she fell out of the Kombi's passenger side door on to the rough gravel surface by the roadside. Wearing only green board shorts and a pale blue T-shirt, she felt the sharp-edged rocks and stones cut into her knees as he straddled her waist and pinned the front of her body to the ground.

She detected the salty taste of blood in her mouth as he attempted to bind her ankles with electrical tape, but Joanne fought back. Even though she was lying on her stomach she managed to kick out with her legs and what was left of the movement in her arms.

She tried to hit him in the crotch but he avoided her. 'I was reaching above trying to grip his testicles, struggling and moving about,' she said in court.

Clearly the attacker had not anticipated such resistance but he needed to keep her still for a moment so that he could completely secure her. And there was only one option.

Reaching around to the front of her head he punched the right-hand side of her face with his clenched fist. Joanne was momentarily stunned by the ferocity of the blow to her temple and lay there motionless. Her attacker seized the opportunity, pulled her up from the ground, unsuccessfully tried to wind some tape around her mouth, which ended up entangled in her hair, and marched her towards his own vehicle.

He grabbed the back of her neck with one hand and placed the other firmly behind her shoulder to steer her in the right direction. His large hand prevented her from turning her head to look for Peter as she staggered from the side of the Kombi towards his truck.

'He had his hand around my neck directing me. I didn't look. I couldn't see.'

Though curiously she was able to catch a glimpse of the 'shiny, tubular bull bar' at the front of his four-wheel-drive vehicle, which had a khaki canopy connected to the rear tray by laces and metal holes.

As they approached the side of the truck, her attacker lifted up a corner of the canopy and reached inside for a canvas sack which he proceeded to place over her head.

Blinded by the hood and bruised and battered by the assault, Joanne was pushed into the passenger seat of his truck and sat there motionless while she considered her next move.

Thankfully the canvas bag had been dislodged from her head as she was thrown into the vehicle. Although it was still dark outside an inside light made her vaguely aware of the dog she had noticed earlier as the gunman waved them down.

It was sitting next to her in the cab, apparently untroubled by the presence of a stranger. The dog, which she described as brown and white, neither licked nor smelt her, but stared resolutely ahead. Strangely the animal made no noise or displayed any sign of aggression.

Joanne, however, was near to breaking point. Shouting and screaming she demanded to know what her assailant wanted of her. Was it sex? Was it money?

'Keep quiet or I'll shoot you,' he replied.

She was quiet for a moment and then she asked him if he was going to rape her, and if he'd shot Peter. 'Have you shot my boyfriend?' she cried repeatedly.

'No' was his unemotional response.

Precisely what happened next was unclear, as Joanne's original story and subsequent account were slightly ambiguous.

Somehow she found herself lying in the back tray of the vehicle. But how did she get there? Obviously traumatised and confused, she recalled later that 'he somehow pushed me into the rear'.

But in another account she gave to a police artist shortly after the attack she made it clear that there was an opening behind the passenger seat which she was trying to access. She also remembered seeing a red fire extinguisher supported on a platform just behind her.

Unaided it would have been difficult to manoeuvre her body, with her hands still bound behind her back, from the front passenger seat through a small opening in the rear of the cab, but somehow she performed the task.

Did the two accounts expose an inconsistency in her story or was her memory simply clouded by the unthinkable drama of the previous few minutes? It would not be the first time that Joanne's on-going recollection of the horrific events that night would appear to contradict previous statements.

....

CHAPTER 3

THE ESCAPE

As Joanne lay on her stomach paralysed with fear in the back of the truck she had time to regain her senses. She felt what appeared to be a mattress beneath her body.

She managed to turn her head, which was pointing towards the cab, and as her eyes became accustomed to the darkness she was able to make out the dim shape of a window or a doorway behind her.

The night was deathly silent, the only noise her heavy, fitful breathing.

Desperately she listened out for other road users, hoping that a passing motorist might come to her rescue. Then she heard the unmistakeable sound of scraping gravel. It could have been a spade or it might have been an object being dragged over the uneven, dirt-strewn roadside.

Was it Peter's body being moved, she wondered? No, it couldn't be. The gunman had already assured her that he hadn't killed her boyfriend. But what if he was bluffing?

Her imagination was in overdrive. What would he do to her? Would her final moments be slow and torturous or short and merciful?

It was too horrendous to contemplate. How had she got herself into this position? More crucially, what could she do to escape?

Joanne looked around and realised she was lying under some kind of canvas canopy. She started to slide her body along the floor.

'I rolled over onto my bottom, my legs in front of me, and I edged forward.'

There was a point towards the end of the canopy which was 'slightly lighter'. She assumed correctly that it was an opening. If she was quick and quiet she could climb through, jump down onto the road and disappear.

'I was upright at that time. I hung my legs over the tray with my hands behind my back, looked around, couldn't see anything and jumped down.'

It was not a silent landing. The sound of the gravel under her feet 'made a loud noise' and she was afraid he would grab her before she got away.

Joanne ran as fast as her legs would carry her, but with her wrists still tightly bound behind her it was difficult to maintain her balance and she was afraid of tripping over a rock or branch.

She sprinted, jumped and staggered through the undergrowth for about 30 metres, eventually finding a bush to hide under, but she knew it would not be long before he discovered her gone. In fact he was already coming after her.

'He didn't say anything but I could hear his footsteps

and the crunching of dry grass and branches. He had a torch and I could hear him looking for me.'

As he came closer Joanne curled herself into a ball so he would not see her cowering under the vegetation. How he failed to notice her, concealed as she was only a relatively short distance from the road, seemed incomprehensible.

Perhaps he didn't want to find her. Maybe he had already satisfied his appetite for violence and could not be bothered dealing with a troublesome young woman as well. Whatever the reason the gunman retreated.

Joanne cannot remember how long he stalked her.

'It may have only been a couple of minutes but to me it felt a very long time.'

Occasionally other traffic would pass, but she was too far away to raise the alarm.

Pamela Namangardi Brown and her partner Jasper Jimbajimba Haines, of Ti Tree, were heading south along the Stuart Highway in their old Holden Commodore station wagon after spending the day with relatives at Ali Curung, a small Aboriginal community south of Wauchope.

Pamela, who was in the passenger seat, remembered passing two cars on the roadside north of Barrow Creek, an orange Kombi and a white car with a high body, which drove out on to the bitumen.

There was nothing suspicious about them.

'There's a road you can use to go out hunting around there so I assumed that's what they'd been doing,' she said.

Jasper also recalled seeing the Kombi and a four-wheel drive with lights on.

'There was a canopy on the back,' he added.

Later Jasper was to reveal that the last time he

glimpsed the truck in his rear-view mirror it was heading north and was a good 400 metres in front of the Kombi. This was to prove to be an important point because Joanne never reported seeing the truck being driven north, only the campervan, which was found dumped a couple of hundred metres away.

But because there was nothing untoward about the sighting on that night, the Aboriginal couple decided there was no need to pull over. People often camped by the side of the road in the Northern Territory, and if anyone was in trouble surely they would have waved them down, he reasoned.

If only Pamela and Jasper had known the truth of what was going on in the pitch-black bush. If only they had stopped to enquire if they were needed. If only Joanne could have made them hear her silent pleas for help.

As it was she crouched petrified under the moonless night sky, hoping her attacker would give up his search.

She knew he had gone back to the roadside when she heard an engine being started. At first she thought he would use his headlights to resume the search but instead he drove the vehicle north.

It sounded like the Kombi. Twenty minutes later he returned on foot to the other vehicle. Once again there was the unmistakeable sound of gravel as though he was 'dragging something heavy' across it.

Was he loading Peter's body into the back, she wondered. Although it was too painful to dwell on, what other explanation could there be?

They had been lovers for five years, a young couple who grew up in the same part of England's north, who shared a similar history and the same accent, but whose relationship had been cut short on a lonely highway in the middle of outback Australia.

How could it come to this? One moment they were idly smoking a joint while watching the setting sun and barely an hour later their world had fallen apart, exposing a chasm so terrifyingly bleak, a scenario so implausible, that it defied imagination.

The only difference was that this one was anchored in reality.

Suddenly Joanne heard the sound of a second engine, which she assumed was the truck. She watched its lights and followed the vehicle as it did a U-turn in the road and headed south.

Joanne sighed with relief. She was alone and no longer fearful that the rustling noise of her moving in the undergrowth would alert her attacker.

She needed to remove the handcuffs and she had an idea. Perhaps the cable ties that formed the loops around her wrists were far enough apart to bring her arms around from her back to the front.

Slowly she contorted herself so as to ease her lower body through her arms, a manoeuvre which proved to be remarkably simple in the circumstances.

'I just lifted my hands from underneath my bottom and lifted my legs through — it was very easy,' she admitted.

So easy that one wondered why she had not tried it before. Or perhaps she had.

With her hands in front, Joanne was much more mobile. It allowed her to reach into a hip pocket in her shorts for a tube of lip balm which she used to grease the inside of her handcuffs. Hoping that the lubrication would be sufficient to slip them off, she spread the balm around her wrists but to no avail.

She gripped the tape with her teeth hoping to slide the ties off, but the cuffs remained steadfastly tight, the plastic cutting into her flesh as she struggled to free herself. Gradually it dawned on her that she was a prisoner in one of the world's biggest open spaces, a cruel irony which only made her feel worse.

There were no walls or iron bars to contain her but she was as much a captive as a convict in a cell.

As Joanne lay frightened and frustrated in her bushland hideout she looked up. There are few more spectacular sights than an outback starlit night but this evening the cloud had turned the sky into an inky black. There was no moon or Milky Way to gently light the landscape and the air temperature was falling rapidly.

Joanne was cold and miserable. The temperature was down to 15 degrees Celsius and she had no idea how long she had been there or how much longer she would be forced to stay. She didn't even have a watch to monitor the time.

'I was so very frightened and so freezing.'

And while the gunman and his vehicle appeared to have departed there was no guarantee that he would not return. If he came back at dawn he would obviously find her. In daylight she would be a sitting target, unable to conceal herself.

After all, she was the only witness capable of identifying the man who had killed Peter Falconio. Her testimony, if he was arrested, would send him to prison for life. There was every incentive to find her and silence her for good. Every reason to slay the one woman who saw the killer. Without Joanne's evidence there was little or no chance of the vehicle being identified and the murderer being caught and convicted.

Why then did he give up the search and appear so content to let her go? Why had the gunman not used his dog to sniff her out? Surely it would have alerted its master to another human being in that limited area?

Joanne's mind was buzzing with questions which had no immediate answers. But one thing was certain. Against seemingly insurmountable odds she had managed to evade her captor and now she was determined to make one last dash for freedom.

No one knew exactly how long she sat there pondering her plight before summoning the courage to move closer to the road, but it must have been at least four hours. There had been hardly any traffic that Saturday night, which is usually the quietest day for commercial transport shuttling north and south between Darwin and Alice Springs. Like many professional drivers, most Territory truckies like to have their weekends off.

A few smaller vehicles passed her in the distance but they were probably cars or utes, she reckoned, and she could not be sure whether the gunman might be among them. Joanne needed to be certain that if she waved anybody down they would be reliable men of the road and could be trusted.

In the still of the outback night she had grown to recognise the different engine sounds. By now she could tell a car from a lorry, a three-litre sedan from a prime mover, so she waited patiently for the distant tell-tale groan that would almost certainly herald the imminent arrival of a road train.

But how would she stop it? Would the driver see her? What if the truckie, taken by surprise, swerved to avoid her, only for his trailers to clip or run her over? Road trains take hundreds of metres to halt and for their snake-like cargo to turn.

This then was her dilemma. To run to the roadside when she heard the right engine noise and accept the risk, or to stay cowering in the scrub and face an even more uncertain fate.

It was around 1 a.m. Joanne Lees, 27 years old, cold, petrified and nursing minor cuts and bruises, had no choice. There were headlights on the horizon accompanied by the gentle roar of a heavy engine. It was now or never.

'I thought I would have to be brave and get some help for Pete.'

She staggered to her feet and ran.

CHAPTER 4

....

THE RESCUE

Truckies Vince Millar and Rodney Adams were settling in to their lengthy journey from Darwin to Adelaide. Both knew the road like the back of their hand and each was used to the shift pattern they had adopted — five hours on and five hours off.

Vince had taken over the wheel at Tennant Creek, allowing Rodney to climb into the bunk behind the front seats for a snooze. Tonight they were pulling three trailers roughly 40 metres long and had just filled up with 200 litres of fuel. It was about 10.30 p.m.

Their next stop was Barrow Creek, roughly halfway between Tennant Creek and Alice Springs, some 500 kilometres south. Vince was averaging 90 kilometres an hour in his Bulls Transport prime mover. Though a boring drive, particularly at night, it was important to keep his wits about him and concentrate on the road ahead. Steering a road train requires a level of skill and operational experience that only comes with years of practice. After nearly five hours in the driver's seat Vince was looking forward to the changeover at Barrow Creek, where Rodney would take the wheel and he could enjoy a nap.

Around midnight he saw the 300 kilometres sign to Alice Springs which meant that Barrow Creek was only 20 minutes away. They had no plans to stop in the pub. They would just swap seats and continue down the Stuart Highway.

Their strict timetable meant there was no opportunity to spend the night in a comfy bed. They just kept driving. It was like this all the time. This was their life, backwards and forwards between Adelaide and Darwin with one night a week at home if they were lucky.

But this evening would be different. An event they would never forget was about to unfold in front of them. A person who would unleash a chain of events that would thrust them into the international spotlight was about to make her first appearance.

Just after the road sign a lone figure jumped out from the roadside spinifex into Vince's path, holding her arms up high above her head so the driver would see her wrists were bound.

He was so close and so surprised that he hardly had time to swerve to avoid her. With three trailers on the back he feared he might have skittled her.

'After she had gone past the front of the cab I thought she had fallen under the wheels,' he admitted.

Even though he slammed on the brakes it still took nearly a kilometre to bring his massive load to a standstill. As the road train lurched and screamed its way to a halt Rodney woke up in his bunk and asked what was wrong.

Vince couldn't believe what was happening and pretended that he was just going to check the tyres. Rod lay down and over the noise of the idling engine was unable to comprehend the mumbled message from his mate a few minutes later: 'I think I've run someone over.'

Clearly worried that something awful had happened, Vince leapt down from the cab and looked for a torch in the tool box. It wasn't there but the headlights were on, casting just enough light for him to see if there was anything — or anybody — under the wheels.

Vince had no doubt what to expect. 'I was looking for a body, whether it be an arm or a leg or a bit of clothing.'

But there was nothing, apart from the road train's huge tyres and the skid marks they'd left. Perplexed, he gazed around for another explanation. It was at that point that he became aware of the sound of hurried footsteps.

'I looked down to the end of the second trailer and heard this clip-clop coming down the road and some sheila saying, "Help, help."'

She was on the other side of the truck and he couldn't see her at first.

'I put my head down and said, "Hey, settle down. Come here."'

Breathless and distraught, the young woman crouched and crawled crab-like under the chassis, practically throwing herself at Vince, who was unsure what was going on.

'I grabbed her and threw her back away from me, like sort of protecting myself, if she had sort of anything on her because you just don't know . . .' he explained.

Then she started screaming: 'Help me! Help me! Look I'm tied up.'

Vince stared at her hands but wasn't quite sure what bound them. He guided her to the front of the prime mover so he could examine the problem more closely in the headlights.

She was a mess. Apart from the plastic cable ties around her wrists, there was black sticky tape around her neck, in her hair and some around her legs.

'Geez! Hang on a minute,' he exclaimed before ordering Rod to get up and help. 'I think I've got some sheila out here tied up. Come and give us a hand.'

Rodney, still half-asleep in his bunk, was aware of a woman's voice and in the interests of decorum chose to don a shirt, something he rarely did in the cab. Reaching down for his thongs, the preferred footwear of most long-distance drivers, he climbed down from the truck and walked around to the front. Rodney was taken aback by what he saw and heard.

'Joanne was almost hysterical. Apart from the ties around her wrists there was tape around her neck and matted in her hair.'

Rod went to the tool box and got the wire cutters out. Vince held her arms while his mate sliced the handcuffs off. Then he tried to pull the tape from her hair.

'I started to remove the tape and said, "This is going to hurt, you'd better do it yourself. You know your own pain tolerance,"' Rod added.

Joanne Lees was free at last. Now she had to cope with the mental anguish.

'My boyfriend's gone, I can't find my boyfriend,' she shouted in despair.

Still uncertain about what had happened, her two saviours tried to calm her down. They placed the severed ties in the tool box for safe keeping, helped her into the cab and proceeded to reassure her.

'Joanne was mumbling something about a Kombi van. She was weeping and crying,' Rod recalled.

The two men started discussing what to do and where to go.

'Alice Springs had the nearest police station but Joanne suggested there was another at Ti Tree,' Vince said.

Joanne continued to talk about Peter.

'She was in a state of panic but in the warmth of our truck she fell apart,' said Rodney.

'Please don't leave me,' she pleaded.

'With her head on my shoulder she sobbed, "I want my mum,"' added Rodney. 'It really broke me up.'

She also wanted to find her boyfriend and her van, so Vince offered to have a look around. He decided to move the road train to the side of the road, jump down from the cab and disconnect the trailers. He was intending to drive up and down the road in the prime mover to see if he could find anything, but before he had a chance to move off his eyes were drawn to a pile of dirt on the road about 15 to 20 centimetres high.

'There were a few swirls and I thought, "That's strange." It was unusual to see a pyramid of dirt on the bitumen.'

They also saw two recently formed tyre tracks near what appeared to be a white gate further up the road. That also struck them as unusual for such a remote spot.

For a moment they considered investigating further but decided against the idea in case the truck got bogged.

By now Joanne, who was sitting in the middle on the engine cowling and seemed a little calmer than before, had begun recounting the extraordinary events of the past few hours to her new-found friends.

'She was saying some bloke waved her over and there were sparks coming out of the back of the van, and then she started talking about how this bloke had a gun, had held it to her head and tied her up,' said Vince.

'What the bloody hell are we doing out here looking for a bloke with a gun!' he exclaimed. 'We're going. It's too dark.'

Vince did a U-turn, reconnected his load and headed south, not sure what to do next.

At Barrow Creek he was encouraged to see the lights were still on in the roadhouse, despite the hour. Inside, landlord Les Pilton and a few guests were celebrating the new year in July, a curious antipodean tradition similar to the mid-year yuletide festivities recreated in such wintry locations as the Blue Mountains west of Sydney. A week earlier they'd held a Christmas party for the same reason.

It was about nearly 2 a.m. Les was on bar duty and the party was winding down. Some builders had been working for him over the previous few weeks and they'd invited a few of their friends and family up from Alice Springs for the weekend.

He heard the road train pull up outside and recognised Vince immediately when he walked in. Les had been the proprietor of the Barrow Creek Hotel for 16 years and knew most of the truckies who made their living on the Stuart Highway.

Les Pilton is aware of everybody and everything in these parts. Little happens without his knowledge. As unofficial local historian, he also holds the keys to the telegraph station in case tourists want to look inside.

The building is now a monument to the Northern Territory's violent and troubled past when white pioneers clashed with indigenous tribes. In 1872 two telegraph employees, John Franks and James L. Stapleton, were killed in an attack on the station by local Aborigines and, as recently as 1928, some 70 Aborigines were massacred by a posse of whites after an old dingo trapper was murdered by Aborigines on Coniston Station.

Remarkably some of their Aboriginal descendants are still around. The Tara community, about 12 kilometres northeast of Barrow Creek, has a population of 80, and some 120 members of the Pmatajunata tribe live 35 kilometres away at Stirling Station.

These days the local indigenous people are more welcome at Barrow Creek but there remains an element of segregation. Few Aborigines enter the pub, preferring to be served their maximum six beers a day through a hatch in the wall.

While such traditions would not be tolerated in politically correct, metropolitan Australia, no one complains here. For Les Pilton, who doesn't have an ounce of racism in his body, and the rest of the community, both black and white, they are accepted facts of Northern Territory life.

Les was tidying up and waiting for the last guests to head for bed when Vince strode in. The landlord glanced up with his usual welcoming smile and knew immediately that something was wrong. Vince had a worried look and asked if he'd seen anyone driving an orange Kombi with a white roof.

'I told him we had a passenger and explained her story.'

Les tried to telephone Ti Tree police station, but it appeared to be unattended and he got the answering machine instead. He had better luck with Alice Springs and he handed the phone to Vince to tell the duty officer more.

Outside Joanne was sitting in the cab with Rod and refusing to budge.

Silent and trembling slightly, she was bent forward with her head in her hands. Les and the truckies attempted to coax her down, but she wouldn't move.

'She was terrified,' said Rodney.

Eventually the three men convinced her that she would be safe with them, and after several minutes of quiet persuasion she agreed to climb down from the cab. With Rodney close to her left-hand side, she walked slowly into the pub and sat on a bar stool near the front door.

'Her head was bowed, she was hunched up and so very frightened,' added Les.

He offered her a stiff drink but she settled for a cup of tea instead.

Les noticed her face was swollen, though whether this was the result of a blow or tears he could not be sure.

And there appeared to be a misunderstanding over the way her hands had been tied. Les insisted in several subsequent media interviews that Joanne had told him the attacker had bound her wrists in front of her body, and this was how she'd undone her leg strappings and run away. They were remarks that were to lead to further confusion in the days and weeks that followed as contradicting stories emerged about the manner in which she had been handcuffed.

Meanwhile, Vince was talking to the police again. The duty officer had to be sure this wasn't a prank call. He spoke to Joanne briefly to confirm the details and then set about calling and putting together a team of off-duty officers to make the 284-kilometre journey to Barrow Creek. It would take at least three hours to get there.

Aware of the drama, others had started assembling in the bar. Catherine Curley, then aged 20 and working at the hotel as an apprentice chef, had gone to bed about 12.45 a.m. but was woken more than an hour later by someone knocking at her bedroom door in one of the outside chalets.

It was Vince. 'Something's happened,' he said, 'you'd better get up.'

The time on her bedside clock was 1.50 a.m.

'I got up straight away, dressed, left the shed and went over to the hotel.'

A few of her friends were at the bar, including a New Zealand builder known as Matta and another guy called Rosco. Catherine also noticed a stranger, a 'scruffy' woman with untidy hair and scratches on her legs and arms. Had there been a car accident, Catherine wondered.

The woman was obviously upset and kept asking about Peter.

'Where's Peter?' she would sob as tears welled in her eyes.

'We still couldn't quite work out who Peter was,' explained Rodney, who by this time had produced a first-aid box with some alcoholic wipes to attend to Joanne's injuries.

Catherine thought it better to take her to the ladies' loo so she could clean herself up. 'As well as the scratches there were marks around both wrists,' she added.

The two young women walked along the hallway which separates the bar from the bedrooms and the toilet area at the back of the pub.

'She was still fairly shaken.'

'I can't believe this is happening,' Joanne muttered as she wiped away the tears.

On her return Les suggested that she take a nap after the ordeal she had been through.

'She was really traumatised,' he observed.

He had already lit the fire to warm her up, though the dogs in the pub, an Alsatian belonging to Les and a blue heeler puppy owned by Catherine, probably appreciated the flames more as they lay beside the hearth. Joanne, who had a pet dog of her own back in England, hadn't seen a blue heeler before arriving in Australia and noted its speckled markings.

Still reeling from the shock of the past few hours, Joanne accepted the offer of a bed and was shown bedroom number seven. It was not the Ritz but she had more concerns than creature comforts at this stage and at least she was safe.

There were three single beds surrounded by green walls from which to choose. Above her there was a single ceiling fan and on the floor a grey carpet and mottled white mat and a small chest of drawers. Not that she had any possessions to put in them. Her only clothes were what she was standing in.

Keeping the bedroom light on and demanding the door be left ajar, she dozed but couldn't sleep and after a short rest decided to return to the bar.

The police arrived at 4.30 a.m. There were many questions. Those caught up in the drama were separated and interviewed individually. Joanne's story was so convincing and the horror of the attack so graphic that police knew they had to act quickly if the killer was to be caught. How had he made his getaway? Did he head north to Tennant Creek or south to Alice

Springs? Or maybe he had taken one of the many dirt roads that weave across the outback. Just possibly he could still be in the vicinity.

They ordered roadblocks up and down the Stuart Highway as far north as Katherine and as far south as Kulgera on the South Australian border. The police also blocked roads as far east as Avon Downs on the Barkly Highway near the Queensland border and west to Top Springs on the Buchanan Highway. They had Joanne's rough description of the man and his means of transport so they knew what to look for.

Even the air space around Barrow Creek was turned into a no-go area. Police prohibited private planes and helicopters within a 20-kilometre radius and 5000 feet height of the crime scene while they carried out their own aerial search.

And they needed forensic evidence, including any incriminating blood or saliva that might have been transferred from the killer to Joanne's clothes.

While taking a shower she had already found a long hair which wasn't hers. Could it have fallen from the attacker or his dog? Or maybe she simply picked it up in the cab of the road train.

She gave it to Les's partner, Helen Jones, for safekeeping. It was the beginning of a friendship that was to blossom in the dark days ahead as Joanne began to rely on her for support and encouragement.

Helen's kindness and generosity in that first week had known no bounds. She treated her like a daughter and was happy to give her some of her own clothes when the police required Joanne's entire wardrobe for forensic examination.

A 50-year-old mother of three whose first husband had died, Helen understood the emotional turmoil she must have been going through. Joanne was in deep shock, and drew her legs up around her as she cowered on the bar stool.

Concerned that she might want to tell her family back in Britain what had happened, Helen asked Joanne if she wanted to telephone home. 'But she couldn't bring herself to do it,' she recalled.

When the time came for Joanne to be taken to Alice Springs late that Sunday afternoon, Helen went with her, offering her a bed in Les Pilton's mother's house as a sanctuary away from prying eyes and the gathering media army who were after her story.

Joanne's account of her miraculous escape from a madman in the middle of the Australian outback, and the tragedy of her boyfriend's brutal murder, had already aroused the interest of news organisations in Australia and around the world.

Eight-and-a-half hours behind Northern Territory time, the news was being extensively reported on the Sunday morning television bulletins 19,000 kilometres away in Britain.

In Barrow Creek it was late afternoon, almost 24 hours after the terrible events of the night before, yet unbelievably Joanne had still not telephoned her parents back in Almondbury, on the outskirts of Huddersfield, or Peter's family, who also lived in Yorkshire.

While it was impossible to make a mobile phone call from Barrow Creek, Les and Helen had already offered her the use of the pub's landline, but she declined their offer.

'She just couldn't bring herself to phone because she was so emotionally het up,' recalled Les. 'She was so worried about finding Peter that she couldn't worry about talking to her folks as well,' he added.

Helen confirmed that Joanne didn't ring home until she got to the police station after she had visited the hospital in Alice Springs early Sunday evening.

If Joanne was too distraught to speak to her mother and father and could not bring herself to telephone Peter's parents, why hadn't the police made contact? For a young woman who, hours earlier, had wanted her mum, it seemed surprising that there had been no verbal communication between them.

Joanne's parents had seen the TV news that Sunday morning and, knowing their daughter and Peter were in the Alice Springs area, had feared the worst. They had even called Peter's family, several kilometres away in New Mill, to share their concerns.

It was not until her stepfather, Vincent James, walked into Huddersfield police station a few hours later that his fears were confirmed.

It had taken nearly a day for the dreadful news to filter through and Joanne had still not called home. Was it the shock? Was she hoping against hope that Peter might be still alive? Or perhaps she had yet to come to terms with the awful reality.

CHAPTER 5

....

SOUL MATES

The grief of a young life cut short was about to grip two families on the other side of the world. Joan and Luciano Falconio were going about their Sunday morning at home in Hepworth, on the outskirts of New Mill, when the telephone rang.

It was Joanne's stepfather Vincent, who wanted to know if they'd seen the television news about a couple being attacked on the Stuart Highway in Australia.

Joan knew Peter and his girlfriend were in the area because he had contacted home only a few days earlier, but she couldn't bring herself to believe it might be them. 'It can't be them, it can't be,' she prayed.

At first the two families were unable to find out more details of the attack or the names of those involved, so Vincent turned to the police for help. He walked up to the front desk at Huddersfield police station and relayed his concerns. The station sergeant went away

40

and returned shortly with the grim details. Joanne was alive but Peter was missing, feared dead.

'I just fell on my knees,' said Joan when she heard the news.

Peter was their third son, born 20 September 1972, in Harrogate. His arrival meant another brother for Nicholas and Paul. Mark, the youngest, was born five years later.

Luciano, an Italian migrant, had settled in Yorkshire after marrying Joan. The family moved to Doncaster and then New Mill, a picturesque village near Holmfirth, where the long-running BBC television series *Last of the Summer Wine* is filmed.

Back in the early '70s when the Falconios were bringing up their young family, few Britons considered taking a holiday in Australia. Most students went straight from taking their exams to a full-time job. Youngsters could not afford to take off a 'gap year' to backpack around the world.

While the swinging '60s had made it more acceptable for young people to travel overland to North Africa, and even India or Afghanistan for the truly adventurous, most young British holiday-makers preferred a package tour to European tourist haunts such as Ibiza or Benidorm than Marrakech or Kabul.

In October 1973, another Middle East war was about to engulf the planet in an oil crisis, Richard Nixon was hanging on to the United States presidency and Princess Anne was about to marry Captain Mark Phillips. Across the other side of the globe Sydney was celebrating the official opening of its opera house, which had taken 15 years and over $100 million to build.

The Falconio family was moving up in the world. Luciano had taken over a newsagency business in New

Mill and rented a flat next door to accommodate his young brood.

They were a tightly knit family and even when the children got older and left home they remained in close contact, frequently phoning and dropping around to their parents' home for a meal.

Even today the surviving brothers, Nicholas, Paul and Mark, live near each other.

'We see each other regularly and have tea at least once a week,' says Paul. 'We don't live in each other's pockets but we've been close all our lives, keeping in contact and sharing the same friends,' he adds.

Peter had gone to Wooldale Primary School on the outskirts of New Mill followed by Holmfirth High, where he is remembered by the staff as a 'smashing kid'.

'I can't think of anything bad to say about him. He had loads of friends. He never had an argument with anyone. He was a very gentle person, not violent at all. Just a likeable, decent fellow,' says Paul.

They are sentiments echoed by Luciano, who talks about his 'wonderful boy — and not just because he was my son. He was very clever and very loving to everyone.'

His mother Joan speaks about a 'happy young man who was interested in everybody and everything — a lovely child who grew up to be a lovely man'.

As a little boy he liked to play with Meccano but didn't share his brothers' interest in football. 'He wasn't that much into sport but as he got older he enjoyed skiing,' says Paul.

Peter also enjoyed his food and after taking a catering course became an accomplished cook. It was a skill that was to endear him to Joanne and her family, who lived several kilometres away in Almondbury.

Joanne and Peter met at a nightclub called Visage in 1995. Her family lived in a semi-detached, pebble-dashed council house which they later bought from the local authority. Its back garden overlooked the playing fields of Almondbury High School, where Joanne had been a pupil. With a block of scruffy council flats next door, it was the sort of working-class area that any young person with upwardly mobile aspirations would have wanted to leave at the first opportunity. And Joanne, who was a clever girl, was keen to improve herself. After leaving Almondbury High she enrolled at Huddersfield's Greenhead College, regarded as one of the best sixth-form colleges in the country.

Her mother Jennifer, who remarried when Joanne was in her teens, did her best for her and Sam, her younger brother who was more than 10 years her junior.

When Joanne's mum died in Huddersfield Royal Infirmary at the age of 54 about a year after the murder, those who knew her felt the cause of death may have been as much emotional as physical. For many years she had suffered from ill health including rheumatoid arthritis, but the strain and worry of the previous 12 months and her affection for Peter prompted those close to her to conclude she may also have died from a broken heart.

Vincent, then in his early-60s, admitted that his wife had found it difficult to handle Peter's disappearance and the media coverage it attracted. Coping with the anxiety and uncertainty had not helped her condition.

Jennifer fell for Peter's easy-going manner and the Latin charm he had inherited from his father. She remembered the pledge he'd made to her when he took Joanne to Brighton with him. 'Don't worry, I'll look after her,' he promised.

'We couldn't have hoped for a nicer boy. We were really pleased she had a boyfriend like that. He was part of the family. We thought the world of him,' Jennifer admitted.

Mr and Mrs James were also impressed by Peter's cooking skills, which he had passed on to Joanne. When she came home for Christmas one year she cooked the turkey dinner, prompting her stepdad to suggest they should buy Peter a bottle of Champagne in gratitude.

He was not without his faults. Peter wasn't the best timekeeper and Joanne would get mad with him if he turned up late, but he would invariably make light of it and everyone would end up laughing, Mrs James recalled shortly before she died.

She always had high hopes for her daughter and Peter was a bonus. Jennifer felt that his education, ambition and family background would help Joanne up the social scale to a more middle-class existence than the life she'd had in Almondbury.

So there was an inevitable mix of sadness and pleasure when the happy couple waved goodbye to Joanne as she stood at the front door of her modest semi-detached house on that cool, damp November day in 2000, just before they headed for the airport and the start of their global jaunt.

'Mums are always teary when their daughter leaves home but Peter assured me he would look after her and he did.'

Jennifer wished them both good luck and told them to enjoy themselves.

Joanne turned, smiled and urged her mum not to worry. 'We'll soon be back. After all it's only a year,' she reminded her.

She didn't realise then but it was the last time Jennifer would see them together. The next time she would meet her daughter would be shrouded in sadness, her most vivid memory of the young man she hoped Joanne would marry, his endearing smile at the front doorstep that November morning.

For Vincent, who was also close to the couple, the next few years would be equally harrowing as he coped with a double loss — his wife's death and Peter's disappearance. He would always love his stepdaughter but it would never be the same blood-bond that Jennifer and Joanne had enjoyed. In the years that followed he would talk to his stepdaughter on the telephone and occasionally she would visit him in Almondbury but it was a long-distance relationship which was hard to sustain. Though Joanne was never far from his thoughts.

Even today a school photograph of his stepdaughter is placed proudly on the mantelpiece and he has much faith in her ability to get on with life.

'The past few years have been devastating for her but she's a very strong-willed person,' he insists as he ponders the teenage years she spent at home while studying for her general certificate of secondary education which she passed aged 16. 'She got her GCSEs and took a few part-time jobs after leaving school, including one at a bacon-packing factory. Not that I can remember her bringing some home,' he says, smiling.

She also got a job behind the bar at the Beaumont Arms, a well-known local hostelry which used to be called The Kirkstile Inn.

Joanne had a wide social circle, who remember her as 'happy-go-lucky and outgoing'. But she was always very protective of her privacy, which her friends, who were invariably extremely loyal to her, would respect. It was a personal trait that sometimes annoyed those who knew Joanne at school.

'You either liked her or loathed her,' said one. 'She had this tendency to either bring out the worst in people or make you feel a life-long friend.'

Among those who have known Joanne the longest is Stefka Zbyszkew, who was a near-neighbour for more than 20 years. Now aged 50, Mrs Zbyszkew, the daughter of a Ukrainian migrant, remembers her own daughter being taken out by Joanne when she was a baby.

'All I can say is that she's the nicest person you could ever wish to meet. She'd always stop and help anybody. You can take it from me. When I had my daughter who's now 23, Joanne would always want to take her out in the pushchair. She really loves small children.

'When people say they don't believe what she said happened in the outback I know for a fact she's telling the truth,' Mrs Zbyszkew insists.

It is that sort of loyalty which is to be found in many of Joanne's friends. But equally there are others, only prepared to talk on condition of anonymity, who hint at another side to her character.

'Weirdo', 'strange', 'dreamer' are but some of the epithets used to describe her.

CHAPTER 6

....

LEAVING HOME

In the late '90s Joanne leapt at the opportunity to join her boyfriend in Brighton, on the south coast of England, where he was studying for a degree in building and construction management. Peter had already been a student there for two years and clearly missed his girlfriend.

Brighton was a much more cosmopolitan town than Huddersfield, offering an intoxicating mixture of music, clubbing and the pleasures of the flesh. Not for nothing was it once known as London-by-the-sea, where day-trippers could combine a paddle on the beach with the harmless fun of Brighton's other attractions, including the Palace Pier, the amusement arcades and the Volks Railway which ran along the seafront.

Only an hour on the train from London, it also drew a wide cross-section of Britain's artistic elite, including writers such as Terence Rattigan and actors like Laurence Olivier.

But that was in the '60s and '70s. Now Brighton boasted a much more hedonistic lifestyle, where drugs and dance parties were an accepted part of the vibrant south-coast town's youth culture.

For Joanne and Peter, who grew up in the more straight-laced and conservative confines of provincial Yorkshire, Brighton was a liberating experience. They drank, they partied and they revelled in each other's company, the first opportunity they'd had to live together as lovers.

But they also worked hard. Peter was keen to complete his studies with a good grade so he could go on to prove himself in the outside world and Joanne needed a job to keep them financially afloat.

She found full-time employment with the travel agency Thomas Cook, which stimulated her dreams of visiting foreign parts. She grew accustomed to Brighton's large population of backpackers and overseas students dropping by to seek advice on holidays and international airline schedules.

Fiona Stevenson, who worked with Joanne in Thomas Cook's North Street branch in the centre of Brighton, remembers a young woman who relished her job and the company of travellers. 'She was a really lovely, lovely person,' she recalls.

Peter, meanwhile, had his head down, engrossed in the minutiae of building and construction. He had impressed his personal tutor and course leader at Brighton University, Dr Kassim Gidado, who regarded him as a 'very determined young man' with a dazzling professional future.

Peter was so keen to start his new career that he combined his final-year studies for a Bachelor of Science degree in construction management with a job at Laing, the large British construction company, whose bosses were so impressed with him they found him a full-time job.

But while academic and professional advancement were important to Peter, he also longed for the opportunity to travel. He and Joanne had already enjoyed a few foreign holidays together, including trips to Italy and Jamaica, but they both hankered after a much longer period away.

They had talked about Australia and some of their friends had been there. Why not take a year off and embark on a working holiday down under, they thought. They were certainly young enough. Still under 28, they were eligible for an Australian working-holiday visa, which would allow them to earn some money while travelling and they could visit so many other countries on the way. Too young, they felt, to settle down and have a family, the whole world beckoned.

Paul Falconio sensed their excitement when he visited them in Brighton and realised the travel bug had bitten since they'd left Yorkshire. 'They were really looking forward to going off to Australia and weren't apprehensive about the idea at all.'

Their itinerary would take them to Nepal, where they planned to go trekking, and then on to Malaysia, Singapore, Thailand, Cambodia and Australia, before returning via New Zealand and Fiji.

Come October they were quitting their jobs and packing up their belongings in their rented apartment near Brighton seafront. They had saved a fair amount of money and spent the last few weeks before their departure saying goodbye to friends and finalising travel arrangements. There were clothes to buy as well, including lighter tops and trousers for the more tropical climate and tough walking shoes.

Finally they had their tickets and their bags packed. All that remained was a short excursion to Yorkshire to farewell their families and store the small collection of furniture, and other knick-knacks they had acquired during their time together, in a spare room at Peter's parents' house in Hepworth. It was November 2000.

Mrs Falconio knew she would miss them. 'They were soul mates, really happy together and nice to have around,' she said.

Having waved goodbye to their families, Joanne and Peter flew via Vienna so that they could stop over in Nepal, the Himalayan kingdom squeezed between India and Tibet and arguably one of the most hauntingly beautiful nations on earth. Thirty years earlier the Nepalese capital of Kathmandu was on the hippy trail. Nowadays it was common for travellers of all age groups and social persuasions to pass through the idyllic mountain landscape before moving on to other cultures, other lands.

The pair trekked by day and were usually too exhausted but to sleep by night. It was hard to phone or email home, but Peter would always call when he could. It was a habit which stuck during the months ahead.

After the frenetic pace of life in the weeks leading up to their departure, Joanne and her boyfriend discovered that for the first time in many months they had a lot of spare time for each other. And they were in no hurry. Australia was still another two months away and they had Singapore, Kuala Lumpur, Bangkok and Phnom Penh to sample.

Like most backpackers they stayed in budget accommodation and soon learnt the rules of the road, sometimes the hard way.

While waiting in an immigration queue in Cambodia Peter was pickpocketed. He lost a lot of money, as well as credit cards. The couple were devastated by the theft but while wondering how to overcome their misfortune struck up a friendship with other travellers who helped them out.

They were the sort of lessons that most young tourists soon learn while on the road — always keep your valuables in a safe place or risk losing them. And when all else fails, help and comfort appears from the most unexpected quarters.

Other people she met in the immigration office that day revealed they were travelling in the same direction and offered their support. What seemed an unmitigated financial disaster turned into a minor hiccup compared with the tragedy that was to unfold several months later.

By the new year Joanne and Peter had their sights set on Australia. They had enjoyed their time in Asia but were looking forward to living in a western culture again and, more importantly, earning money. Their savings, though healthy, did not allow for a prolonged period without replenishment so they were eager to find a job once they arrived in Sydney.

The pair flew into Mascot airport on 16 January 2001, the height of the Australian summer when temperatures regularly hit the high 30s. Like most backpackers arriving in Sydney they needed a swim and headed straight to Bondi, where they also found somewhere to rent. It was a small place in North Bondi which they shared with two other people, a Dutchman and his five-year-old daughter.

After two months in Asia they wallowed in the relaxed beachside lifestyle and spent hours splashing

around in the ocean. This was what it was all about —
sun, sand and surf.

Sydney, with its population of four million and robust
local economy, also offered plenty of employment
opportunities, especially for backpackers who were not
so choosy about the work they did. Unlike young
Australians they could not fall back on the welfare
system to support them, so there was no alternative but
to find a job.

Peter got one at a furniture company called January's
but Joanne was a little more selective. She liked the idea
of working in a shop and because she enjoyed reading
set her mind on a bookshop.

Quite why she targeted Dymocks, a basement retail
outlet in George Street at the heart of Sydney's city
centre, is unclear, but she was so determined to gain a
sales position there that she called Gary Sullivan, the
manager, every second day for a fortnight until a
vacancy came up.

Joanne had caught the eye of a few male employees
who encouraged him to take her on and she soon
settled in.

'One of the blokes said she was a "bit of a looker —
you'd better give this girl a chance",' he said, laughing.
'She was very outgoing, popular and had a bubbly
personality.'

Everyone enjoyed her company. Paul Jones, another
fellow worker, described her as a breath of fresh air and
different to other temporary staff who passed through.
Joanne made deep and lasting friendships and quite
clearly cared about those she worked with, he said.

Staff were actively encouraged to sample the
merchandise and give their own recommendation on
the content for the benefit of customers. Among the

titles Joanne reviewed was a book called *After You'd Gone* by Maggie O'Farrell, a seemingly depressing choice for a fun-loving youngster. It was about the loss of a loved one and dealt with the plight of a woman in a coma after her partner had died.

Gary realised he had chosen wisely in employing Joanne and soon came to know her well. He was also introduced to Peter and heard they were very close.

'He used to come into the shop occasionally and help out with stocktaking or moving some furniture around. He was a fairly quiet sort of person.'

Gary understood they had been together for a long time and believed Joanne expected him to propose at some romantic spot during their travels.

What Peter didn't know was that his girlfriend of nearly six years was so enjoying the company of her new circle of friends that deeper relationships were emerging with one or two of them.

Often Joanne and fellow workers would gather for morning coffee or lunch at Earls in a rear lane behind Dymocks bookshop, and it was there that she met Nick Riley, another British backpacker.

A regular in the backstreet cafe, he would often meet Joanne for a drink in the nearby Angel bar after work. Sometimes Peter would join them, unaware that Nick and Joanne would soon become much more than friends.

Peter had his mind on other matters and was heavily involved in preparations for the next stage of their journey, an ambitious drive through central Australia and the eastern states, which would take three or four months. Because of his background in construction and the building industry he was a meticulous planner and wanted to ensure that they were well prepared for such an arduous expedition, which might take its toll on their vehicle.

Aware of the reputation for reliability of the Volkswagen Kombi, he looked around for a second-hand model. Eventually he found one at the Kings Cross car market, a sale yard long favoured by the backpacking community. Here young tourists finishing their epic Australian tour might park their van for several days for someone like Peter to come along and make an offer.

After a bit of haggling a deal would be struck and the vehicle would have a new owner. Peter thought he'd done particularly well to buy his orange Kombi for $1200. It needed a bit of work done on it but the engine seemed sound enough and with a few additions to the interior they'd be off and running.

Over the next few weeks he set about transforming the inside of the vehicle, putting his own stamp on the fixtures and fittings by installing a spotlight in the back so they could read while lying down at night. He also fixed a safe deposit box in the front, where they could hide their money, passports and other valuables in a secure container. And he built a shelf under the dashboard, where they could place maps, drinks and cigarettes. It also became a convenient spot to place their store of cannabis while travelling.

Peter was partial to his joints and seemed to have established contact with a supplier in Sydney to meet his needs. Joanne on the other hand was only a very occasional smoker, though conceded that she wasn't a complete innocent when it came to drugs. While in Sydney she took half an ecstasy tablet, she admitted later.

As the date for their scheduled departure in June got closer, Joanne's fondness for her new-found friend in

Earls cafe became more intense. Nick invited her over to his place in Newtown, an inner-city suburb which is popular with students, being close to Sydney University.

First they'd go out for a few beers at the Cooper's Arms, where they would meet up with his friends, and sometimes they would go on to Kelly's, a nearby Irish pub. Invariably the night would end in the first floor bedroom of the large house he used to share with other backpackers in Brown Street.

Peter remained oblivious to the relationship and the real purpose of those Thursday evening assignations. Joanne merely told him she was staying the night with a girlfriend, an explanation that Peter never seemed to doubt, such was the trust he had in her.

Nick, who had been introduced to Joanne by one of her fellow shopworkers, Tim Ford, another Englishman, was a smart, jack-the-lad character who had an eye for a pretty girl and enjoyed a good time. A young man who worked hard and played hard, the university graduate from Reading, west of London, had experience in finance and IT but was never happier than when he was able to crack jokes and knock back a few beers during happy hour at the Cooper's Arms.

But for Joanne's impending travel plans with Peter, it is quite possible the relationship might have developed further. Those who knew Nick at the time say he seemed to calm down a lot while in Joanne's company and was quite smitten with her.

Certainly the pair had no intention of allowing distance to get in the way of their friendship after Joanne left Sydney and he headed back to Britain. While the physical side of their relationship might have to be put on hold, cyberspace would allow them to keep in regular contact courtesy of a confidential email address. And just in case anybody else happened to stumble on their messages, Nick would have a pseudonym — 'Steph', a name sufficiently androgynous to be explained away as one of Joanne's many on-line friends of either sex.

Not that Joanne considered this a serious affair. To her, he was more a ship that passed in the night, an acquaintance whom she just happened to fancy and who was more than happy to reciprocate the favour.

Later she would refer to him as 'a friend from Sydney' with whom she had a relationship. But when pressed about the sexual side she refused to 'classify it as an affair or a relationship'.

However, 'Steph' must have meant something to her because as their email correspondence progressed, she raised the possibility of meeting up with him again in Berlin when they returned to Europe.

Peter never knew his girlfriend was cheating on him. Mutual friend Tim Ford, who often slept on Nick's downstairs couch and was aware of Joanne's infidelity, said it was never an issue.

All the time he was friends with Peter and Joanne he never saw anything amiss between them. 'They were wonderful together — the perfect couple,' he always insisted.

And he knew that Joanne was hoping Peter would pop the question some time during the final leg of their journey home through the South Pacific.

CHAPTER 7

....

SYDNEY TO ALICE

The couple had been in Sydney for precisely five months, a comparatively short period but long enough for them to establish a wide social circle. They almost felt like locals now and were sad to leave, especially Joanne who was a keen and popular member of the staff at Dymocks bookshop.

Indeed, such was her popularity that the rest of the retail team presented her with a gold necklace with an image of Australia on a pendant to wear around her neck as a going-away gift. Joanne was touched ('they are all very kind,' she later told her family) and vowed to keep in contact with them all. Maybe she would even drop by to see them again on her return to Sydney before flying back to Britain.

On Monday, 25 June 2001, Peter and Joanne piled the last of their luggage into the Kombi, filled up the petrol tank and began the long, slow drive out of Sydney. Up the busy Parramatta Road, through the city's sprawling western suburbs, past Liverpool and on to the freeway heading southwest to Canberra. They'd not motored this far out of Sydney before and the wide open spaces made a refreshing change from the heavily built-up urban areas of Bondi, Manly and the city centre where they had spent most of the past five months. Soon they were in the Southern Highlands, a gently undulating rural area where small country communities such as Bowral and Mittagong might have reminded them of the little towns and villages they had left behind back home in Yorkshire.

A few kilometres on from Berrima they might have noticed a sign pointing to the Belanglo State Forest on their right, the scene of another horrific crime that had Australia in its thrall for much of the 1990s. It was here that serial killer Ivan Milat brutally murdered seven young hitch-hikers after picking them up on the Hume Highway.

Like Joanne and Peter they were backpacking south to the state of Victoria, though unlike the British couple they did not have their own transport and relied on the generosity of passing truckies and motorists to give them a lift. This turned out to be their undoing, as they were lulled into a false sense of security by Milat's perceived Aussie charm, only to fall victim to his violent intent as he set about their cold-blooded murder in a peaceful Belanglo glade.

This was the other side of Australia, a society whose warm and welcoming exterior concealed an evil and malevolent underbelly, a nation with its fair share of rednecks and crazies for whom innocent young travellers were easy prey.

Joanne and Peter had probably heard all the stories of the murders, the muggings and the backpackers who went missing in this vast continent, but like most tourists believed it could never happen to them.

Captivated by the landscape and the wide, open sky, they had their mind on other matters, including skiing in the Snowy Mountains on the New South Wales–Victoria border.

The first snowfalls of winter had already given a white coating to the ski trails and both were keen to try out the slopes. Skiing is not a sport normally associated with Australia, but when the weather allows, resorts like Thredbo and Perisher Blue are transformed overnight into an alpine paradise with all the apres-ski you can handle.

After a few days in the Snowies Peter and Joanne drove on to Melbourne and the start of the Great Ocean Road, a winding two-lane highway which hugs the Victorian coastline and offers some of Australia's most staggering vistas, including the Twelve Apostles, stack-like formations carved out of the cliff and shaped by centuries of wind and rain from the Southern Ocean.

Mostly they would camp by the side of the road or in one of the many tourist camp sites which are dotted along the far south coast of Australia. There was never any shortage of places to stay, and as they made their way closer to Adelaide Joanne and Peter were growing accustomed to their nomadic lifestyle. They were free to do what they wanted when they wanted and there was nobody to order them around.

In Adelaide, the so-called city of churches, they checked into a camp site and plotted the next stage of their route. Joanne sent an email to her mum, step-dad and teenage brother Sam, as well as the family dog Jess, to tell them where they were.

'We are currently in Adelaide but head up to Alice Springs tomorrow — hopefully it will get warmer from there on,' she wrote. 'We are travelling around in the camper van which gets a bit cramped at times and it involves a lot of driving, but we are getting to see a lot of Australia.'

From Adelaide the road ran north to Port Pirie, Port Augusta, and Woomera, site of a former British rocket testing range and recently more infamous for a government detention centre which housed illegal migrants and asylum seekers.

The landscape was beginning to change, as well. After the lush, green south, this part of Australia was more arid, almost like a moonscape in some parts. Joanne mentioned it in one of her postcards home, telling her family that it was the place they filmed *Mad Max*.

At Coober Pedy, an old opal mining town, it often got so hot that locals were forced to live underground. Tourists could even stay in a subterranean motel. Such sights were so foreign to them that it seemed this part of Australia was another world, and the further they drove the more aware they became of the alien environment.

They were several hundred kilometres up the Stuart Highway now, a long, straight monotonous thoroughfare with only road trains and the occasional tourist to jolt them out of the hypnotic effect the route was having on them. Through Marla, Kulgera and then west at the hamlet of Eridunda along the Lasseter Highway to Yulara, the gateway to Uluru.

Regarded as one of Australia's most spectacular natural monuments, Uluru stands 348 metres high and is considered a sacred site by Aborigines. Tens of thousands of tourists climb the massive rock each year though its indigenous custodians discourage visitors from scaling it because, according to Aboriginal folklore, it is criss-crossed by spiritual pathways which should not be traversed.

It is not known whether Peter or Joanne either climbed Uluru or took a stone from the site as a souvenir of their visit, but they would almost certainly have been aware of the superstition that those who did often suffered bad luck.

Over the decades thousands of small rocks and soil samples innocently removed as mementos have subsequently been posted back by foreign holiday-makers who have reported personal misfortune after taking little bits of Uluru home with them.

After spending a day or two in the area, the couple moved on to another well-known local attraction, Kings Canyon, in nearby Watarrka National Park. Surrounded by ancient sandstone walls which soar as high as 100 metres to a plateau of rocky domes, the canyon is a sanctuary for plants and wildlife.

They also met up with some other travellers, a Canadian couple who accepted a lift with them. 'They were hitch-hiking on the side of the road and we spent several days with them,' Joanne recalled.

They got on well together as they ambled back to the Stuart Highway and on to Alice Springs.

Mark, one of the Canadians, helped to repair a steering problem on the Kombi. He found some cable ties in the back of the van and used them to fix the steering rod. The vehicle was beginning to show its age and the heavy mileage over the past month had only added to the wear and tear.

They reached Alice on 11 July and decided to use the next few days to get the VW looked at and attend to some housekeeping. Peter called in to a local accountancy firm to finalise his tax return. He was hoping to get a rebate so was disappointed to learn that he owed the tax man money.

Around this time Joanne decided to book a return flight from Brisbane to Sydney, after Peter had told her he wanted to spend a week in Papua New Guinea, once they completed the Queensland sector of their jaunt.

The plan was to meet up again in Brisbane, from where they would fly out of Australia and return home via New Zealand, Fiji and the US. But that was still a long way off and the more immediate challenge was to get their means of transport roadworthy.

VW specialist Rod Smith, who had his own workshop in Alice Springs then, remembers the couple bringing the Kombi in for repairs. He wasn't too optimistic about them reaching Darwin in the vehicle's current state but they declined a full service.

Rod advised them the van would backfire a lot but they decided to press on regardless the next day.

It was their last night in Alice Springs so they decided to go out and enjoy themselves. Friday evening in the beer garden at Melanka Lodge backpackers was regarded locally as the social highlight of the week and the bar was teeming with young travellers.

Reports that Joanne and Peter had a lovers' tiff there were later denied, but several eye witnesses claim to have seen the pair having a blazing row during the evening. Perhaps it was another couple. Joanne insisted they were getting on fine.

Come the next morning, any strain in their relationship had been put aside as they made their way to the Alice Springs Camel Cup race day. It was bright and sunny, perfect weather for such an outdoor event which attracts thousands of spectators.

Along with the ticket, Joanne and Peter were given adhesive stickers to wear on their T-shirts. The slogan read 'Try hugs, not drugs'.

Mindful of the easy availability of narcotics at big public events, police and welfare agencies were keen to dissuade young people from buying or using drugs. It's a big problem in rural Australia where the absence of more socially-acceptable entertainment only adds to the monotony of life in the outback, where pot is the mind-altering substance of choice, closely followed by petrol-sniffing.

Hard drinking is also popular, but being legal, alcohol does not offer the same scope for making an illicit fortune from its sale and supply.

In the world of drug peddling, events like the Camel Cup provide a perfect opportunity for pushers to go about their business. They know there will be plenty of potential customers within a relatively small area and a high cash return for the supplier.

Bradley John Murdoch was probably aware of the financial potential but he rarely stopped during the long drive home to Broome, except to buy fuel and refreshments. With so many people in Alice for the races he could have done a bit of selling in pubs and bars around town.

Australia's red centre was an important staging post in his outback drug-run from South Australia, where the cannabis was grown, to Broome. It was a pretty good business too, turning over about a million Australian dollars a year.

It was not known for certain whether he attended the 2001 Camel Cup, but it would have been tempting for a man with a bundle of cash. He could have wagered several hundred dollars or more before heading home via the Buchanan and Duncan Highways, a long dirt road which starts just south of Daly Waters and cuts across the desert to Halls Creek, before joining the Great Northern Highway which connects to Fitzroy Crossing and eventually Broome.

Sometimes he'd go via the Tanami Track, which begins just north of Alice Springs, but either way it was a hard ride, about 1800 kilometres in all. Murdoch had travelled them all many times before and knew every inch of the way.

It would not be known until the trial itself that Murdoch did not attend the Camel Cup that year.

CHAPTER 8

....

DID HE DO IT?

By the time Big Brad, as he was known, got back to Broome in the early hours of 16 July 2001, the search for Peter Falconio was well underway. He'd driven non-stop from Broome, fuelled not only by a spare tank of petrol in the back of his white Landcruiser HJ75 ute, but also a ready supply of cannabis and speed.

Murdoch had become partial to both in recent years, smoking up to 10 joints a day and snorting amphetamines to keep him awake. The speed stimulated his brain and nervous system, making him feel alert and confident, but also agitated and aggressive. It was a potentially lethal mix, but he needed to get home quickly and the drugs seemed to make the journey easier. They improved his concentration as he bounced and bumped his way across that gruelling outback terrain.

Big Brad had spent much of his working life traversing the desert roads of Western Australia and the Northern Territory. Once he'd driven cattle trains and on other occasions trucks full of explosives to the Argyle diamond fields. Employers trusted him because he never let them down, completing marathon round trips on time and with the minimum of fuss.

Sometimes he would swap life on the road for a job that would allow him to stay in one place. Though not a qualified mechanic, he knew a lot about engines and was a handy man to have around on farms or in vehicle repair shops.

That's how he met up with Brett Duffy, who ran West Kimberley Diesel in Broome. He had worked on and off for him since 1998 and occasionally lived in a caravan out the back of the workshop. It was a convenient arrangement having someone living on site, as it provided added security.

Murdoch also benefited. There was a toilet and washing facilities and Big Brad was meticulous about the way he kept himself.

'You'd walk into the toilet before work and Brad would always be there with a pair of clippers, trimming his moustache or beard,' Brett Duffy told the court.

And the same applied to his ute which he was always cleaning and improving.

'Basically Bradley's vehicle was his home and he had everything in it that he required,' Brett added.

The two men got on well and sometimes went fishing together. Murdoch had few close mates and valued Brett's friendship.

Over the next three years Brett learnt not to question Murdoch's frequent disappearances for weeks at a time but became suspicious when he saw how much cash he had on him. Murdoch, who was a casual employee, always had wads of money in his fat wallet.

Brett suspected more but didn't think it was his business to poke his nose into other people's affairs. Broome is one of Australia's last frontier towns, where men who have a past go to disappear and where locals know better than to question each other's activities.

Deluged by the monsoon rains for nearly half the year and a popular tourist town for the rest, Broome, like the climate, has two faces. Firstly there is the legitimate business provided by tourists and the pearling industry and secondly the darker side which few will openly discuss.

The criminal undercurrent, not easily discernible, hides itself in smoky bars and pokey back streets where men do deals with a stubby holder in one hand and a roll-up in the other, while their weary womenfolk with their Winfields and cheap cask wine look on disapprovingly.

It was in this world that Bradley John Murdoch felt at home, a town where people didn't pry and instinctively recognised those who were best left well alone, like Big Brad.

You didn't mess with Murdoch, who was known to carry a gun in a dark leather holster concealed under his shirt near his chest. And he had to know you well before he accepted you into his company.

James Hepi, a 35-year-old Maori, shared a duplex with Murdoch in Forrest Street, Broome, and became a close business associate. The two men ran a thriving drugs trade, buying and packing cannabis from Hepi's property near Sedan in South Australia and selling it throughout the Northern Territory and northwestern Australia.

The pair made regular trips between Broome and Adelaide and Murdoch modified his vehicle to ensure his illicit cargo remained hidden in its cache should he be stopped by the police.

It was also important to protect himself from others of criminal intent, fellow drug peddlers who might see him as a threat to their own territory, or users who might be tempted to rob him of his valuable consignment.

That's why he always carried a firearm, sometimes a .357 Magnum or maybe a smaller .22 revolver if he didn't want to draw attention to the weapon under his shirt. He possessed a modest arsenal of guns which gave him a feeling of power and which he would show off proudly to his inner circle of mates back home in Forrest Street.

Despite the fact that firearms had got him into trouble in the past, he enjoyed the authority they gave him and the respect and fear they commanded from others.

Murdoch had not killed anyone so far but he came close to it one day at Fitzroy Crossing, more than 200 kilometres east of Broome on the Northern Highway to Halls Creek. A crowd of boisterous Aborigines had been celebrating the result of a football grand final on 20 August 1995 and had blocked the road bridge across the Fitzroy River.

Murdoch, who was pretty inebriated himself, was furious, especially when they subjected him to hoots of derision. He had always had a problem with Aborigines, ever since he was beaten up by a group of Aboriginal kids in Northampton, WA, where he grew up.

In spite of his build — he weighed more than 102 kilograms (16 stone) and stood 196 centimetres (6 feet

5 inches) tall — Murdoch was no match for so many but vowed to return later and give them a lesson they would not forget.

Shaking with anger, he drove to Brooking Springs cattle station where he had been working and helped himself to a .308 bolt action rifle and a .22 Magnum. He then retraced his path to Fitzroy Crossing, where the locals were still partying, and fired indiscriminately at their cars. Miraculously nobody was hit, apart from a woman who suffered a minor injury from a piece of flying metal.

Murdoch's style of retribution, while earning him a grudging respect from some, could not go unpunished. Even in an area where lack of police resources meant that the law was not always imposed as it should have been, the authorities could not turn a blind eye to his action.

The police launched a search for him and next day he surrendered, pleading guilty to the shooting charge as well as the theft of two firearms. His racism and hot temper had finally got the better of him, earning him a prison sentence of 21 months.

Bradley John Murdoch, who was born on 6 October 1958, had always been a loner. Ever since his childhood in Northampton, just north of Geraldton on the West Australian coast, he was happy to keep his own company. His two brothers were more than a decade older so they had little in common, and he had few schoolfriends apart from Phil Cragan and his brother Colin, who attended Northampton Primary with him.

Later the youngsters found themselves together again when both families moved to Perth. Murdoch was 13 but left school as soon as he could. Already he showed signs of a defiant streak which got him into trouble with the police on a couple of occasions.

His parents, Nqance and Colin Murdoch, a warm and respectable couple who both worked hard — she was a hairdresser and he a mechanic — were obviously worried about their son and were heartened by his decision to settle down and get married in the early '80s.

Murdoch was only 21 but although his wife bore him a son, the relationship broke down after several years and he had little contact with them afterwards.

He decided to head north and, like so many men whose marriages fall apart, began a semi-nomadic lifestyle which took him wherever the work was. Picking up driving or mechanical jobs, he roamed from Geraldton to Broome to Derby and inland to the outback cattle stations which always wanted casual labour.

Once he tried to set up a truck repair business at Halls Creek on the Great Northern Highway, but his hopes were dashed when Aborigines placed a land claim on the site. The rejection of his plans unleashed further resentment towards local indigenous people whom he had little time for. Murdoch's inherent dislike of blacks grew into unmitigated racism and reinforced the hostility he felt towards authority in general.

When he moved to Broome in the mid '90s he tried to put the past behind him. He liked the place because there were other men like him to drink with and people left you alone if you didn't want to talk.

Some, intimidated by his appearance, instinctively gave him a wide berth. His heavily tattooed arms left no doubt about his racist leanings. On his left arm was a picture of an Aborigine hanging by his head from a tree with his legs engulfed in fire. And on the right there was a Ku Klux Klan figure pointing at the Aborigine to his left. Skulls and a black clown's head like a joker also featured in the tattoos, which started at his wrists and spread to the top of his shoulders.

Murdoch's piercing stare and toothless sneer only added to his aggressive pose.

Yet, according to the few who got to know him well, the frightening countenance was in sharp contrast to the loving, caring qualities that sometimes showed themselves.

Brett Duffy's wife Rosa, who saw Murdoch most days when he worked at West Kimberley Diesel, said he always took time out to speak to children, including her own little boy.

'He liked to talk to them about their books and toys and especially enjoyed playing with them on their PlayStation,' she added.

'He's a really intelligent guy with very nice handwriting. And his grammar is good too. He also loves reading, especially westerns and similar paperbacks.'

When not at work, Murdoch was usually to be found sucking hard on a cold stubby. He began his shift early so that he could knock off by 3 p.m. to escape the mid-afternoon heat which cloaked Broome in a blanket of high humidity and made hard physical labour almost impossible.

His watering hole of choice was the Famous Beer and Satay Hut in Walcott Street, a couple of roads away from his home. Not so much a pub, more an open-air bar where a cooling breeze would waft across the counter, the Satay Hut offered pleasant surroundings and the company of like-minded blokes who enjoyed their beer, their ciggies and the occasional illicit substance.

Dave Gibson, one of the regulars, remembered passing the time of day with Big Brad at the bar, only for him to disappear for weeks on end. 'He'd tell me he was going barra fishing and would be away for a while to lay his nets. But I now realise this was merely an excuse for his trips to South Australia,' Gibson told me.

When he became bored with the Satay Hut Murdoch would call in at the Roebuck Bay Hotel Sports Bar, Broome's busiest pub and a drinking den favoured by both locals and backpackers.

He would always sit at the top corner of the bar closest to the western-style swing doors, where he could keep one eye out for anyone who might require his 'services' and the other on the scantily clad girls behind the bar.

The Roebuck's main attraction is its barmaids who wear skimpy bikinis as they go about their business. There is no pretence at political correctness here. Drinkers ogle and guzzle in equal measure.

Occasionally a roar goes up as a punter celebrates a winning horse on the Sky Racing television screen. 'You beauty!' goes the cry while the losers scatter their TAB tickets on the floor and go back to trying to catch the barmaid's attention long enough to order another beer.

This is serious drinking territory, where the tables are draped in black plastic to catch the spillage and the only acknowledgement of food is to be found in the automatic snack dispenser at the back of the Roebuck's cavernous interior.

Murdoch preferred the Satay Hut but there was no doubt that there was a lot more action at the Roebuck. He could park his Landcruiser alongside all the other utes outside and could stay relatively anonymous in the crowd.

Life was starting to look good for Big Brad, who had plenty of money in his pocket and no shortage of lady friends to keep him company. Despite his appearance he could still attract the women and what's more they liked him.

Rosa Duffy, who knew quite a few of his girlfriends, insists that while Murdoch was no angel he was always a gentleman when it came to the fair sex.

And Julie Anne McPhail had personal experience of his respect for women. Hadn't she crossed the Nullarbor with him in June 2001? And hadn't they camped only a few yards apart and he hadn't laid a finger on her?

'He was a complete gentleman,' she said in court.

Even though they were both pumped up with drink and drugs as they made their way in separate cars from Perth to Adelaide, Murdoch never made a pass.

'I was a heavy drinker in those days and was able to hold quite a bit, and because I was also on speed I had a heightened alertness, so I remember everything that happened,' she explained.

Julie had recognised Murdoch from her days in Broome when she worked behind the bar at the Coffin Cheaters clubhouse, which was run by a group of local bikies. Now their paths had crossed again on the long drive east and they were both happy to complete the journey in convoy. At night she would follow his ute, which had stronger headlights than her own car, and he would sleep nearby when they chose to rest.

When they crossed over the border to South Australia they camped at the Head of the Bight near the Nullarbor Roadhouse.

'I needed a sleep so I took my swag out of the car, placed it on a rock and lay down. Brad placed his ute a little further away to give me shelter from the wind and slept in the back.'

Next morning Murdoch offered her a coffee and they continued their journey, stopping every few hours for a drink and another line of speed.

Julie was happy to have him around. And he provided an added degree of protection because he had a gun. They talked about his love of firearms and she revealed how she had always hankered after a small ladies' revolver with a mother-of-pearl handle.

Murdoch couldn't offer her precisely what she wanted but he did just happen to have a small, silver-barrelled revolver on him and he was happy to sell it.

'He offered me a shot but I declined — I didn't feel comfortable — so he fired a round off into the bush himself.'

Julie decided the revolver wasn't quite her style and the two continued their journey, eventually parting company in Port Augusta as she turned right to Adelaide and he headed for Swan Reach to meet Hepi on his property near the banks of the Murray River.

But before they left each other she had a word of advice: 'When you go back home to Broome you must stop at the Barrow Creek pub on the way because it's so unusual. I know the landlord, Les Pilton. It's known as the Pilton Hilton.'

He thanked her for the tip and drove off.

Hepi had moved to South Australia on a more permanent basis and was pleased to accommodate his business partner prior to his return journey north. There was a workshop at the back of the house and Murdoch liked to tinker there.

Once Hepi interrupted him while he was messing around with three black plastic zip ties and a roll of '100-mile-an-hour' duct tape. He had wrapped the tape around the ties to make a pair of handcuffs.

'I asked him what he was doing,' Hepi told the pre-trial hearing. 'And he put the shit in the bin.'

The month was June 2001.

CHAPTER 9

....

BURIED IN A SPOON DRAIN?

Even in winter the desert tracks cannot be guaranteed and the middle of 2001 had been particularly wet, making it a slow, arduous journey for the most experienced of drivers with the biggest vehicles.

Murdoch certainly had the skill and his Landcruiser, with its big wheels and deep tracked tyres, had often got him out of trouble. In the outback, where there may be no help for hundreds of kilometres, you needed transport that would not let you down and supreme confidence in your own ability. You had to look after yourself and be resourceful in the desert. And when problems arose you needed the means to solve them.

Apart from a spare tank of fuel, Murdoch also carried plentiful supplies of water and digging equipment should his vehicle get stuck. Except for his dog, Jack, a bull terrier-Dalmatian cross, he mostly travelled by himself, though sometimes he took a close mate along, among them Brian Johnston who had shared the duplex in Forrest Street.

Slightly built with short, dark hair and an earring, Johnston was known as the Sheriff in Broome, not because of the authority he wielded but because of his liking for old American westerns. On one occasion he returned from Disneyland in the United States with a couple of fake sheriff's badges and a cowboy-style waistcoat which he wore around town.

Johnston, who was unemployed and didn't pose a threat to Murdoch, accompanied him on at least three occasions on the long journey south and back again.

Once he helped Big Brad buy another Landcruiser, which he purchased from a man named Jason Reynolds in Adelaide in March 2001. Murdoch already had two other vehicles, an old HJ47 series Landcruiser and an F100, but he fancied another.

It was a 1993 model, a former Telstra ute with a white tray top and Desert Dueler tyres. It also had a 45-centimetre-high rim around the tray, which was about a metre wide.

There were poles behind the driver's cabin and a long window at the back of the front seats.

While it was feasible for an adult to lie widthways across the rear tray, Jason made it clear in court that it would have been impossible for a human being to climb from the driver's cab directly into the back of the truck.

Not that he discussed such requirements with Murdoch at the time. The new buyer wasn't even worried about a gearbox whine, explaining to Jason that he planned to place a larger diesel motor in it anyway.

The price was $16,500 but they settled on $16,000 which the purchaser paid in cash.

Brian Johnston remembers thinking that his mate had got a good deal.

'The vehicle was in pretty good nick. It had a canvas covering, a bull bar and big white spoked wheels with chunky tyres,' he told the committal proceedings.

The F100 was left behind in South Australia when the pair made the return journey north in the newly-acquired HJ75.

After three such trips, Brian got used to travelling in close company with Murdoch and the eating habits he adopted on the way. There was always iced coffee and chocolate mint flavoured milk on board, partly for his delicate stomach.

'Brad suffered from indigestion and the flavoured milk seemed to settle him down.'

Sometimes they'd stop and have a barbecue. Murdoch liked his modern conveniences and creature comforts, packing the ute with camping furniture and lots of cooking utensils.

'He had a double-burner primus stove as well as a table and chairs, which he'd place by the side of the road.'

He also carried a fridge, an Esky, 20 litres of water and plenty of non-perishable food. Everything was packed into plastic tubs or tanks, which were themselves stored neatly in the rear tray so they would form a flat surface on top. He liked to roll his swag out on them when he slept.

If he passed a roadhouse he'd splash out on a steak or toasted sandwiches. There was never any shortage of money. Murdoch invariably carried several thousand dollars on him.

And to complete the picture of domestic bliss, Jack would sit obediently in the back of the ute while his master munched away.

'He was a pretty friendly dog,' said Brian. 'Not noisy, but fairly smart. Brad told me he was a Dalmatian-blue heeler cross with blue spots — not black or brown.' A description slightly at odds with earlier accounts of the breed.

'Occasionally Jack would want to get out and if there was a park or open space he'd be let out for a run. But it always had to be somewhere away from the road so the dog was safe,' he continued.

Although Murdoch loved Jack, he demanded absolute obedience in return. And on the rare occasions that the dog did something to upset his master, retribution would be swift.

Sometimes he would beat the animal with a broom or a torch, raining so many blows on the dog that he would cower in terror. No wonder Jack usually did as he was told. When he sat in the front seat of the truck he stayed there. Even when there were others around he refused to be distracted, fearing the wrath of his master should he move.

Jack was trained to do as he was ordered, a habit that may explain why he virtually ignored Joanne when she was thrown into the cab of the gunman's utility.

On the desert roads Murdoch and his vehicle would have raised few suspicions. Dressed in Stubbies, a flannelette shirt and double-plugger thongs, he looked like thousands of other outback travellers in their mud-spattered four-wheel drives.

That's what he intended. To go about his business unhindered and unnoticed.

It was also why he placed a peaked cap on his head whenever he entered a truck stop to pay for fuel or snacks.

'He didn't like to be recognised,' recalled Brian.

Nor did he like his movements monitored. Murdoch feared he could be tracked by his mobile phone calls and would carry several different SIM cards to throw people off his trail. Fellow travellers like Brian would be used to buy these cards for his phone, so he could avoid making calls in his own name. Under Australian law SIM cards can only be purchased on the production of some form of ID.

Such was his paranoia over being caught for the drugs he was carrying that Murdoch went to extraordinary lengths to avoid detection. Deals were done in utmost secrecy and only with those who could be trusted.

Dealing and peddling in the quantities of cannabis he was carrying was a serious criminal offence and he had no intention of being found out. After being sentenced to 21 months' imprisonment a few years earlier after the Fitzroy Crossing incident, Murdoch had no desire to be banged up for a lot longer.

That was one of the reasons he carried a gun, to help him out of trouble. His weapon of choice on the outback routes was a .38 revolver which was small enough to conceal in a hidden cavity in the long-range fuel tank at the back. If he thought he'd need to access it quickly, he'd place the firearm in a calico bag behind a panel on the inside of the driver's side door.

But Big Brad Murdoch didn't look for trouble. His aim was to get each journey over as quickly as possible so he could return to the relative anonymity of Broome and his then lover, Beverley Anne Allan.

Why would he do something stupid which might draw attention to him or his vehicle? No point in getting stopped by the police for a minor traffic offence, he reasoned.

Even in the outback where you could remain relatively obscure, security surveillance cameras could not be ignored. Every service station had one, especially in larger towns like Alice Springs, and he didn't want to be caught on camera for something he did or didn't do. That's why the cap was useful and a pair of glasses as well. You never knew what the cops would fit you up with if they wanted to, he reckoned.

Can't trust anybody, he thought, least of all the bastards in blue.

By the time Murdoch got back to Broome on 16 July after his trip to Alice Springs, he was 'very strung out', according to Beverley, a 42-year-old single mother who had been going out with him for the previous nine months.

He told her it 'hadn't been a really good trip' and he'd had a 'few dramas'.

Someone had been following him all the way and he had to find out who it was and 'deal with it', she explained to the court.

There had been police roadblocks set up to find the attacker of a missing backpacker and he'd been forced to go the long way home.

Their relationship, which was under strain, had always been a 'one-way' affair, with Murdoch only ever seeing her on his terms. His latest behaviour didn't bode well for the future.

On the surface Murdoch tried to act normally. On the Monday morning he dropped by to see Brett Duffy at West Kimberley Diesel, to pick up a set of Caterpillar batteries which he had ordered on the previous Thursday over the telephone.

Rosa Duffy assumed he had been in Broome since then, because nobody usually kept that brand in stock locally and they had to be specially ordered in. If he had been on one of his frequent trips away she thought he would have purchased the Caterpillar batteries elsewhere.

He also appeared relaxed enough when he arrived that Monday morning. There was nothing to suggest he had been involved in any kind of weekend drama, but in other parts of Broome people were beginning to gossip.

The word around town was that the artist's impression in the news of the bloke who'd attacked the young British couple at Barrow Creek looked awfully like Brad Murdoch. And the sketch of the attacker's vehicle seemed similar to Murdoch's ute as well.

Big Brad decided to lie low for a week while he began to alter the look of his ute. He told Hepi, 'It wasn't me,' even before the New Zealander could ask him about the Barrow Creek incident, but Hepi was unnerved when Murdoch himself later raised the question of dead bodies: Out of the blue he discussed the best way of getting rid of human remains.

'Bury them in a spoon drain by the side of the road,' he volunteered. 'And cover them with dirt. The soil's a lot softer there.'

Spoon drains are man-made run-offs designed to carry flood water off the road during heavy rain. They are a familiar feature of outback highways, especially north of Alice Springs.

Why was Murdoch talking about bodies and how to dispose of them? Was it his warped mind or was there a more sinister explanation?

Hepi pursued the matter no further. 'I didn't think I needed to kill anyone to carry on what I was doing,' he told the pre-trial hearing.

CHAPTER 10

....

IS JOANNE A SUSPECT?

I remember the first fax. It was sent by Northern Territory police at 7.45 a.m. on that Sunday morning, 15 July 2001. Headlined 'WARNING TO TERRITORY DRIVERS', it advised motorists not to use the Stuart Highway after an incident at Barrow Creek the night before. A woman and her boyfriend had been pulled over by another driver who was 'armed and dangerous'. She had escaped but there were grave fears for her missing companion.

'Police believe the driver, described as a Caucasian male with a moustache, also had a dog with him,' the news release added, warning that he should not be approached and recommending road users delay their travel until the incident had been resolved.

Three hours later a second fax arrived, providing further graphic detail of the attack and the man responsible.

'During the incident an English tourist was taken at gunpoint and tied up.'

The alleged offender had dark, straight, shoulder-length hair with grey streaks, a droopy moustache with corners tapering down below the mouth, heavy bags under his eyes and a deep Australian accent, it revealed.

Though the full details were yet to emerge, this had all the makings of a major crime story. Within 24 hours newspapers, radio and television stations across Australia and around the world were reporting what became dubbed 'The Outback Ambush', and media organisations were despatching their correspondents to Alice Springs on the first available flight.

Seats for a direct service were at a premium. It was the end of the school holidays and most planes were fully booked. In my case the only way to get there was an early Monday morning service from Sydney to Brisbane, a connecting flight to Darwin and then a southbound plane to Alice, a total journey time of nearly 12 hours.

The level of interest in the plight of Joanne Lees and Peter Falconio was immense. Here was a 27-year-old female backpacker confronted by every woman's worst fear. Threatened by a man with a gun, she was tied up and forced to hide for several terrifying hours at night in the middle of nowhere, not knowing whether her assailant wanted to rape or murder her.

And all this after her boyfriend had apparently been shot dead and his body dumped elsewhere.

There could be few more horrifying scenarios. And yet amazingly the plucky young woman had somehow fled her captor and survived to tell the tale. All the dramatic elements were there. First the surprise attack, then the brutal murder, followed by the fear she felt while being hunted by a madman and finally her amazing escape and eventual rescue.

Such stories wrote themselves. The plot was so extraordinary you couldn't make it up and for the first few days no one dared to question the veracity of Joanne's account.

It seemed churlish in the extreme to doubt what this poor young woman had gone through, and press and public alike rallied to her support. There was a groundswell of sympathy. Even Prime Minister John Howard offered words of comfort.

Yet 19,000 kilometres away alarm bells were beginning to ring. Newspaper editors and TV producers sensed they might have been through a similar situation before. There were vague recollections of a crime committed in Britain a few years earlier when a young woman named Tracey Andrews claimed her fiance had been killed in a road rage incident.

In fact she herself had stabbed him more than 30 times in the face, neck and back after a row near their home in Worcester.

No one had suspected the 29-year-old woman's involvement at the time, but later she was arrested and subsequently found guilty of his murder and sentenced to life imprisonment.

Not that anybody had officially raised the possibility that Joanne Lees might have been responsible for the death of Peter Falconio, but reporters needed to know whether police regarded her as a suspect. This was a delicate area and one which would almost certainly attract criticism when raised.

But wasn't it a fact that most murders were carried out by a close relative or friend of the deceased? And wasn't there something odd about Joanne Lees' reluctance to speak openly about her ordeal? Normally victims of crime do not have to be persuaded to talk in front of the television cameras if they think it will help police to catch the criminal; but not this time.

Joanne was apparently too traumatised to face the media and it would be another 10 days before she agreed to make a statement in person.

It wasn't the only issue that raised suspicions. Soon other questions were being raised about the crime.

How did she manage to get her bound wrists from behind her back to the front of her body?

How was it possible she remained undetected in the bush when her attacker, reportedly holding a torch and accompanied by his dog, came within a few feet of her?

And how come there was no sign of the gunman's footprints in the undergrowth?

Then there was the blood spill on the road, just half a litre and apparently no sign of spatter. Wasn't it a rather small amount to have come from a fatal wound?

And most mysterious of all, how did she manage to climb from the cab of the attacker's ute into the rear tray while she was tied up? Not many vehicles similar to the one she described had access from the cab to the back tray, and even if this one did, it would have been hard to manoeuvre herself from the front seat with her arms behind her back and her legs wrapped in tape.

Such questions began to dominate private conversations in the rapidly growing media camp that had set up base in Alice Springs. Sooner or later they would have to be asked and answers sought.

Finally the moment came during one of the daily press conferences held at police headquarters.

'Is Joanne Lees a suspect?' a reporter enquired bluntly.

'No,' Commander Max Pope replied.

Did she have her passport and was she free to go?

'Yes,' he confirmed.

'Are there any gaps in her story?'

'No.'

It was to become a familiar police response in the days and weeks ahead with detectives insisting there was no reason to disbelieve Joanne. At least that was the official line.

Until then I had also accepted Joanne's version, but an unexpected call from a police source started me wondering. The contact revealed that a scientifically based examination of her statement had found problems. It didn't mean she was lying, but the way she answered questions suggested she might not be revealing the whole story.

I was intrigued and, although I had no access to the statement itself, decided to investigate the technique being used. It is called Scientific Content Analysis and involves a set procedure for the minute examination of speech patterns. Although SCAN, as it is known, has its critics it is widely used by police forces and investigation agencies around the world to establish whether witnesses or suspects are lying.

What particularly aroused my interest was not so much the fact that SCAN had raised doubts about the truth of Joanne Lees' statement, but that the police were apparently sufficiently uncertain about the accuracy of her story in the first place to employ the services of specialists to analyse what she said.

This contradicted the public line they were peddling and cast a new light on the way they were dealing with the investigation. Or was it some kind of double bluff? Could their outward support for Joanne be designed to lull her into a false sense of security? Were they secretly waiting for her to make a mistake?

SCAN was devised by Avinoam Sapir, a former Israeli police lieutenant who teaches the technique to police, customs officials, military personnel and even bank investigators in Europe, the United States, South Africa and Australia.

It purports to be able to establish whether the subject is being truthful, what information he or she is concealing and whether or not the person being questioned was involved in the crime.

It does not cover body language or eye movement, but concentrates on speech patterns which might offer tell-tale signs of deception.

For instance a truthful person will include other apparently inconsequential detail when explaining what happened, while someone who is being deceptive may hold back or alter important information. This often leads to gaps in the story, inconsistencies or perceived contradictions.

In other words a truthful statement will often include irrelevant detail while a deceptive statement will usually contain the bare bones and may avoid addressing the central issue.

Those who try to divert the narrative away from the actual crime to those events surrounding it often have something to hide, according to the SCAN philosophy. The technique is not infallible. There can be other explanations including speech problems caused by a previous mental condition, but generally Scientific Content Analysis identifies areas of evidence which might benefit from further examination.

We do not know the extent to which Joanne's statement aroused such suspicions among Northern Territory detectives, but she was certainly reluctant to speak in detail about the attack in public.

In one of the few media interviews she gave afterwards, she talked to Mark Wilton of the *Centralian Advocate*, Alice Springs' local newspaper.

Mark's advantage was that he knew Les Pilton's partner, Helen Jones, who used to work in the paper's advertising department and was now acting as Joanne's flatmate and unofficial minder in the accommodation that Les had kindly offered.

Mark, who was understaffed and had a newspaper to produce that Tuesday afternoon, had been waiting patiently for the young Briton's exclusive account, which Fleet Street and the Australian media were also anxious to hear about. An experienced reporter who knew this could be the scoop of a lifetime, he was keen to extract every spine-tingling detail of her story.

'He needs to be captured because I don't think he would hesitate to do it again,' Joanne told the *Centralian Advocate*. 'Everyone can use their imagination about what it was like for me that night, but I was determined to escape and I feel very lucky to be alive.'

Joanne recounted the events leading up to the incident. 'We stopped and refuelled at Ti Tree and watched the sunset, and after we'd been driving again for some time, a vehicle drove up alongside us and Pete slowed down, at first thinking it was going to overtake.

'But he drove alongside us, his interior light was on and it was a four-wheel drive with a dog. The man pointed to the back of our vehicle and motioned for us to stop. We then stopped and he pulled up behind us. Peter got out of the car and went to the back of our van and the two were talking amicably and I thought everything was okay.

'Peter then came back to me and asked if I would rev the engine, so I moved to the driver's seat and I revved the engine. I revved the engine again and I heard a bang. I thought it was something to do with the fault the man was saying was wrong with the Kombi.

'The next thing I looked out of the window. He then came up to me and opened the door and told me to switch off the engine and pushed me to the passenger side.

'Looking back, whether we stopped or not, I believe that he would have shot our tyres or done something anyway. I honestly can't believe this man would have let me go,' she concluded.

While Joanne clearly hoped that her interview with the *Centralian Advocate* might help to catch the killer, her eagerness to help the police with their search did not extend to agreeing to a full press conference, even though officers were keen to persuade her otherwise. So why was she so unwilling to co-operate with the media as a whole? Was she afraid of the inquisition she would undoubtedly encounter? If so, why?

As each day passed the police investigation team came under increasing pressure to produce their star witness. She had helped an artist to produce a Comfit picture of the man police were hunting and the vehicle he was driving. All that remained was her first-hand description of the attacker and her personal account of what he did.

Why, if she was so desperate for the apparent killer of her boyfriend to be caught, was she not willing to appear in front of the cameras to reinforce the message being circulated by police as the nationwide manhunt continued?

No one had a satisfactory explanation, least of all the police who were dealing with a growing and ever more curious media contingent.

Shown here on his graduation day, Peter gained a Bachelor of Science degree in construction management at Brighton University before he and Joanne hit the tourist trail down under.

Happier days as Peter and Joanne enjoy the holiday of a lifetime travelling around Australia.

The lonely stretch of road on the Stuart Highway where Peter Falconio would lose his life.

The scrub just off the highway where Joanne escaped the gunman and hid for several hours. With her hands bound behind her back, her body grazed and bruised, she feared the dog might find her, but inexplicably the gunman didn't let him loose.

Police inspect Peter and Joanne's Kombi campervan the day after the terrifying attack.

Jasper Haines and Pamela Namangardi Brown remembered driving past an orange Kombi and a white truck with a high body that night. But Jasper also said he saw the vehicle heading north, contradicting Joanne's version of events.

Barrow Creek Hotel proprietor Les Pilton and partner Helen Jones looked after Joanne in the aftermath of the incident. Helen was dismayed when she was later accused by Joanne of 'getting off on someone else's tragedy'.

The blue heeler at the Barrow Creek Hotel that Joanne claimed was similar to the dog owned by her assailant. However, in the pre-trial hearing it became apparent that Murdoch's dog Jack, although it was a mixed breed, looked more like a Dalmatian to the naked eye.

The Barrow Creek Hotel, where truck drivers Vince Millar and Rodney Adams took a distraught Joanne after picking her up on the Stuart Highway on the night of the attack.

Twelve days after Peter's disappearance, an emotional Luciano Falconio, accompanied by son Paul, leaves a media conference in Alice Springs holding a reward poster.

A Comfit picture of the suspected gunman released a few days after Peter's disappearance. The length of the suspect's hair would prove to be a controversial issue.

Video footage of the murder suspect's vehicle, a Toyota Landcruiser, taken at the Shell truck stop in Alice Springs hours after Peter's disappearance.

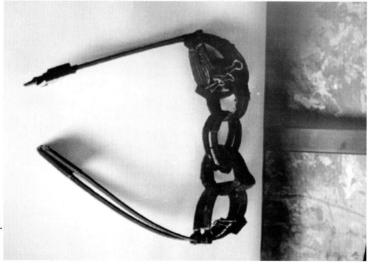

The handcuffs allegedly used by Murdoch to help restrain Joanne. DNA found inside the tape wrapped around the cable ties would prove to be a crucial piece of evidence.

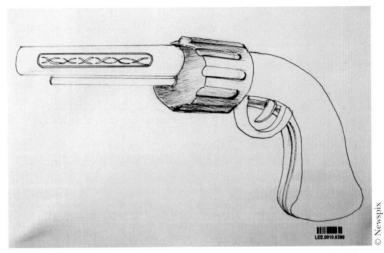

The police sketch of the suspected murder weapon, as described by Joanne. But did the gun's distinctive scrolling bear a similarity to the design on the side of their Kombi?

Peter and Joanne's Kombi, bought at the Kings Cross car market in Sydney for $1200. The distinctive markings are visible on the driver's door.

Commander Bob Fields, an old-fashioned copper who realised the value of the press in an investigation like this, had tried to satisfy the demand for information. The limited amount of detail he was able to give to reporters was imparted in good faith and presumably based on interviews with Joanne. Yet the accuracy of those early accounts was later called into question.

First he said that 'the female tourist heard what she thought was a gunshot'.

Two days later in the interview she gave to the *Centralian Advocate*, she went out of her way to point out that at no stage did she think she'd heard a gunshot.

Commander Fields said the attacker 'was searching for her with his torch and dog — just an incredibly terrifying further aspect to what had already happened', he added.

Yet as the investigation progressed the dog was 'airbrushed' out of Joanne's account of what happened as she hid in the bush. Had Commander Fields been wrongly advised by his witness or had he misinterpreted her early account?

Meanwhile, any hope of finding Peter Falconio alive was rapidly diminishing.

'Obviously we don't want to speculate but I'd have to say, nearly 36 hours after the incident, there's no sign of him and we absolutely fear the worst,' he admitted.

The search for the apparent killer was also difficult.

'I'd hate to use the expression "a needle in a haystack", but that's what we're dealing with at this stage,' he added.

While it was easy to sympathise with the challenge facing Commander Fields and his colleagues, questions were also being raised about whether the Northern Territory police were up to the job.

The first indication of a police stuff-up in the early days of the investigation emerged on 17 July, three days after Falconio's disappearance, when there were reports of a man fitting the description of the attacker being filmed on a surveillance video at a Shell service station in Alice Springs.

In a town like Alice the rumour mill works overtime when something important happens and it does not take long for local gossip to reach the ears of the *Centralian Advocate*.

On this occasion the newspaper had got wind of the security footage being made available to detectives on the day after the attack, so why hadn't it been released for public consumption? If the police were so keen on tracing the driver and his ute, why hadn't it been made available for transmission on the television news?

At a press conference held on the Tuesday after the attack, the *Advocate* confronted Commander Fields about the existence of the video.

'Someone has informed our newspaper there is a tape of this guy you're looking for filling up at the Shell 24 hour,' said a reporter. 'Has the tape been handed to you?'

Perhaps a little taken aback by the question, Commander Fields insisted he had no knowledge of the footage.

Either he genuinely didn't know or he was playing for time. But as was later to become apparent there was a video and its existence would raise further questions about the efficiency of the police investigation.

While detectives were being evasive about the service station security footage, they were clear about one thing — the truth of Joanne's story.

There was no doubting the young woman's evidence.

'I don't want to go into the details of the crime scene but the account she's given us is consistent with what's there and certainly there is a suggestion at the scene that her companion is either injured or, worse still, been murdered,' he conceded.

But where was Joanne? Apparently she was not up to facing the media. She was still suffering from shock and nursing cuts and bruises.

And the police were being more than supportive.

'I praise that woman for what she did,' said Commander Fields.

'How she got out of that situation is totally beyond me. She had no physical injuries of any significance but she was tremendously traumatised by the event.'

It was only natural that Joanne attracted everyone's sympathy. Not only had she survived an appalling experience but her boyfriend was almost certainly dead.

'I don't want to sound callous, but all indications seem to show that something terrible happened to him,' Commander Fields acknowledged.

But why? What was the motive? If it was sexual why had the would-be rapist not pursued his search for Joanne? If it was robbery, why had the couple's valuables not been stolen? Why had they been specifically targeted? Or was it just a random crime that nobody could explain?

Even Commander Fields agreed he had not discovered a motive.

'But I am firmly convinced no action on the part of either of these victims caused this incident,' he emphasised.

On the other side of the world, Joanne Lees' and Peter Falconio's families were not only perplexed but distraught.

At home in Yorkshire, Peter's brother Paul said they were going through hell. 'We are just sitting tight and praying,' he added.

His mother, Joan, told local reporters, 'We're trying to be positive and not think the worst. It's all we can do.'

Paul and Peter's father, Luciano, agreed they should fly to Australia as soon as possible.

Joanne's family was equally devastated by the news. Her mother, Jennifer, said they were hoping for a miracle. Jennifer was not well enough to travel so her husband, Vincent, decided to fly to Australia on her behalf. His travel plans were delayed by the fact that he did not have a current passport, forcing him to drive to Liverpool to get one.

The Falconios were the first to arrive in Alice Springs, followed a day later by Joanne's stepfather.

None of them had given up hope that Peter would be found alive, least of all Luciano. After a 27-hour flight from London via Sydney, he pointed out that he would not have made the journey if he thought his son was dead. 'I would not have come so far if Peter was not alive,' he insisted. 'I'd be staying at home,' he said at a hastily convened news conference shortly after their arrival in Alice Springs on the Wednesday.

There had been no time for the Falconios to meet Joanne, who had been described as upset and disoriented after her ordeal. But at least she was alive. Luciano's main concern was finding his boy. 'I'm looking forward to seeing Joanne but I'm looking more forward to seeing my son,' he said.

Peter's girlfriend had also been helping detectives with a re-enactment of the crime. Police found an orange Kombi similar to the couple's as well as a white ute to make the restaging as authentic as possible.

She was asked to climb into both vehicles and demonstrate what exactly happened. It was a highly emotional experience for her and at one stage she bent forward with her head in her hands to wipe away the tears.

Outside on the road she showed how the gunman bound her arms and legs. A gun was produced as well as a canvas bag to place over her head though it was considered too much to ask her to be tied up again.

By replaying the sequence of events and re-examining the timeline, investigating officers hoped to jog Joanne's memory. Was there a crucial detail she had overlooked? A remark, a feature of the gunman's vehicle or something about his clothes which might lead to his identification?

Afterwards police were forced to concede the re-enactment had been fruitless. It might have given them a more precise picture of the incident but it produced no more clues.

The next day Luciano and Paul were taken to Barrow Creek to see the crime scene for themselves. For several minutes they were left alone as they tramped through the scrub, Paul offering his father a supporting arm as they trudged through the thick undergrowth, trying to visualise what Peter and his girlfriend must have gone through.

Even by the standards of the Yorkshire dales this was a remote place. Apart from the police vehicles there was no sign of human habitation. No crops, no fields, no fences to suggest the hand of man. No phone or power lines along the roadside. No hint of civilisation. What a lonely and dispiriting corner of the earth in which to die.

'A place that I have never seen before, a desert-like place is how I would describe it,' said Paul.

He and his father must have realised the hopelessness of the situation. On the surface they remained positive about finding Peter alive.

'From a few things I saw it gave us hope that Pete is still out there,' Paul said.

Luciano nodded. Faith was his only consolation. 'I hope we will find my son, that's all I want to say because I want to go back with him.'

But their haunted look and body language said more than words.

Someone tried to console the two men by remarking that Australia wasn't such a bad country really.

'I know,' replied Paul on behalf of his father. 'I'm just sorry I'm here in such circumstances.'

In his hand was a sprig plucked from a wattle tree as he wandered through the bush. It was some kind of tangible link with Peter's final moments. Paul closed his fingers around the leaves and placed them in his pocket to take home.

Like the Falconio family, everyone, including the police, seemed to be clutching at straws in their hunt for the man responsible for such evil. As the search for the gunman continued a $250,000 reward was offered for information leading to his arrest.

Countless red herrings and rumours of possible sightings caught the public's attention. Reports of men and vehicles fitting the killer's description flooded into the Northern Territory police hotline.

In Sydney, a driver behind the wheel of a truck with a canopy bearing an astonishingly close resemblance to the vehicle Joanne had described was arrested in the middle of the morning rush hour. The trouble was there were countless four-wheel drives like this in Australia and especially the Northern Territory.

Then someone remembered seeing a movie on Imparja TV, the Aboriginal television channel, on 24 June. It was called *Breakdown* and told the story of a couple whose car had a mechanical failure on a remote highway. The husband stayed with the car while his wife accepted a lift from a passing lorry driver, who abducted her.

Police ordered a copy of the film to examine the plot for any possible similarities with the Barrow Creek incident. But they quickly discounted the theory that the gunman had been inspired by it.

'Of course it was an abduction but the manner in doing it was totally different,' police pointed out to reporters.

Back in Alice Springs Joanne was lying low in the safe house she had been sharing with Helen Jones. Maybe it was Helen's English accent that helped to consolidate their relationship — although born in Ireland, she had moved to Britain in her teens before emigrating to Australia.

Such was the pressure on space that the two women had to share the same bed. And because Joanne's clothes had been taken away for forensic examination, Helen felt compelled to buy her something to wear.

It was an unusual relationship in the circumstances. Although Joanne was still deeply troubled, Helen helped to keep her sane. 'We'd wake up and talk and then make a cup of tea, snooze and then she'd wake up again,' Helen told me later.

To help take Joanne's mind off things, Helen took her to see her baby grandson, Patrick, believing it would be good for her to relax in a family atmosphere. She didn't tell her son David whom she was bringing and when they arrived he was taken aback.

'Crikey! That's Joanne Lees. What's she doing here?' he asked.

'I explained we needed a bit of a change, so we all had a pizza, a glass of wine and talked about our families,' Helen said. 'Joanne was charming and we just sat around talking about home.'

Helen deliberately tried to avoid conversation about the attack.

'The police had said they'd rather we didn't discuss it and I was quite happy with that. I didn't want to upset her because every time the phone rang she asked, "Is it anything to do with Peter?" and to me that was just more distressing,' Helen explained. 'So we tried to keep off the subject.'

At one point during the evening Joanne offered to change a light globe which had blown.

'I hate being on top of a step ladder and she simply volunteered, "Oh I can do that,"' Helen recalled.

It was only when Joanne held baby Patrick in her arms that her face gave a hint of sadness, said Helen. Joanne loved kids and perhaps one day might have a family of her own: with Peter, she'd hoped. Holding little Patrick had suddenly brought it all home. The ramifications of what happened a few days earlier were only just beginning to sink in.

No wonder she found it difficult to even consider fronting the media. She was emotionally exhausted and mentally scarred. Despite police attempts to persuade her to talk publicly about the attack, Joanne was adamant. She feared breaking down in front of the cameras and losing her ability to speak coherently.

Thanks to the presence of Paul Falconio a compromise was eventually reached. She would write a statement and he would read it out. It was not an altogether satisfactory arrangement in the eyes of the media who wanted to put questions of their own to Joanne, but it was better than nothing.

Six days after the incident Paul sat in front of a battery of cameras and, with his hands shaking, placed a photograph of his missing brother and his girlfriend beside him on the desk.

Curiously the six-paragraph statement made little reference to the attack itself but concentrated on the search and some of the rumours that had built up around her.

'I don't want to lessen the severity of what happened, but I believe there has been speculation I was sexually assaulted but this did not occur,' she said, adding, 'I consider myself very lucky to have escaped and to be okay.'

Joanne thanked all those who had telephoned the police with possible leads and urged the public to continue to do so. But her appeal, while plainly heartfelt, also contained a thinly veiled warning to the press to stay away from her: 'I'd like to ask people to concentrate their efforts more on trying to find Pete than trying to speak to me.'

While she acknowledged the police were doing their best, it was the media she seemed more concerned with.

Oh, and by the way, she emphasised, she had no intention of selling her story.

While there had been offers of money from some of the tabloid British newspapers and one or two Australian commercial television programs, her response was perhaps understandable. Yet as it would later transpire, Joanne was not completely immune to the temptations of chequebook journalism.

....

DNA THE ONLY CLUE

A week into the investigation and it was becoming ever clearer that the police were getting nowhere. The only breakthrough so far had been the discovery of a tiny smear of blood found on Joanne's T-shirt.

DNA analysis proved that it did not come from either Joanne or her boyfriend. It could have been left by the attacker although the sample was so small it might have been transferred to her clothes by someone she had merely brushed against earlier.

And if it had been left by the assailant why was there no more? If he had bled during the struggle it was reasonable to assume that other quantities of skin or DNA might have been found on Joanne's clothes or body, but there was none.

However it got there it was important to match the DNA with its source, if only to exclude the person from police enquiries. But that would be a long and exhaustive process. In the meantime detectives had to broaden their investigation and adopt more unorthodox techniques.

Despite the extensive police search of the area surrounding the crime scene, little of value had been found apart from a single shoeprint, which, it was established, came from Joanne, and the Kombi which had been dumped about 200 metres away.

Detectives enlisted the services of Aboriginal trackers including Ted Egan, who had helped the police on many previous occasions. His ability to find criminals and people who got lost in the outback was legendary.

In the 1980s he had been used to locate a killer who had shot a man and injured two police officers at Harts Range, northeast of Alice Springs. More recently he had flown to Germany to track three dangerous criminals who had escaped from prison. He found two of them.

Seventy-year-old Ted based his tracking ability on skills taught to him by his mother. He looked for stones that had been moved or foliage that had been disturbed in his search for clues.

Perhaps it was his age or the scarcity of evidence, but Ted's powers seemed to be on the wane when he visited Barrow Creek a few days after the attack. His principal discovery was what appeared to be a jack mark, suggesting the attacker's vehicle might have had a flat tyre, but the rest of his findings seemed inconclusive.

There were also many reported sightings of a man similar to Joanne's description of the driver, among them a long-haired drifter named Chris who appeared to be a dead ringer for the supposed killer and who admitted being in the area at the time. He even had an almost identical ute with a canvas canopy and had been camping near the Stuart Highway a few days previously.

But after he was shown to Joanne and DNA tests were carried out, police eliminated him from their enquiries.

Was this the same man whom two employees from North Concrete in Alice Springs had seen a couple of days earlier at Ti Tree rubbish dump?

Kevin Graham and Graham Somerville were doing some construction work at Ti Tree and had to dispose of their empty cement bags at the local tip on the day before the attack. On arrival they were surprised to see a person sleeping on a swag in the back of a ute. They never saw his face — only his legs, which protruded out of the back.

More intriguingly they did see his dog — 'a blue or red heeler but definitely not a Dalmatian', as Kevin later stressed to police.

'I recall the vehicle was a white Landcruiser with a green canopy. We must have stood about a hundred metres from it and thought it was a strange place for someone to camp,' Kevin told me later.

And then there was the dead dog found at Neutral Junction Station, north of Barrow Creek and east of the Stuart Highway. Ostensibly there was no connection with the attack, but the discovery of the large, brown, mixed-breed animal, which had been shot, naturally aroused police interest, given Joanne's account of the dog in the ute.

The find was considered important enough for Bill Tower, the Northern Territory's longest-serving crime scene examiner, to take a look.

He found tyre tracks leading to where the dog had been dumped but the body did not fit the description of the one he had been given.

'It was much bigger than a heeler and had large feet,' Tower said.

But why would a farmer shoot a pet dog so far away from their house and not bury it? Unless it was a wild dog which had been bothering livestock.

Perhaps it was a camp dog owned by local Aborigines? That didn't add up either because indigenous people don't usually shoot or kill their pet animals who are regarded as part of the family.

How the dog got there and why it was killed were two questions which would remain a mystery.

As the days wore on, the hunt for the man who shot Peter Falconio intensified. More police were drafted in and the Northern Territory government, conscious of the negative publicity the crime was generating at home and overseas, needed results. The Lindy Chamberlain case of the early 1980s had done enough damage to the Territory's image and the government did not want a repeat performance.

Money and resources poured into the task force set up to investigate the case but little progress appeared to be made. In the vague hope that Joanne might have overlooked an important fact, perhaps unwittingly blocking out crucial details because of post-traumatic stress, police enlisted the help of a hypnotist.

A top Sydney psychologist was brought in to hypnotise Joanne but the procedure uncovered nothing new.

'We hoped it might shed new light on the incident,' Assistant Commissioner John Daulby admitted. 'But sadly no new information was gleaned.'

A week after the attack I spoke in detail on the telephone with Commander Max Pope, one of the officers closest to the enquiry. Perhaps understandably, there were key areas of evidence which he did not want to disclose at that stage in the interests of the on-going investigation, but few could mistake the lack of progress.

The following is a transcript of the interview:

RM: 'I believe she saw the gunman holding the gun when he came back to the front of the Kombi. Did she recognise that gun? Did she know what sort of gun it was?'

MP: 'She has given us a description of the gun.'

RM: 'Was it a revolver or was it a shotgun?'

MP: 'Once again we're not going into the details of the gun.'

RM: 'What about the amount of blood found at the scene of the crime? I know you've confirmed that blood was found there and that DNA from Peter was in this blood. Can you say what sort of quantity of blood was found there?'

MP: 'All we're saying is that a quantity, we haven't drawn an assumption on whether or not it was sufficient to be life threatening or not, we've just said there was a quantity of blood and we've left it at that.'

RM: 'Was it dried blood? Was there blood spatter?'

MP: 'It was a pool of blood.'

RM: 'So there wasn't the sort of blood spatter which you would normally get with a gunshot wound or anything like that?'

MP: 'I can't do that one either.'

RM: 'Given that Joanne has not given a press conference, can you say whether the police have advised or urged her to talk publicly about what happened?'

MP: 'We have left that up to Joanne to decide what she decides to do with the press and it was Joanne's decision yesterday to release that statement which the brother Paul Falconio read out.'

RM: 'Are you intending to interview her again this weekend?'

MP: 'Look, Joanne comes to assist us whenever we call.'

RM: 'Has she expressed a desire to go back to the UK yet?'

MP: 'Not as yet.'

RM: 'I'm just trying to think through the logic of the killer, the gunman. Have you wondered what might be the motive for him to conceal the body when he's openly dumped the Kombi near the roadside? Why wouldn't he leave the body near or in the Kombi? What would be the motive for burying the body somewhere else?'

MP: 'Why he did these things is in his mind only, and for us to speculate upon isn't much good. It is totally within his mind for the reasons he did these things.'

RM: 'Are you involving anybody else, such as psychologists, in the interviews you do with Joanne?'

MP: 'Look, all I'd say about that one is that we're using all resources available to us.'

RM: 'What's happening with the search? Will you scale it down?'

MP: 'We're still concentrating some of our efforts in that area. We're making sure that we haven't missed anything in that region. You're aware that we initially searched a square kilometre area and expanded that out with a high level search so we can be sure that we haven't missed anything.'

RM: 'Were you surprised that you only found Joanne's footprints near the scene of the crime and no others?'

MP: 'Not when you consider that she'd run 25 to 30 metres off the road and in that whole distance we only recovered three partial footprints. So it's an indication how the lie of the land is and how the tracks are retained, so no it's not surprising.'

RM: 'Were those footprints near the road or actually in the bush?'

MP: 'I don't know that. I know very close to the road the surface is very hard. I can't tell you what distance they were found in.'

RM: 'And as far as you're concerned, are you still 100 per cent convinced that Joanne is telling the truth?'

MP: 'Well, what we're saying is that the information we've taken from the scene supports what she's told us.'

RM: 'Does that suggest an element of doubt?'

MP: 'It may for you . . .'

RM: 'Is Joanne bearing up to her ordeal quite well?'

MP: 'Yes, it's been a very traumatic time for her considering the circumstances and she's bearing up well.'

RM: 'Is she in contact with Peter's father?'

MP: 'There has been contact but I'm not quite sure how frequent and what level it is.'

RM: 'Are you happy about Joanne's mental stability? Apart from the trauma she's gone through, are you happy about the way she's reacted to your questioning?'

Pause.

MP: 'Look, I don't have any difficulties. As I said, Joanne Lees has come to us, provided a statement, she's been supportive of providing information and the evidence at the scene supports her story.'

I went over this interview many times after it was conducted on 21 July 2001 and often wondered why Max Pope paused before responding to that final question. Maybe he was simply stopping for breath or to collect his thoughts.

And why did he not offer a description of the gun, which Joanne remembered had a scrolling design engraved on it? Someone out there might have recalled a firearm with such a distinct pattern and shed some light on its owner.

As for the 'high level search' to make sure 'we haven't missed anything' at the crime scene, the subsequent discovery of tape and lip balm in the undergrowth made a mockery of such claims. How was it that such a thorough examination of the scrubland where Joanne hid failed to uncover such significant items? Why did it take another three months for police to stumble across such vital evidence, which would give added credence to her story?

Such unanswered questions only served to reinforce the media's determination to access the woman at the centre of the case, but still she refused to speak at a press conference. Slowly the sympathy which she had been offered by reporters in the early days of the investigation was turning into suspicion.

And in the absence of Joanne it was the police who had to field the hard questions.

The negative nature of those questions was inevitably reported back to her and may partly explain the growing animosity with which she viewed the media and her antagonism to reporters. It might also be the reason why she appeared so obstructive during the one and only time she made herself available for questioning in front of a television camera in Alice Springs.

....

CHAPTER 12

JOANNE AGREES TO SPEAK

leven days after the incident at Barrow Creek
Joanne Lees agreed to a carefully staged press
conference in Alice Springs. To be exact it was not a
news conference in the accepted sense of the term,
more an opportunity to read a prepared statement and
reply to three questions which she had chosen from a
list of 13 previously provided by journalists.

There were other restrictions too. Only one reporter
was allowed to be present — a young woman from the
Australian Broadcasting Corporation — plus a television
cameraman and several press photographers.

Initially Joanne had demanded that no members of
the British press be present, such was her contempt
for Fleet Street and the perceived innuendo that she
might have somehow been involved in her boyfriend's
disappearance. Police media officers recognised that
there would be an almighty row if they excluded
the UK media given the level of British interest in the

story, so extended the ban to Australian journalists as well.

Predictably such demands were not welcomed by the huge media contingent now camped in Alice but it was better than nothing. At least Joanne's voice would be heard for the first time.

It had taken the combined persuasive powers of the officers leading the enquiry, as well as the personal intervention of the Northern Territory Police Commissioner, Brian Bates, to convince her to co-operate.

Bates flew to Alice Springs and spoke to Joanne over a cup of coffee before she eventually relented, but even then she made it clear any public appearance was to be organised on her terms.

Demonstrating all the practised media-management skills of a Hollywood star or powerful politician, she demanded to know the questions beforehand. Reporters compiled a list of topics about the case they would like her to address, including:

- Can you talk us through what happened?
- How are you coping?
- Have you any idea why you and Peter might have been targeted?
- Exactly how near did the attacker and his dog get to you when you were hiding in the bush?
- How come he left no footprints?
- What feelings do you have about your assailant?
- Can you talk about the last day you spent with Peter and your time at the Camel Cup?
- There have been suggestions that you had a row with Peter at the Camel Cup. Is that true, and if so, what was it about?

- Did you have a feeling that you were being watched?
- Did you and Peter plan to marry?

However, Joanne rejected all of the above, agreeing only to discuss the doubts that had been raised about her story and her reaction to the press.

First Joanne, who had asked a local hairdressing salon to open early so that she could be attended to before other customers arrived, read out a typed statement which she had written herself.

Looking slightly nervous, she was determined to get through the media appearance without breaking down. Only once did her composure look like cracking and that was when she addressed her words to the man who had taken her beloved Peter.

Staring down the barrel of the one TV camera lens present, she declared, 'If I could say one thing to the man who did this, I would ask him to let police know where Pete is.'

She said she had asked detectives to only give her positive news and remained hopeful of finding her boyfriend alive.

'I am confident everything that can be done is being done, and I am hoping one of the leads police are following up will lead to Peter being found,' she added.

Barely able to conceal the mounting anger she felt about the doubts that had been expressed over her story, Joanne said, 'Anyone who has spoken to me or had any contact with me . . . no one doubts me, only the media have asked questions about my story.'

And that, of course, was one of the issues. Perhaps if she had talked openly and without restriction about her experience at an earlier stage, the press might have laid off and the rumour mongers might have remained silent. For whatever reason Joanne had apparently developed a deep suspicion of the media whom she continued to lambast.

'I find it so overwhelming and intimidating. I've got a problem with all press. They distort the truth and doubt my story. They misquote me, making up stories and accusations,' she claimed.

It was a classic example of blaming the messenger for what had happened. While the media en masse can be intimidating and sometimes frightening for those caught up in the maelstrom of news gathering, Joanne's verdict on the treatment she had received was largely without foundation.

In fact in the early days of the case, newspapers, radio and television on both sides of the world had gone out of their way to be fair and sympathetic in their coverage of Joanne's plight. While some of the questions the police were asked by journalists might have seemed insensitive, it was important to raise the doubts if only to dispel them.

Certainly not all the news coverage was completely accurate, but that was more the result of insufficient detail to explain the whole story rather than a deliberate attempt to smear Joanne's name. It is said that newspapers are the first draft of history. As a result, errors are often made in the turmoil of a developing story, especially when combined with the demands of a looming deadline.

This is no excuse for distortion or inaccurate quotes but in the rush of daily journalism it is inevitable that misunderstandings or mistakes occasionally occur.

What should have been of greater concern to Joanne were the conspiracy theories circulating in internet chat rooms, and being discussed around every office water cooler, questioning her account of the attack.

While the media always has to worry about being sued for getting things wrong, ordinary people talking among themselves have no such legal bounds and the Falconio case was generating a huge amount of malicious gossip. Even today a Google search for the name Peter Falconio or Joanne Lees will produce an endless supply of theories, both defamatory and supportive, about what happened on the Stuart Highway.

Like the Lindy Chamberlain case two decades earlier, everybody had their view about the woman at the centre of the case and whether she was telling the truth. Some argued that Joanne was being victimised and her name blackened by vicious innuendo. While others reasoned that her story just didn't add up. They weren't sure she was lying but her account didn't ring true.

When a case attracts such diametrically opposing opinions about a person's guilt or innocence, fact can quickly be overtaken by fantasy. When everybody has their own view about what might or might not have happened the conclusions can frequently be extreme and well wide of the mark. It also suggests an overwhelming uncertainty about the truth.

Even with the benefit of a massive database of evidence surrounding the case, I wasn't sure what actually happened. I had many ideas and scenarios which might have explained the mysterious sequence of events, but there was always a niggling doubt. And the same applied to nearly everybody I spoke to.

As soon as I convinced myself about the plausibility of one theory, further information persuaded me to think otherwise. Like many who had followed this case I was consumed by a desire to find the answer. It was a quest that took me to Yorkshire, Brighton, Broome, Adelaide, Darwin, Alice Springs and, of course, Barrow Creek. Yet I still didn't know for sure.

This was not to suggest that Joanne was lying. Even she may not have been privy to the entire story. What if she was an unwitting accomplice to what turned out to be Peter's carefully orchestrated disappearance? After all, she never saw Peter's body and the police could only assume he was shot. The pool of blood discovered on the roadside was hardly evidence of a life-threatening wound. So could it have been part of a cruel hoax to fake Peter's death, a trick which Joanne had no knowledge of?

But what would be the point? Had Peter discovered the affair which Joanne had been having with Nick Riley back in Sydney and secretly conspired with others to leave her in the middle of the Australian outback? It was a possible explanation but why go to such extraordinary lengths to effect his disappearance when he could have had a row and simply walked out on her?

And wouldn't such a conspiracy have been totally out of character? Here was a kind and responsible young man from a respectable middle-class family in Britain, a lad who might have liked a joint but had no known criminal links or aspirations.

But just suppose there was more going on behind the scenes. Was he more deeply involved in drugs than was realised? Had a deal gone wrong? Had there been an argument over money? Did he fear for his life?

Not so, insisted the police, who remained convinced it was an opportunist killing carried out by an evil and violent man. There was no evidence to support the many and wild theories that abounded, they said. Even to suggest such possibilities would quite clearly give offence to his law-abiding family back home in England.

But wasn't this the same Peter Falconio who once asked about life insurance fraud and how easy it might be to fake his own death?

Even the police had received anonymous correspondence alerting them to Peter's questions on the topic. In February 2002 detectives working on the case received a letter claiming that Peter had asked for information about the best way a death could be faked. The London *Daily Mail* received a similar tip from a former workmate, which prompted newspaper speculation that Peter Falconio was still alive.

As unbelievable as such rumours sounded, it later emerged that a man had reported seeing and speaking to Peter somewhere on the coast of eastern Australia, although police were unable to find sufficient evidence to support his story.

Such claims, whether sightings or rumours of life insurance fraud, were both hurtful and agonising for the Falconio family, who dismissed them as mischievous and offensive.

Mrs Falconio said that suggestions her son had faked his own death were 'absolutely disgusting'. 'My son isn't here to defend himself, is he?' she told the *Mail*, adding that no one had ever had a bad word to say about him. The speculation and the gossip only served to heap more sadness on a family who were still trying to come to terms with their loss.

It was impossible to even contemplate a treasured son putting his family through so much misery by faking his own death. Yet in the weeks following Peter's disappearance there were several other reported sightings, the most convincing of them coming from a couple in Bourke, a country town in the far west of New South Wales.

Exactly eight days after the Barrow Creek incident a young man seemingly identical to Peter Falconio walked into a service station at Bourke, accompanied by an older man and a woman.

Robert Brown and his partner Melissa Kendall remembered it well because they were amazed by the eerie similarity between the man standing in front of the counter and a photograph of Falconio on the front page of that morning's Sydney *Sunday Telegraph*.

It was about dusk on 22 July 2001 and the couple were preparing to close the filling station, which was owned by Robert's parents, as they subsequently related in court.

Melissa, who was later to be appointed assistant registrar to the court at Bourke, was the first to see him. 'A gentleman walked in and asked for the toilet key. He was about 180 centimetres, well-built, clean shaven and with an injury to his face just between his mouth and chin,' she recalled.

She recognised him instantly and went out to the rear kitchen behind the counter to tell Robert, who was cleaning up.

'I was washing a few bits and pieces ready to shut up when Melissa came out the back and told me my old mate in the paper was in the shop,' he said.

She pointed to the photo in the newspaper and they examined it for a good 30 seconds.

Two minutes later the young man, sporting short-cropped, bleached-blond hair, returned from the toilet and handed back the key to Robert, who by this time had gone out to the counter to take a look for himself.

Stunned by the likeness, Robert stood open-mouthed while Peter Falconio's double asked for a bottle of Coke and a Mars bar.

'If it wasn't him they were twins,' he insisted afterwards.

In the four years since that reported sighting, Robert, who now works as a teacher's aide in Bourke, has never wavered in his view. 'I served Peter Falconio myself and spoke to him briefly,' he declared. 'I was in too much shock to do much about it. I just said, "Is that it, mate?" and he replied, "Yes," handed me the money and I gave him the change.'

A couple of minutes later a second man appeared, wearing a dirty, off-white T-shirt and blue jeans. He had blackish-brown, shoulder-length hair and was in his early 40s.

Melissa admitted to feeling 'quite scared' by his appearance.

He bought a packet of dog biscuits and paid for them with a $50 note.

'I didn't say too much because I wanted him out,' she added.

After filling up their vehicle with petrol, they drove to an adjoining side lane, where they parked for several minutes.

Both Robert and Melissa wandered outside to surreptitiously observe the odd-looking trio and, so as not to draw attention to themselves, made it appear they were calling their blue cattle dog.

'I didn't want to stare because I thought they might shoot me,' he admitted.

But he had no doubt that Peter Falconio was part of the group.

'I just couldn't believe it. They were shoulder by shoulder, whispering and talking among themselves. It looked like they were three people going on holiday,' he said.

Robert thought he could detect a slight accent in the man who seemed like Peter but he wasn't sure whether it was Yorkshire.

Melissa was too shocked to take it all in. Though she did remember the small, dark green ute they were driving with drop sides around the rear tray and a dog sitting on some luggage in the back.

'I just couldn't believe what was happening. I thought it was them, but I didn't know what to do,' she added.

Sadly neither Robert nor Melissa raised the alarm at the time, otherwise police might have been able to resolve their suspicions by intercepting the vehicle on one of the four sealed roads going out of Bourke. That is, assuming the ute was heading towards Cunnamulla to the north, Brewarrina to the east or Nyngan or Cobar to the south. Maybe it was equipped for outback travel and was heading west along the numerous dirt tracks which snake across the desert towards Tibooburra, White Cliffs or Broken Hill.

We will never know because it wasn't until the next day that Melissa mentioned the curious events of the night before to a friend whose husband was a local police inspector. He subsequently took a statement from her but little else could be done.

I pondered this reported sighting on many occasions and went back to Melissa to ask her to go over the details again. She remained adamant that the man she saw that day was Peter Falconio and Robert agreed.

Even more tantalisingly, the couple also revealed afterwards that police told them there had been a reported sighting of Falconio a few days earlier at Lightning Ridge, the outback opal mining town a couple of hundred kilometres east.

Robert and Melissa are fine upstanding members of the community. They are what the legal fraternity would describe as highly credible witnesses. They also had time to study their subject and compare his face with the image in the newspaper. Even though his hair colour was different to that in the *Sunday Telegraph*, his facial features were apparently identical.

This was no momentary glimpse. Robert was able to look at Peter Falconio's double for a full two minutes and outside the service station for another five.

And what of the man with the unkempt appearance and the shoulder-length hair who accompanied him? Didn't he look uncannily like the man drawn by the police artist based on Joanne Lees' description of the gunman?

While it was easy to dismiss such outlandish suggestions, it is often the unexpected that provides the best leads and I had learnt from past experience never to reject theories simply because they seemed implausible. Truth is frequently stranger than fiction.

In the mid-1960s, didn't Great Train Robber Ronnie Biggs work undetected as a carpenter at the Channel Nine studios in Melbourne before his cover was blown and he escaped just in time to South America?

And didn't John Stonehouse, a British Labour government cabinet minister, re-emerge in Australia after leaving a pile of his clothes on a Miami beach in 1974 to fake his drowning? He was caught after several months living under an assumed name in Melbourne with his former secretary, Sheila Buckley.

Both Biggs and Stonehouse were known to millions, yet still they managed to evade detection, in the Great Train Robber's case for five years.

If the Bourke sighting of Peter Falconio had any shred of accuracy about it, one might have asked why he should turn up as bold as brass in a public place, seemingly unperturbed by the fact that his picture had been plastered all over the front pages. Or was he unaware that his face had suddenly become so well known?

If, for whatever reason, he had been deliberately lying low, it was quite possible that he had not seen a television or newspaper for several days. If he had taken the Oodnadatta Track south of Alice Springs, he could have made his way east across the desert roads without coming into contact with another human being, let alone any print or broadcast media. Of course this also assumed he had a plentiful supply of food and fuel with him, but as Bradley John Murdoch was to demonstrate, driving long journeys within Australia was eminently achievable if you had the know-how and the back-up. It would be even easier if there were three of you.

If there was any chance that Peter Falconio was still alive, where would he be staying and would he still be hiding out?

As recently as late 2004, I spoke to a man who claimed to have been told quite categorically that Joanne's boyfriend was alive and well and working as a chef in Queensland.

Michael Harre, who works for Central Radiators in Alice Springs, said a customer on his way to Darwin had

119

told him that he had seen and spoken to Falconio only a few weeks earlier, but the police were not interested. 'Apparently they had bigger fish to fry,' he said.

And where exactly was Falconio supposed to be working?

Mount Isa, the central Queensland mining town.

The Mitchell Highway north of Bourke connects directly to the Landsborough Highway, which leads straight to Mount Isa. Hadn't Falconio also done a catering course in England?

....

CHAPTER 13

MYSTERY OF THE MISSING VIDEO

If Joanne thought her appearance in front of the media would take the heat off her, she was quickly proved wrong. Her look, her manner and the way she talked continued to raise questions about her story. Reporters, and more especially the public, continued to have their doubts.

The Sydney *Daily Telegraph* even went so far as to play a video recording of the press conference to an associate professor of psychology at Sydney University, Dr Dianna Kenny, to critique her performance.

Her verdict was that Joanne looked 'very uncomfortable'.

'It wasn't a convincing statement, it sounded very rehearsed,' she told the newspaper at the time.

'There was a very strong attempt to control herself — and she was attempting to come across as bland. She wasn't at all convincing when she said she was confident that Peter was still alive. [And] when she said she has asked police to tell her only happy things, that's very naive.'

Dr Kenny stressed it was important not to jump to conclusions when people didn't come across in the media as they might expect. 'We don't know exactly what she's going through in the middle of the night. My gut reaction was "this is strange" but she was in a very strange situation.'

Such comments reinforced what many people were thinking. While happy to give Joanne the benefit of the doubt, their suspicions had not been entirely put to rest.

For the young woman at the centre of such intense media attention and speculation, it was all getting too much. There were reports of her being upset over the amount of police questioning. Some of the daily grillings since the attack were believed to have lasted up to 18 hours, giving her very little time or opportunity to come to terms with the tragedy and, more especially, the loss of her boyfriend.

British and Australian newspapers claimed that Joanne found the non-stop interrogating confusing, repetitive and painful and that she had been offered very little in the way of legal help or counselling.

When she was eventually allowed to see a psychiatrist more than four days after the attack, he described her as still in 'survivor mode'.

Back home in Britain Joanne's mother, Jennifer, expressed concern that her daughter was not being adequately cared for. She said her husband, who was by now in Alice Springs, had been allowed only limited time with her and that their conversations were always in the presence of police.

A Northern Territory media officer conceded that

she might have been subjected to an 'over-long period of questioning', but insisted she was never forced to stay.

Later, Joanne attempted to play down the perception that she had been critical of the police or that detectives had been heavy-handed. Once again Paul Falconio was asked to be her spokesman, calling a press conference to make clear that critical comments attributed to Joanne had not been made by her.

'We know that Joanne worked long hours with police during the initial stages of this investigation but she was extremely anxious to assist police,' he said. 'We believe it was very important for police to gather all the information they could in the first few hours to help them catch the offender.

'Since arriving here, police have briefed us daily on the progress of the investigation. We are confident they are making every effort to catch the offender.'

What was going on? Was the confusion over Joanne's relationship with the police merely a misunderstanding?

Certainly she was free to come and go as she pleased, but the length of the interviews had done nothing to ease the impression that she was being treated more as a suspect than a victim.

To add to the confusion there was the continuing mystery of the missing surveillance video, which police had earlier insisted did not exist. Nearly three weeks after the *Centralian Advocate* brought up the question of the security footage from an Alice Springs truck stop purportedly showing a man and a ute remarkably similar to those described by Joanne, police at last admitted they did have the tape after all.

Confirmation of the tape's existence drew gasps of astonishment from those who had accepted the previous police statement that there wasn't one.

Assistant Police Commissioner John Daulby explained the three-week delay on the grounds that the video tape had to be sent away to be enhanced. Local attempts to make the picture clearer had failed.

Detectives were trying to create a better image of the vehicle's registration plate in the hope that it would reveal the identity of the owner, but this too failed. Once you have a badly degraded image, little can be done to improve the quality and police were forced to accept that the black and white, fuzzy scenes of a man and his ute were the best that could be achieved.

The story of the tape and what happened to it was the subject of much rumour and innuendo. At one stage there was a suggestion that the original image, which might have been clearer than the one police obtained, had been erased from a computer hard drive linked to the garage's surveillance system, but this proved unfounded.

It was Val Prior, who managed the Shell truck stop at the time, who eventually explained what happened. 'The police came round on the Sunday evening after the attack and took the VHS cassette, which recorded everything, away with them,' she said.

There was no hard drive containing a clearer image of the registration plate. In fact the surveillance cameras were more of a deterrent and rarely provided details of a vehicle's registration plate. 'You'd struggle to get a number from the video tape,' she admitted.

But there was still no excuse for police not disclosing the truck stop image of the suspect and his vehicle earlier. Consider how it might have changed the course of the case and the progress of the investigation had the images been made public within days of the attack. Even the release of murky pictures might have assisted the police enquiry if they had been made available to the media earlier.

So why weren't they?

Assistant Commissioner Daulby's explanation that they had to be sent interstate so they could undergo better technological enhancement did not convince digital image specialists, who argued that simple Photoshop software would have been sufficient to improve the footage. That is, assuming the images could have been enhanced in the first place. A VHS tape of a shot from a non-broadcast quality surveillance camera would allow little or no scope for improvement, regardless of the technology used.

Why did it take the police so long to find this out? Could it have something to do with suggestions that the original cassette was mislaid and only turned up three weeks later?

Police did not confirm this explanation, which would have been a major embarrassment for them. But sources close to the investigation subsequently told me that there was strong evidence to support the rumour that it was left on a detective's desk and lost for a time.

There was also the question of whether the man in the footage was originally identified by Joanne as the gunman. First she reportedly told detectives that it wasn't. But nearly a week later she apparently changed her mind, telling a news conference that there was 'a very good possibility' that it was.

This was in marked contrast to Assistant Commissioner Daulby's statement that although police were very keen to speak to the man in the video, 'we are not saying he is the gunman.'

Daulby added that UK media reports quoting Joanne's family as saying she believed the man in the surveillance footage was the gunman were false. 'Joanne has never said, "that is the gunman,"' he declared.

By now even those who had been closely covering the case for the best part of a month were confused. What would have made Joanne change her mind, if indeed she had? Could the uncertainty have had something to do with the disparity between the description of the gunman she had first given to police and the face in the video?

Then she had spoken of her attacker as a man with shoulder-length hair, but the figure in the service station had much shorter hair. Certainly he had a cap and what appeared to be a long droopy moustache but the long hair, unless it was hidden under his cap, was nowhere to be seen.

While the value of the security video still had to be established, the police had made one major breakthrough, which could not be disputed.

During the examination of Joanne's clothing, forensic investigators found a tiny smear of what appeared to be blood on the back of Joanne's T-shirt. It had not come from Peter or his girlfriend, suggesting that it might be linked to the gunman.

Further analysis identified the DNA as coming from a male person, but police emphasised they could not be certain it came from the attacker. The results would be compared with databases in Australia, New Zealand, America and Britain in the search for a positive match.

DNA profiling has been heralded as the most important discovery in the history of forensic examination. It allows the positive identification of any individual from the smallest body trace. The minute sample left behind on the back of Joanne's T-shirt was no hindrance to the scientific investigation.

All human cells contain the nucleus which bears the coded information unique to every individual in the form of deoxyribonucleic acid, better known as DNA.

This was the first significant lead in the hunt for Peter Falconio's likely killer. All detectives had to do was to establish a positive match. Many of those questioned by the police agreed to provide a DNA sample voluntarily, but it was not compulsory.

When detectives came knocking at Bradley John Murdoch's door in Broome he convinced them that he had nothing to do with the events at Barrow Creek and quietly got on with his life. After all, even his vehicle was different to the one shown in the truck stop video. And as for Murdoch himself, he looked nothing like the bloke being sought by police. It would be another year before he came into their sights once more.

CHAPTER 14

SHREWD BUT SINISTER

If Murdoch had one passion in life it was his love of utes. He'd had three of them in recent years including his latest purchase, the former Telstra truck he bought in Adelaide, an HJ75 Landcruiser. Big Brad was always improving them, adding to the bodywork or tinkering with the engine.

Around Broome he was always popping into auto shops or engineering firms to discuss his latest plans and ordering new parts.

Several skilled tradesmen got to know him well, including Michael Somerville, who ran Karella Welding. Early in 2001 he built a boat trailer for Murdoch who was so impressed with the work he returned with further orders. Somerville worked on the old F100 as well as the recently purchased HJ75 which had a shorter rear tray than usual and was in a bad state of repair.

On 27 July 2001, Murdoch brought the vehicle to be modified.

'I extended the tray to the full Landcruiser length in preparation for a canopy to go on and put a new flap bar around the edge. I didn't build the canopy because Brad wanted an aluminium one which he'd purchased the material for at a specialities shop in Perth,' he said in court.

Over the next few months Murdoch made further modifications to the vehicle, some by his own hand, and when he did not have the expertise he would employ the services of others.

'Brad was a mechanic so he was always playing with his vehicle,' said Somerville.

After Murdoch had the tray extended and a new canopy built, the back of his ute was like a steel cage. The sides and rear were surrounded by security mesh which was secured by lifting up the dropsides and locking them into place.

Edward Egerton-Warburton, who had worked at West Kimberley Diesel with him, recalled how the mesh couldn't be opened without the dropsides being lowered. The canvas curtain at the back could be fixed in the open position but the mesh would remain in place, firmly secured to the dropsides.

It was a perfect spot to keep a dog on long journeys because it could see out of the vehicle but not escape. Once the mesh cage was secured it would be extremely difficult for anyone to get out of the rear of the truck — 'not without breaking the mesh', Egerton-Warburton explained in evidence at the pre-trial hearing.

Equally, because a long, rectangular fuel tank was bolted on to the back of the cab and the top of the canopy extended over the roof, it was impossible to climb from the front to the rear.

'There was no access directly between the cab and the tray,' he insisted.

It was an ideal vehicle in which to camp out, for when stationary it was possible to unlock the dropsides which would release the security mesh, allowing the sides of the canopy to be lifted up and propped open with the aid of support rods.

Murdoch spared no expense in an effort to make his vehicle more comfortable and better suited to the driving and weather conditions. As part of that procedure he also installed tinted windows.

William Butterfield, who owned Kimberley Kool Windscreens in Broome, said Murdoch paid $290 for a screen and tinting on his Landcruiser and still has the invoice to prove it.

Wayne Holmes, who ran a powder-coating business, revealed how Murdoch called in during June 2001 and asked him to powder-coat six wheels on his HJ75. 'They were fat wheels, about 10 inches wide and I powder-coated them a charcoal-metallic colour and did the same to the bull bar. The vehicle was in excellent condition and had either been resprayed or freshly detailed,' said Holmes at the hearing.

And so it went on. Robin Knox, who worked at Broome Exhausts, revealed how Murdoch brought his vehicle in on 22 August 2001 to have some work on the exhaust carried out. The two men had met previously at the Roebuck Bay Sports Bar, where Murdoch had discussed the possibility of fitting a big box exhaust to the Landcruiser.

When he drove into Broome Exhausts in his HJ75 on that Wednesday morning, Knox was surprised at the good condition of the vehicle. 'It had been cleaned right up, which is unusual for a Broome car because you get a lot of red dust. But there was no dirt at all, not even under the chassis. It was spotless,' he told the hearing.

Murdoch's attention to his vehicle was no surprise to those who had regular dealings with him and who were aware of his obsession with cleanliness and the pleasure he derived from adding extras to the bodywork. At least that was how he wanted it to seem. In truth he needed to transform the look of his HJ75 so it could no longer be mistaken for the vehicle in the security footage.

Warren Minshull, who owned a mechanical repair business in Broome, was also familiar with Murdoch's vehicles and would regularly serve him when he came in to buy parts.

He'd come into the workshop to purchase oil filters and recovery gear and Minshull recalled how the rear tray of the HJ75 had green matting on the floor, like Astroturf. The canvas canopy was green and white and there was a black bull bar on the front.

Minshull said Murdoch didn't mind spending money on his vehicle which was always 'spot-on clean'.

'He was a typical Aussie wearing double-plugger thongs, blue shorts and a blue singlet,' he added, but he was not someone you could warm to. 'He was always on his own, a bit of a loner who didn't seem to have any mates,' Minshull told me later.

And there was something sinister about him too, the sort of guy you wouldn't want to upset. 'He always seemed a pretty shrewd bloke whom you wouldn't want to rip off.'

Brothers Steve and Greg Mills got the same impression. They run NorWest Diesel in Broome and recalled how Murdoch had had an unpleasant streak, particularly when he disagreed with something.

Greg remembers how Murdoch once took great exception to the fact that Steve had repaired motorcycles owned by local members of the Coffin Cheaters Club. 'Brad used to belong to a rival gang called The Rebels and didn't like Steve working on their bikes. I remember him warning him to stop doing the work or else — "you c..t!"'

Murdoch's tendency to unleash a torrent of abuse on those he perceived to be acting against him suggested a man who was both irrational and easy to provoke. When left to his own devices at work he was happy enough, but when someone upset him the ugly side of his character was quick to emerge.

On one occasion a young couple sunbathing on the beach were menaced by Murdoch and his dog, which bit the man. The incident was mentioned to Loi O'Dore, a self-employed upholsterer who had dealings with Murdoch on several occasions and whose name was mentioned in the local media, prompting the couple to ring him about their own experience.

O'Dore, a Frenchman who is better known around Broome as Jean-Louis, owns Tropical Upholstery which manufactures canvas canopies for vehicles. He had put some curtains made out of green PVC on the back of Murdoch's HJ75. Later, in the middle of 2001, he did some more work on the canopy and it was on this occasion that Jean-Louis mentioned to Murdoch that he had seen a similar vehicle to his on the television news.

By now the Landcruiser appeared somewhat different from the earlier model he'd brought in. 'It looked a lot newer and was done up with a custom-built, aluminium frame, powder coated green and with mesh sides.'

Like many others in Broome, Jean-Louis had heard the rumours about Murdoch being in Alice Springs around the same time as the Barrow Creek incident and couldn't resist raising the matter.

He mentioned the truck-stop surveillance video and pointed out how it resembled the first vehicle he'd worked on. Murdoch seemed unfazed by the implications and openly admitted that it could have been him because he had been up there at the time and may have stopped at the service station for fuel.

'He said the police had spoken to him about it and he had told them it wasn't him, so I didn't think any more of it.'

Murdoch's explanation seemed to satisfy those who were brave enough to enquire. People don't ask too many questions in Broome, but Jean-Louis, perhaps because of his French background, was the exception and did not feel quite so bound by local ways.

And anyway Murdoch's vehicle always seemed to be a work in progress and few could remember precisely when crucial changes to the bodywork were carried out. If he had deliberately set out to change the look of the HJ75 after 14 July 2001, he could be reasonably certain that it would not raise too many suspicions, given the modifications made to it in the past.

Murdoch, who always paid in cash, was good for business. Local boatbuilder Stephen Galvin, who owned Galvin Aluminium Fabricators, built the canopy to go on the Landcruiser's rear tray.

'It was a fully enclosed canopy, solid at the front and rear. The whole structure, including the front and rear, was welded onto the tray and there was a steel plate shaped to the cab of the car and the roof welded

133

onto the back. The roof and the front were solid and the sides consisted of security door mesh,' he revealed in court.

It was a profitable week's work. Mr Galvin was paid $900 for the job, all in paper money. By now Bradley Murdoch's HJ75 was like new.

'The paintwork and the interior was good, the vehicle had been fitted with new springs and shock absorbers as well as a turbo charger and it was in good condition generally,' said Galvin.

A week later he pulled up behind Murdoch at an intersection and was impressed by the look of the sparkling white vehicle and its new green canopy.

Murdoch looked pleased with himself. Within the space of a few months his Landcruiser had undergone a dramatic makeover and he felt confident that any lingering doubts people might have over his alleged links with the disappearance of Peter Falconio would soon be forgotten.

He could resume his role as the successful bloke around town whose 'business interests' occasionally took him to South Australia and always guaranteed a ready supply of cash in his pocket.

Even his physical appearance was nothing like the suspect in the video. Now clean-shaven apart from an occasional moustache, his close-cropped hair and smart work clothes were totally different to the stooped, capped figure shown walking out of the Alice Springs service station.

Only those who knew Bradley Murdoch well recalled the hat he used to wear but which was now no longer part of his wardrobe.

Myles Sadler, who had known him in Perth and Broome, claimed he used to wear caps a lot, including one with a logo on the front, bearing the name of Cummings, an engine manufacturer.

Was this the same peaked cap caught on the surveillance video and the one Joanne Lees maintained her attacker was wearing when he tied her up at Barrow Creek?

If Bradley John Murdoch thought he could relax after the intense activity of the past few months, he was wrong. Some still had their suspicions and it would not be long before one of his closest friends would bring them to the attention of the police.

CHAPTER 15

....

JOANNE GOES HOME

A month after the incident at Barrow Creek, Joanne Lees returned to Sydney, accompanied by Peter's brother Paul. She had decided not to go back to Britain for the time being in the hope that police might find her boyfriend or the gunman.

At Sydney airport security personnel escorted them off the plane and on to the tarmac, where they were whisked away in a waiting car so that they did not have to walk through the arrivals lounge.

Joanne went back to her old job at Dymocks, where she spent much of the next three months. It was reassuring to be back with her former work colleagues and the friends she had made while living in Sydney with Peter. They supported her and protected her from prying eyes and the occasional press photographer who tried to snap her in the basement area of the George Street bookshop.

In Alice Springs the police investigation continued but there was no concealing the lack of progress. There had been a brief period of media speculation following the discovery of a man's body near the roadside some 60 kilometres south of Alice Springs, prompting speculation that it might be Peter. But it turned out to be an unrelated murder, for which a man was later convicted. Detectives established beyond doubt that the killing of Stuart Rhodes, a local chef, had nothing at all to do with the Falconio case.

By September the largest criminal enquiry in the history of the Northern Territory was being scaled down. Members of The Regulus, the name given to the task force set up to find the man who carried out the Barrow Creek attack, still beavered away in the Heenan Building at Alice Springs, but despite the enormous public response generated by the publicity and the $250,000 reward there were still no significant leads.

It was not because of lack of information. Over the previous three months police had received a flood of tips which produced 5600 lines of enquiry. Detectives eliminated no fewer than 200 potential suspects and 350 vehicles similar to the one driven by the attacker.

The calls continued to come in at the rate of a dozen a day and Assistant Commissioner Daulby remained positive about the outcome. 'Obviously we're very optimistic we'll find him [Falconio] and we will find the offender — we've got to be,' he said, pledging the investigation would continue to get top priority.

But it was also obvious they had made no clear headway. As fast as the tips and clues were followed up, they would be eliminated. It was impossible to ignore the fact that the gunman's trail was growing colder by the day.

By the middle of November Joanne, who was desperately hoping to hear of a breakthrough from the

Northern Territory police, felt she could wait no longer and decided to head home to Britain.

In a rare interview just before she left Australia, she told her home-town newspaper, the *Huddersfield Daily Examiner*, that it would not be easy to leave. 'It will be a big step for me. I feel close to Peter while I am here and I feel I can be of more help to the police,' she said.

And there was no mistaking her frustration about the lack of progress in the police investigation. 'I can't understand how no one knows the person responsible,' she said. 'I don't know what the police are doing now. They only tell me positive news but they speak to Paul [Peter's brother] every week.'

Back home in Britain, her mother, Jennifer, whose health was failing, was clearly looking forward to her daughter's return. 'She's bearing up but we really won't know how she is until we see her. It'll be strange for her coming back to Britain and it will be heartbreaking without Peter,' she admitted.

After briefly visiting her family in Huddersfield, Joanne returned to Brighton, where she and Peter had lived together. She still had friends there and it was a big enough town for her not to be noticed.

Joanne was keen to avoid attention. The hatred she felt towards the media now embraced nosey members of the public who stared at her in the street. She craved anonymity and avoided clubs or pubs where she might be recognised.

For a time she stayed with an air hostess friend before renting a flat in nearby Hove.

As the weeks went by Joanne would find solace on long walks around Brighton, where the blustery winds from the English Channel seemed to blow away her worries and appeared to invigorate her.

Then in March 2002 came a bombshell. Incredibly, after all her anti-media comments and her pledge never to sell her story, Joanne agreed to appear in an ITV documentary about the case in exchange for a payment reported to be about £50,000 (then $135,000).

The ITV series, *Tonight With Trevor McDonald*, is one of Britain's most-watched current affairs programs, and the producers spared no expense or effort in their pursuit of the story.

Apart from the generous payment to Joanne for her exclusive services, they wheeled out their star reporter, Martin Bashir, well known for his scoop interview with Princess Diana and his controversial profile of Michael Jackson.

Bashir's questioning was fair but tenacious.

'Did you kill Peter Falconio?' he asked Joanne bluntly.

'It's totally untrue,' she replied.

Why was Peter's blood not found on the back of the van where he was standing when shot?

Why did the gunman not leave any footprints in the bush?

How did the attacker's blood find its way onto her T-shirt?

Why didn't she notice Peter's body behind the Kombi as she was led to the ute?

Where was the dog?

And how did she manage to free herself?

These were all highly relevant questions and Joanne did her best to answer them, but mostly her responses were along the lines of 'No idea' or 'I'm not an expert'.

When it came to the events leading up to the attack and the incident itself she was more forthcoming than in previous media appearances.

'I had a funny feeling and really didn't want to stop — I can't explain it,' she said. 'It was just so dark and remote.'

That sense of foreboding manifested itself in the form of the man who drew up alongside them in his truck. 'The man looked aged 40-plus, like a local man. He seemed totally friendly. He kept pointing to the back of our van. He was bigger than Peter, six feet, I'm not sure. He had lots of layers of clothing on. He had long, shoulder-length, grey streaky hair — someone who didn't take much care in his appearance. He looked to me as though he maybe had an outside job.

'There was a red or blue heeler dog, typically Australian dog. Pete told me to wait [in the van]. It was cold and I was just in shorts and a T-shirt. Peter took his cigarettes and went and had a chat with the man. He came back and asked me to rev the engine.

'He said that everything was okay. The door was open. I heard him talking to the man. It all seemed amicable, joking. I could hear Peter saying, "Cheers mate, thanks for stopping."

'I was thinking, "Oh this nice man."'

She said that seconds later she heard a bang and the attacker suddenly appeared at the driver's side window with a gun. 'I saw the gun in his hand, pointing at me, and he started to open the door. He looked big and crouched over. Calm. Not aggressive. Very controlled and commanding.'

Joanne told how he pushed her into the passenger seat and bound her hands behind her back.

'He had a revolver. I haven't seen a gun before. It was a handgun, not very big and I remember it had scrolling in a rectangular box along the barrel. I couldn't smell anything from the gun — later people said that's because you're in survival mode.

'I was asking him, "Where's Peter? What have you done with Peter?" I was screaming for Pete. I just thought that at any moment Peter is going to come and save me.'

Joanne's terror was obvious in her voice as she recounted those dramatic few minutes for the camera. 'He got so mad that he hit me on the side of the face. I just kept thinking, "This is over," and "This is the end of my life."'

'Then he pushed me through a passenger door of his car. I was screaming and screaming but he grabbed me and pushed me through the seats into the back. 'His dog was there, which didn't make a sound; and he just pulled me and grabbed me and pushed me into the back of his vehicle, which had some kind of bed in there or mattress.

'Once I was laid in the back I really thought that was the end of my life. He went round to the side of his vehicle. I kept shouting to him, "What have you done to Peter? Is he hurt?"

'Then he went back to whatever he was doing. And that's when I just thought: this is my chance, I'm going. I slid down the truck and jumped out and ran into the bush. I presumed that he had followed me into the bush with the dog but I never heard the dog. I heard his footsteps crunching the branches and saw the torch.'

Joanne also dismissed reports that she and Peter had had a blazing row on the day they left Alice Springs, pointing out that police had 'mixed us up with another couple'.

And she also claimed that the first phone call to the police from the Barrow Creek Hotel had been treated as a hoax, a suggestion later vigorously denied by Assistant Commissioner Daulby.

However, she did admit she felt partly to blame for what had happened.

'I feel guilty that the man didn't want Pete . . . he just wanted me. He just wanted a female and he had to get Pete out of the way.'

The interview included further veiled criticism of the police, Joanne accusing them of concentrating too much on help from the public in the hunt for the gunman. 'They are concentrating far too much on that. They are sitting back waiting for that phone call and unless they take some action now, that's the only way it's going to be solved,' she said.

Still bitter about the intense scrutiny her evidence had been subjected to, she added, 'I'm just telling the truth and whether people choose to believe me or not, I don't really care. In fact, if Pete was here or if tomorrow he was found alive, he would be so mad because he knows the truth. And I guess it is hard for people to believe, but that's how it happened.'

Few could have been anything but sympathetic for Joanne after watching her relive the attack on television, but what surprised some was the personal criticism she levelled at Helen Jones, who had done so much to help her in the first few days after the incident.

In what appeared to be a totally undeserved denunciation of Helen's motives, she accused her of 'getting off on someone else's tragedy'.

What angered Joanne was Helen's willingness to talk to the media about what had happened, a policy she adopted in the hope that it would jog someone's memory and lead to the early apprehension of the gunman. Even the police encouraged her to talk, reasoning that it might help them to solve the case.

For some reason, however, Joanne was offended by Helen's remarks. The result was a major falling out between the two women. Helen was deeply hurt by the accusation that somehow she might have got a kick out of appearing in front of the cameras. This was certainly not the case, but the unhappy experience had cast a cloud over a relationship that was once so strong.

These days Helen finds it hard to talk kindly about the woman she helped in her hour of need. 'I was upset not just for myself but for everybody else who had put themselves out for her. All we did was try to help,' she told me later.

When Joanne didn't even bother to call in at the pub to say thank you after she returned to Barrow Creek the following year with the British TV crew, it was the final insult.

'If she even did so much as send me a thank-you card now I'd just rip it up and put it in the bin,' Helen confesses.

Such are the bitter recriminations of a woman who provided Joanne with so much support, only to be snubbed several months later.

CHAPTER 16

....

POLICE REFUTE BUNGLE CLAIMS

As the police enquiry proceeded, other less official investigations were taking place in an effort to solve the mystery. It is a time-honoured tradition in major crime stories that when all else fails, a small army of psychics come forward to offer their services and there was no shortage of clairvoyants prepared to provide their unique insight into this case.

Sadly they produced nothing of value. Even a Queensland water diviner caught a bus to the Northern Territory in the hope of locating Peter Falconio's body, but his swinging chain failed to find anything.

Frank Cuda had heard of the $250,000 reward and decided to put his supernatural powers to work. His divining skills directed him to a paddock near Renner Springs, but he found nothing of significance.

One British newspaper, the *Sunday Mirror*, commissioned John Stalker, the former deputy chief constable of Greater Manchester, to fly to the Northern

144

Territory to make his own enquiries into the case. He concluded that Joanne was telling the truth and the gunman was alone.

And he dismissed questions raised about the scarcity of footprints at the scene. The fact that the only footprints to be found belonged to Joanne was not surprising, he maintained. 'In fact the ground is rock hard and covered in small stones. It simply does not give under your feet. I am 6ft 1in and weigh 14 stone. Yet I too left no footprints,' he told the newspaper.

Stalker, who was once the youngest detective chief superintendent in Britain, was a well-respected member of the Crime Squad and not a man who could be easily deceived.

Like the Northern Territory officers his view was that there was no reason to disbelieve Joanne's story and the apparent lack of detail in it. 'In fact, given the trauma she suffered and the pitch darkness in which it happened, the lack of detail is completely understandable,' he emphasised.

During the course of his investigations Joanne sent him a handwritten note which made it clear she had not given up hope of finding her boyfriend alive. 'Please do not refer to Peter as being murdered when we don't know what the outcome will be. We won't give up hope until we know the truth,' she wrote.

The police, however, had little alternative but to treat it as a murder case. All the evidence pointed that way but the apparent killer remained at large.

As the months went by the investigation was costing the Northern Territory government millions of dollars. In a leaked memo, the officer in charge of Alice Springs police, Southern Region Commander Gary Manison, revealed that three per cent of his budget had been eroded by the enquiry. From now on all overtime work had to be approved beforehand and officers on sick leave could only be replaced in critical situations. Even vehicle travel had to be minimised and relief officers could be sent to police stations with more than two officers only when essential. Police chiefs admitted that the workload caused by the Falconio case was the prime reason: but there were no plans to wind up the investigation.

By February 2002 the pressure on Task Force Regulus to produce a breakthrough was intense. Reports of bungling in the early stages of the investigation, especially surrounding the late release of the truck stop surveillance video, left many people questioning the ability of the Northern Territory police.

Such queries were reasonable given that nearly eight months had elapsed since the crime occurred and the gunman had still not been found.

Commissioner Paul White decided it was time to investigate the investigation, though he didn't word it like that. Instead he described it as a review which would allow the main issues to be re-evaluated.

'The overarching objective of the review is to complement the work of the current investigation team by assessing progress to date,' he said. 'As is the case in many long-term, major crime investigations, the review will provide an opportunity to examine issues with a fresh set of eyes. The intended outcome of the review is an independent assessment that will help the investigation team solve this case.'

And who would carry out the review? Jim Litster, a retired assistant commissioner from South Australia who worked on the bombing of the National Crime Commission, and Superintendent George Owen, then officer in charge of road safety. If those closely observing the case had been hoping for a couple of top-flight detectives from interstate to put a rocket under Task Force Regulus they were to be sadly disappointed. While Messrs Litster and Owen had years of police experience behind them, a retired officer and a road safety specialist did not seem to be the most appropriate people to galvanise the Falconio investigation squad.

Yet at least it proved the police had not given up hope of finding the gunman and Commissioner White insisted that despite suggestions to the contrary, the current investigation team remained committed and resolute, determined to solve the case 'notwithstanding the painstaking and arduous task they have undertaken'.

One of the issues to be re-examined by the review team was the way forensic evidence had been collected. Questions over the standard of forensic testing had been raised after a freelance Alice Springs cameraman, Chris Tangey, claimed important evidence revealed by Luminol testing in the Kombi's cab had been dismissed by those carrying out the task.

The use of Luminol has been a long-established practice at the scene of a crime where blood may have been spilt. It is used to identify the presence of blood by making it glow blue in the dark, even when the bloodstain is not visible to the human eye.

It is not an infallible process because Luminol also reacts to other agents which have nothing to do with the human body, such as metal, but it is widely used and often provides valuable clues in the early stages of an investigation.

Tangey had been called in to film a forensic test on the campervan in August 2001 because he owned a Sony

PD150, a semi-professional handycam which was able to shoot in low-light situations.

The Luminol reaction can only be seen in the dark and police wanted to find out if Tangey's camera could record the luminescence on video tape. What followed gave the cameraman sufficient cause for concern that he felt compelled to make the tape available to those with a more specialist knowledge of forensic procedures.

Alarm bells began to ring when he walked into the police forensic compound in Alice Springs to see all Peter Falconio's and Joanne Lees' personal belongings and much of the Kombi's interior furnishings piled up against a wall with no apparent protection.

'There were boots, mattresses, pillows and clothing etc all piled on top of each other and stacked against the wall. I thought, "shouldn't these have been in a plastic bag or something?"' he explained to me.

Then one of the investigation officers, Bill Tower, introduced him to the main forensic officer, Joy Kuhl.

'I suited up and got some shots of Joy mixing the chemicals and Bill turned the lights out. They went over the van bit by bit but didn't find anything to the rear of the vehicle and there was no luminescence.

'So we went to the driver's side door, turned the lights out again and Joy stepped next to the steering wheel and started spraying the Luminol in the cab and there was some luminescence on the dashboard.

'Then about a minute later I turned and noticed through my left eye that there was quite strong luminescence on the inside of the driver's side door and it was in the shape of a hand. I stepped back and still had the microphone on, and Bill said, "What's that reaction on the door?"

'Joy replied, "I don't know what it is. It can't be blood because I went over that this afternoon."'

(This is believed to refer to an earlier test she performed with ortho-tolidine. This is used for screening purposes only, as it also yields a positive result for substances as varied as food, detergents and vegetation, as well as blood.)

At this point Tower turned to the cameraman and observed, 'It's fading away there now. You're probably not getting anything there now, Chris. It's gone.'

'Then it sounded like Joy tried to distract me and remarked, "Look over there."'

Her exact words on the tape were: 'See the metal bar in there.'

But Tangey sensed that Joy Kuhl and the police officer were keen to turn him away from what seemed to be a handprint and focus his attention elsewhere.

'It is my understanding that Luminol reacts to bare metal and human secretions such as blood and sweat. I also believe that after metal has been sprayed with the chemical it can glow for many minutes, whereas a human source will typically fade within 30 seconds to a minute. This is why what appears to be a handprint on my tape is of particular interest as it fades out completely in that very time window, whereas the metallic items don't,' he said.

I viewed a copy of the tape and tended to agree with Tangey's interpretation of what he heard and saw that day. As Tangey's forensic knowledge was minimal, it was always advisable to gain a second opinion in such matters and the Alice Springs cameraman decided to do just that.

He sent a copy of the video to Emeritus Professor Barry Boettcher, a retired head of biological sciences at

Newcastle University. Professor Boettcher's response to what he saw left no doubt in his mind that the shape on the driver's side window looked very much like a human hand. And even if it wasn't it should have merited further testing.

This was potential evidence that was being ignored, Professor Boettcher believed.

'I find it surprising that Mrs Kuhl and Mr Tower appeared not to show any interest in the brightest luminescence found during the taping of the tests on the Kombi,' he declared.

'Had they thought it to be a strong false positive reaction I'd have expected them to talk about it, as opposed to ignoring it altogether. It's very puzzling because the investigators were taking great pains with their enquiries, so it would seem inappropriate that the brightest luminescence should be dismissed in such a casual manner.'

Professor Boettcher's response to the forensic examination of the Kombi and his surprise at Kuhl's lack of interest in the handprint was not the first time he had had cause to question her methods and not the only occasion their conflicting views attracted headlines. Two decades earlier he had cast doubt on her forensic examination of the car in which Lindy Chamberlain was alleged to have murdered her baby, Azaria.

Kuhl's testimony that Lindy and Michael Chamberlain's Holden Torana contained evidence of foetal blood was instrumental in Lindy's conviction for murder. She used a reagent called Behringwerke, but misinterpreted the reaction, which she believed indicated the presence of blood on the floor of the car. In fact, the chemical could react to rust, or in this case sound deadener, in much the same manner.

Even the scientists who produced the chemical pointed out that there had been a misunderstanding, but it did not stop Lindy being jailed for life; although she was subsequently pardoned and her conviction quashed.

Now more than 20 years later Kuhl and Professor Boettcher were at loggerheads again over the interpretation of forensic evidence in a murder trial. The circumstances of the case may have been very different, but the results could have an important bearing on the conviction of the defendant.

Had a vital piece of evidence been overlooked? Or was there a more simple explanation? How did the handprint get there when the vehicle had already been examined for fingerprints? Could the interior of the van have been contaminated by an ungloved hand?

Tangey couldn't be certain but suspected that Tower may have touched parts of the Kombi without the necessary handwear. 'It seems beyond doubt that Tower was not in fact wearing gloves in the examination and is seen to contaminate the interior light switch with his bare hand,' he said.

Tangey had been there and had the camera tape to prove it.

Had Tower not invited him to film the forensic examination nothing of this would have been made public.

Originally the cameraman had struck a deal with Tower that he would provide his services for no fee and that after six months he would be allowed to sell the footage to the media. Six months later, and with no progress in the Falconio investigation, he rang *The Australian* newspaper to alert them to the tape and what it contained.

When the story appeared in the newspaper, the police were predictably irate.

'First they tried to threaten me and demanded I hand the tape back,' he claimed.

'Then Kate Vanderlann, who was running the investigation, rang me with her voice visibly shaking and demanded to know when she was going to get the tape back.'

When Tangey refused on the grounds that it was his tape, he alleged she threatened to charge him under the Electronic Devices Act. Fortunately he knew the law and reminded her that only the Federal Police could prosecute people under that Act and as she represented the Northern Territory police she did not have such powers.

Within minutes he was telephoned by Assistant Commissioner Daulby and Col Hardman, Commander of Northern Territory Crime, who he claimed gave him the good cop, bad cop routine. 'They tried to convince me to release the master tape and insinuated that if I didn't I would be in a lot of trouble,' he said.

Tangey had already given Tower a copy of the tape on a mini-disc which had been loaded on to his computer via FireWire, but now the police were saying they needed the tape again because there was no sound on the earlier version.

The cameraman, fearing a police raid on his house, decided to send the mini-DV cassette containing the footage to Stuart Littlemore, a Sydney QC and former host of the ABC TV show *Media Watch*, who held it in his safe.

After legal representation, the Northern Territory police backed off and Tangey received a letter from the Commissioner confirming they no longer required the tape after all. 'So all of a sudden it was important and then it wasn't. There was undoubtedly a stuff-up of some sort. Either they missed the handprint or it was one of their own.'

This of course is Tangey's version of events. The police view was different, as a statement released by them on March 2002 affirmed. In it Col Hardman said the Luminol test on the Kombi was carried out by a highly experienced forensic biologist (Joy Kuhl) to see if any further biological evidence could be found that had not previously been identified.

'Given the extent of previous examinations we did not expect to find any. The result was that there was nothing further located,' he added.

He said that they had used the video camera to establish whether video was a viable option for providing footage of a Luminol testing procedure to a court in the future.

'As can be seen by the video, this presentation was not useful. While recording, the biologist, who has high expertise in forensic examinations, expresses interest in the way certain parts of the car illuminate during the procedure. She was fully aware that a more specific biological examination had already been conducted and she was aware of the results. When an area of the door illuminates, she points out that she has already swabbed that area. That area has been examined on two occasions by biologists and by fingerprint experts and had not produced any evidence,' he explained.

'The forensic scientists did not interpret any stains or other deposits that could have been interpreted as a handprint.'

Commander Hardman said Kuhl was fully aware that metals and other objects would be illuminated during the process and this had happened. 'While she knew that the illumination seen during the filming was not new forensic evidence, she commented that others who don't fully understand the procedure might think the luminescence were signs of a "blood bath". In fact the Luminol test did not identify anything of additional forensic value.

'Reports to the contrary by persons outside the investigation have no substance and any interpretation of any results from this testing could only be made by a trained forensic biologist,' he made clear.

Was this a satisfactory explanation or were the police prevaricating?

Each side had valuable points to make but questions would remain about the overall performance of the investigation.

Even the official review, the results of which were eventually announced in July, did not make public the findings in any great detail. It merely talked in positive terms about the way police had handled the investigation and even the controversy over the release of the truck stop surveillance video was effectively dismissed.

Assistant Commissioner Daulby said the review team had accepted the reason for the delay and praised the way police had gone about their enquiries. He announced that the review had found that criticism of the police investigation was largely baseless and that officers had acted quickly and appropriately.

While he couldn't hide the fact that the gunman was still at large, he insisted that the mystery would be solved. 'I'm confident we'll catch the killer. I'm confident the answer's out there,' he added.

'We've said all along that this wasn't going to be easy — it's not easy at all. We've worked very hard on this [and] there's still a lot to be done. I'm confident that someone in some point in time will give us that piece we're looking for.'

Was the review and the police response to criticism little more than a whitewash? Many of those following the progress of the investigation doubted the value of an enquiry in which the police investigated themselves.

But former South Australian Assistant Police Commissioner Jim Litster said it was not designed to blame anyone. 'People tend to read more into reviews than should be read into it,' he remarked.

Three years after the drama at Barrow Creek and the subsequent investigation, three of the key players in the saga had left their jobs: Joy Kuhl and Bill Tower retired and Assistant Commissioner Daulby was working in East Timor as a police adviser.

CHAPTER 17

....

HAPPY HEPI

James Tahi Hepi was stopped by police while driving his utility into Broome after completing the marathon 3600-kilometre journey from Sedan in South Australia on 16 May 2002. Detectives were acting on a tip-off that the 35-year-old New Zealander had a load of high-grade cannabis secreted on board and was planning to sell it.

The cannabis was difficult to find at first so they drove the truck back to police headquarters in Broome, where they located 3.65 kilograms of the drug hidden in a 40-kilogram gas bottle placed in the vehicle's rear tray. It was an ingenious place to conceal it because gas containers are notoriously difficult and potentially dangerous to open and could have been easily overlooked by the investigating officers.

In reality Hepi knew the game was up and told the police where it was.

The cannabis had a street value of about $45,000 and he was well aware that a criminal conviction for drug trafficking could not only lead to a substantial jail sentence but the confiscation of his assets. Hepi, who had a property in South Austrlaia, had a lot to lose.

Who had dobbed him in was yet to be established, but the New Zealander had a pretty good idea. His relations with Brad Murdoch were not exactly cordial. They had argued over their 'business' relationship and so there had been very little contact between them recently.

'I wanted to know where the money was and the property and I asked him why he had not met me in Broome,' Hepi recalled. 'He said he'd had trouble getting across a roadblock because of the Falconio murder. The police were waiting [for him] at the border.'

Hepi had his own suspicions about Murdoch's involvement in the Barrow Creek incident. Ever since Murdoch returned home to their Forrest Street duplex on the Monday morning after the weekend attack and volunteered without being asked, 'I didn't do it,' Hepi had wondered whether his housemate was telling the truth.

He knew that Murdoch was a hard bastard who had a violent streak if provoked. But was he capable of cold-blooded murder? Hepi didn't know for sure but after he was picked up by the police on a major drugs charge he didn't care. He realised the information he had on Murdoch may be enough to put him behind bars for life and could provide his own ticket to freedom.

He didn't know exactly where Murdoch was that weekend but he had a pretty shrewd idea. Hadn't he altered the look of his vehicle and changed his own appearance within days of returning to Broome?

And hadn't he seen Murdoch putting together those home-made handcuffs out of plastic ties back in his South Australian workshop? Those intricately manufactured handmade restraints, like those used to bind Joanne Lees' wrists and later described by police as 'three small, inter-linked loops covered with black hundred-mile-an-hour tape', were extraordinarily similar to those he had seen Murdoch making.

Buoyed by the evidence he had against his former business partner, Hepi offered to do a deal with the police, in exchange for a lesser punishment. He would co-operate fully with them in their hunt for the gunman in the Peter Falconio case.

When Hepi appeared at Broome District Court in August, his defence lawyer Gordon Bauman told Judge Antoinette Kennedy that police acknowledged his client's complete co-operation in providing information about a major interstate crime.

A detective in court also passed a letter to the judge explaining how helpful he had been and requesting he be treated leniently. In passing sentence Judge Kennedy reminded Hepi that his admission of guilt on such a serious charge would normally result in a lengthy custodial term, but given his co-operation with police, his previous good record and glowing references, she would give him a one-off chance to remain free.

James Tahi Hepi was given an 18-month prison sentence suspended for 12 months. All that remained was to assemble the evidence to arrest Murdoch.

While much of what Hepi had to say pointed to the guilt of his fellow drugs trafficker, the evidence was essentially circumstantial. The police needed proof and the best way was to obtain a positive match with the tiny sample of DNA found on Joanne's T-shirt.

Getting that DNA presented problems. For a start the police didn't know where Murdoch was, though Hepi was pretty certain he had returned to South Australia where he had become friendly with some neighbours about two kilometres away from his own 30-hectare property in the back blocks of Swan Reach near the Murray River.

Murdoch, fearful that police would get to know of Hepi's hideaway and raid it, had moved in with the next-door neighbours.

Then Hepi had a brainwave. He would arrange for someone to collect Murdoch's cigarette butts in South Australia and have them analysed for DNA.

While it is possible to leave DNA from saliva on a cigarette end, it is not always the case. Sometimes an item has to be touched several times before a person's DNA remains adhered to an object.

Murdoch smoked Winfield Golds and had a habit of flicking his dog ends on the ground where he would stamp them out with his foot. Several attempts to locate the cigarette butts were made but all proved fruitless.

The police still didn't have their DNA but they were closing in on their prime suspect. They knew Murdoch's older brother Gary lived in Perth and asked him to co-operate with their investigation. As a close relative his DNA code would provide important information about his brother's DNA, which they could in turn compare with the sample found on Joanne's T-shirt. If they looked the same they could be reasonably certain that they had their man.

Gary agreed to co-operate and they took a swab on 14 August 2001, but what they hadn't allowed for was family loyalty. Gary tipped his brother off about the police interest in him, which sent Brad Murdoch into a panic.

Already paranoid about the police investigation into him, his only solace was in drugs, which made him even more unstable. His judgement clouded by amphetamines and cannabis, he prepared to meet the police with all guns a'blazing if necessary. He was determined not to go down without a fight and was prepared to die. But first they had to find him.

Three days after Gary's telephone call he moved into a shed behind the property owned by Hepi's neighbours, a 33-year-old woman, her 12-year-old daughter and her stepfather, a 62-year-old former massage-parlour owner in Adelaide.

Anxious not to be seen, he taped the windows with black plastic, telling the girl that police were hunting him for the Falconio killing, which he said he didn't do. He was innocent and they were trying to frame him, he explained.

Later the girl found a magazine article about the Falconio case in the room and she asked him where he had got his T-shirt. Murdoch made a throwaway reference to Falconio but did not elaborate.

The child had already established a friendly relationship with Murdoch, whom she had met on several occasions when he had stayed with her parents. He had always been generous with his time and money, giving her $500 as a present on her 12th birthday and a big hug.

'He had never hugged me before. Sometimes he said I looked nice,' she added.

On one occasion she had helped him sort out his maps and they talked about 'school, animals and other things like that'.

Then, on the night of 21 August 2002, his mood changed. What happened next became the subject of criminal charges against Murdoch, but on which he was later acquitted.

Taking the girl into the spare accommodation at the back of the house he allegedly blindfolded, gagged and bound her hands behind her, before pushing her onto a bed and warning her: 'If you move I'll give you brain damage.'

According to evidence later submitted to a court, Murdoch, wearing a handgun in his shoulder holster, then digitally raped her and later pulled a pair of black pantyhose over her head and raped her.

He then allegedly threatened her mother with a handgun before throwing them both into the back of his Landcruiser where he manacled their hands and ankles and chained them to the wire-mesh canopy. In the dim light they noticed a rifle, ammunition and what turned out to be tins of cannabis.

At one point he hit the mother in the face and threatened her with an electric prod if she didn't have sex with him, before indecently assaulting her, it was further alleged.

'Why are you doing this?' she asked, to which he reportedly replied that they were 'in the wrong place at the wrong time'. He claimed the 'cops had framed him' and he was 'on the run'. They were his 'insurance'.

According to the mother, he was heading to Western Australia to kill a man and shoot himself in the head.

Murdoch and his passengers in the rear of the truck drove around for most of the night and much of the next day. They didn't know where they were being taken or what he planned to do with them.

About dawn that day he'd driven into a truck stop and warned the two women, 'Shut up and don't say anything or you're dead!'

He then produced two parcels containing cannabis from inside the canopy and handed them to another man, a semi-trailer driver who had parked nearby. The deal took 10 minutes to complete before he drove off again, snorting amphetamines and smoking pot as he headed west.

After a few hours Murdoch pulled over into a ditch and tethered them to some fold-up chairs so they could not escape.

'I said to him that he was pathetic wanting to tie my daughter up again when he had a gun,' the mother recalled afterwards. 'He then chained us both to the chairs, went and snorted some speed, smoked some cannabis and checked things in his vehicle. He walked around outside to make sure no one was there and he was checking his guns,' she told police.

According to the mother, Murdoch demanded one of his female passengers give herself to him. Fearful of the consequences if she did not co-operate, the mother volunteered.

'I did not want to have sex with him but I didn't want him to harm my daughter again, so I said I would do it.'

After sexually assaulting the woman, the journey continued.

Eventually Murdoch pulled in to a Shell service station at Port Augusta. This was as far as his passengers were going. To their relief he cut the cable ties around their wrists with a pair of bolt cutters and allowed them to climb out of the rear tray.

Then he produced $1000 in cash and told them to catch a taxi home.

Her hands still shaking from the horror of the past 19 hours, she could hardly hold the change which Murdoch had given her to make the phone call for a cab.

Surprisingly she made no attempt to alert the petrol station attendant of her ordeal, explaining afterwards that she was too scared to involve the public. 'You must understand that from the evening Brad had abducted us back at the house I had gone into shock. I didn't want to involve the public because I knew Brad would have a shoot-out,' she said. 'As far as I knew Brad could have been hiding behind a tree or in the bushes . . . I didn't want to put other lives at risk.'

She claimed that Murdoch had threatened to murder her if she tried to call the police.

'If you ring the police this rifle can shoot up to 500 metres,' he allegedly warned her.

In fact it was another five days before the mother agreed that ther de facto husband should ring a detective they knew on her mobile telephone.

Why it had taken her so long to report the crime led to speculation that the alleged kidnapping and rape may not have happened after all. Curiously the mother did not keep potentially important forensic evidence, which might have contained semen or DNA from the rapist and therefore proof of his identity. She threw away the clothing her daughter had been wearing on the night of the alleged rape because she said she was in a state of shock. Her partner, the former massage-parlour owner, had suggested she dispose of the items in a bin at the caravan site in which they were staying. 'I don't know why we did it — but my partner was upset as well,' she said. 'We weren't thinking straight. We were in shock.'

But it didn't seem to ring true, as Murdoch's lawyer Grant Algie later pointed out. Why dispose of incriminating evidence so soon after the attack? Had she deliberately wanted to get rid of the clothes 'because there would be nothing on them'? he wondered.

And why had it taken five days to inform the police?

'You wanted that long perhaps to try and make sure that you and your daughter had a story that [matched],' Algie suggested.

....

CHAPTER 18

POLICE MOVE IN

At 11.30 a.m. on Wednesday 28 August 2002, Geoff Carson, a detective stationed with police in the Riverland area of South Australia, received a mobile telephone call from the de facto husband of the woman whose daughter had been allegedly raped by Bradley Murdoch nearly a week earlier.

Accompanied by a female officer, he drove immediately to the man's property at Swan Reach, where he was given a detailed account of the rape and abduction that began on 21 August and ended some 19 hours later.

Armed with a full description of the kidnapper, Carson called his superior, Detective Sergeant Mark Boileau, to instigate an immediate statewide manhunt. 'Emphasis was placed on the fact that Murdoch was believed to be armed and would retaliate against police if challenged,' the detective explained in a statement.

By mid-afternoon the search was gathering momentum. Detective Sergeant Boileau had telephoned his counterparts at Port Augusta where Murdoch had last been seen. He also spoke to Senior Constable Robert Michael about the women's story and asked him to retrieve surveillance vision from service stations in the area.

It was during this exercise that Michael and another officer, Probationary Constable Peter Stirling, had a lucky break. After driving to the BP garage in Port Augusta on National Highway One, they noticed a Toyota Landcruiser matching the description of Murdoch's vehicle go past.

Discreetly following in their unmarked police car, they radioed for a registration check on the truck and within minutes had confirmation that it belonged to the suspect.

Murdoch was going shopping. He turned left into the Port Augusta business district and pulled into a car park near Woolworths. Senior Constable Michael and Constable Stirling knew they were close to getting their man, but arresting him in such a public place could be dangerous given the likelihood that he was carrying firearms.

Assuming control, Michael declared the situation a 'high risk incident' and demanded armed back-up from all available officers, who were ordered to wear bulletproof vests.

They were not taking any chances. They didn't want anybody caught up in the cross-fire should shooting break out, so nearby roads were cordoned off. Constable Stirling took cover in a car yard while he watched Murdoch step out of the Landcruiser and unzip the canopy over the rear tray. As he stood there he seemed to be adjusting the front of his trousers as though he might be concealing a handgun down his pants.

He then pulled his jumper down over his waist and walked calmly into the front entrance of the supermarket. Soon the two officers were joined by Senior Constable Mark Cowling, a trained marksman who was armed with a sniper rifle. Minutes afterwards another officer arrived, this time with a 12-gauge, pump-action shotgun.

They were joined by Senior Constable Andrew Dredge, who, along with Probationary Constable Stirling, was to play a key role in the apprehension of Bradley Murdoch.

Their task would be to isolate and arrest the suspect, who was described to them as 'extremely dangerous'. The odds were that he had a number of firearms including a high-velocity rifle and a pistol. If confronted by police there was a strong chance he would attempt to shoot his way out rather than be taken into custody, the officers were warned.

Murdoch was blissfully unaware of the police operation being mounted outside as he pushed his shopping trolley around the aisles. He was too concerned with filling his stomach, buying a hot chicken from the supermarket's rotisserie, as well as a packet of sausages, soup, rice, custard, mayonnaise, cheese, strawberry and blueberry twists, some Cruskits and two litres of long-life milk. A glass ashtray, a tube of Deep Heat, a roll of kitchen foil, some safety pins and four AA batteries also went into the basket.

The purchases offered a rare glimpse of the domesticated side of Murdoch's character, a man with a bit of a sweet tooth and a smoker who liked to use an ashtray on the road.

At 6 p.m. precisely another officer, Probationary Officer Ben Timmins, got on his walkie-talkie to reveal that he could see Murdoch at the check-out. Bystanders were ordered into nearby shops as the officers hid behind large gum trees in the car park.

Murdoch placed everything into two plastic carrier bags and calmly walked through the automatic doors. If he had imagined a Butch Cassidy-style gun battle in his final seconds of freedom he was to be sadly disappointed.

At 6.07 p.m. Senior Constable Michael gave the order to advance, shouting, 'Go, go, go!'

As Senior Constable Sean Everett ran across the car park with his shotgun pointed at Murdoch, other members of the team yelled out, 'Get on the ground!'

Confronted by the uniformed officers, he appeared to reach for a semi-automatic pistol in his shoulder holster but thought better of it as he was repeatedly ordered: 'Don't move! Get down on the ground, get on the ground, get on the ground!'

Everett's heart was racing as he looked Murdoch in the eyes. This was a potentially life-threatening moment for the brave copper who could not anticipate his quarry's reaction, and every second was engraved on his memory.

'He appeared very calm and did not appear frightened by our rapid approach with firearms pointed in his direction,' he recalled in a statement tendered to the court afterwards and obtained by the Adelaide *Advertiser*.

'I would describe his reaction to our presence as calculating. I formed the belief that the suspect was about to produce a weapon from a concealed position underneath the front of his shirt. I yelled loudly, "Get on the f. . .ing ground now".'

After hesitating for a split second, Murdoch removed his hands from the front of his trousers and raised both hands above his head.

'He then turned around and got down on his knees,' Senior Constable Everett said.

'I then directed him to lay on the ground face down. He didn't comply immediately. I then shoved him in the rear lower back area with my foot which caused him to immediately lay face down on the ground. I did this to prevent any further possibility of him reaching for a concealed weapon.'

Realising the hopelessness of his situation, Murdoch had already dropped the plastic bags and within a minute was being trussed up. The 12-gauge, pump-action shotgun remained pressed into his back, while another officer handcuffed his wrists and grabbed him around the legs.

Murdoch was completely immobilised on the ground, allowing Senior Constable Dredge to check him for weapons. In his shoulder holster was a gun containing 10 bullets, as well as a spare magazine with another 17 rounds.

Murdoch was slowly lifted to his feet to come face to face with Senior Constable Michael.

'I'm now arresting you on suspicion of the offences of abduction and rape,' Michael told him. 'You are not obliged to say anything further. Anything that you say will be recorded and may be given in evidence. Do you understand that?'

'Yep,' Murdoch replied.

Thirteen and a half months after the attack at Barrow Creek, the chief suspect was in police custody. All that

169

remained was to obtain Murdoch's DNA so forensic scientists could compare it with the stain found on Joanne Lees' T-shirt.

But first the rape charges had to be addressed. The following morning he appeared briefly in Port Augusta magistrates court and was remanded in custody.

Now that Murdoch was behind bars and charged with a sexual offence, it made it easier for the police to demand his DNA, although early attempts to carry out the test were resisted by his defence lawyer, Grant Algie.

Blood, mouth swabs and even pubic hair had already been taken from Murdoch after his arrest, but under state law tests could not be carried out on them without the permission of a magistrate.

Algie argued that his client's privacy was being invaded and the police motive was clear.

'It is fundamentally obvious that the purpose [of testing the blood], one would cynically suspect, is not in respect to these South Australian allegations. It is for the purpose of sending these samples to the Northern Territory,' he claimed.

But on 6 September 2002, magistrate Gary Gumpi agreed to the Forensic Procedures Application, concluding that it 'may well produce important forensic material'.

Privately the defendant also feared that his DNA sample could be interfered with between the time it left Adelaide and when it was eventually compared with the tiny spot on the back of Joanne's T-shirt now being kept in Darwin.

Certainly it still took some weeks before the Northern Territory police were able to confirm a positive match, but by 10 October they were satisfied they had the right man.

At 1.30 p.m. three detectives from Taskforce Regulus and a forensic crime scene examiner went to Yatala high security prison in Adelaide in the hope of questioning Murdoch, but he maintained his right to silence.

Assistant Commissioner Daulby revealed that police had also travelled to Western Australia over the previous few weeks. 'During that time we gained enough information to warrant further investigation into the man being held in South Australia,' he said.

That man remained a person of interest and they were unable to exclude him from their investigation into the disappearance of Peter Falconio and attempted abduction of Joanne Lees, he added.

Assistant Commissioner Daulby said the taskforce would now focus its attention on the man's activities around Alice Springs and Ti Tree on or around 14 July 2001. 'We'll be moving towards a warrant for his arrest at an appropriate time. I can say that we have conducted enquiries in a number of states in the last number of weeks with regard to his movements and I'm confident we'll achieve that warrant in the not too distant future.'

But it wasn't that simple. The fact that Murdoch was already facing rape charges under South Australian law complicated the legal process. If he were charged over the Falconio case, which trial would take precedence?

If the South Australian case was held first and the defendant was found guilty and sentenced to a lengthy prison term, the Northern Territory justice system might have to wait many years before being able to try him over the Falconio case.

On the other hand, if the rape case was relegated in favour of the Falconio trial, would it be fair to the woman and child who had allegedly been sexually assaulted and abducted?

On the face of it the odds were in South Australia's favour. Under the country's federated justice system each state administers its own laws and given that Murdoch faced the rape charges first, South Australia could argue that it had a legal right to prosecute the defendant first. The fact that the Northern Territory also had an interest in him should, in theory, not have any influence in the matter.

Australian states and territories guard their independence jealously and will do their utmost to put their own interests first. Even people wanted for questioning by police in another state have to be extradited by a court of law. It is similar to the extradition systems that operate between foreign countries, with one nation having to apply to another before a suspect can be handed over.

South Australia's Director of Public Prosecutions conceded that the issue at stake posed a big problem, describing it as a 'really tough call for the state because of the notoriety of the crime'.

'We'll co-operate [with the Northern Territory] as far as we can but there are considerations which militate towards having our trial first,' he said. 'It's a question of balancing those competing interests with the attitude of the victims of the alleged offences in South Australia.'

In the end it was agreed to hold the rape trial first. Afterwards it would be up to the Northern Territory to apply for the defendant's extradition.

The Northern Territory's hands were tied because although there was a warrant out for Murdoch's arrest, he could not be charged in connection with the Barrow Creek crime unless he was acquitted of the sex charges, freed after serving his sentence, or somehow transferred between the two penal systems.

It was to be almost a year before the rape case came to court. On 20 October 2003, Bradley John Murdoch pleaded not guilty to two counts of rape, two of false imprisonment, two of indecent assault and one of common assault.

Even at this late stage his defence team was arguing for the case to be stayed. Grant Algie claimed that there was no hope of his client receiving a fair trial in the rape hearing because evidence would be presented about the Falconio case during the hearing. Equally, if the Falconio accusations were mentioned before he was tried in the Northern Territory it might prejudice Murdoch's chances of a fair trial there.

Judge Michael David agreed to a suppression order in South Australia, but this did not extend to the rest of the country.

Algie made it clear that the only possibility of his client getting a fair trial was for the Falconio case to go ahead first. He also made no secret of his belief that the rape charges had been part of a police set-up. 'The defence case is that the false allegations that are made against Mr Murdoch may well be a product of a desire on the part of the victims or others to set him up for the Falconio murder,' he asserted.

'There are those who had a motive to falsely accuse Mr Murdoch with respect to Falconio and people *were* attempting to falsely accuse and set up Mr Murdoch with respect to Falconio,' he claimed.

The alleged victims and their co-conspirators had failed to get DNA evidence on Murdoch before the 'set-up' so the rape story had been devised, he suggested.

Was he indicating that the police had been involved in a conspiracy, Judge David asked.

'It could be,' Algie replied.

Prosecutor Liesl Chapman told the court how Murdoch was in a state of paranoia in the days leading up to the alleged rape because he knew the police were after him for Falconio. To make matters worse he was also heavily using amphetamines and marijuana.

As the trial progressed, both the woman and her daughter provided graphic evidence of the alleged rape and abduction.

And there were further intriguing details from the mother's de facto partner, who has since died. The man, who admitted he had acted as a 'gofer' for Murdoch on occasions, explained how he had helped him and his partner, James Hepi, with their interstate drug trafficking business. 'I would help them pack the drugs and whatever little things they wanted done, [then] they would collect it up, parcel it up and off they'd go.'

The man, who could not be named for legal reasons, said he had invited Murdoch to stay with him on his property after they both fell out with Hepi.

'Brad sort of got suspicious of James,' he said. 'James reckoned he was sick and he wasn't, so Brad had to do the drug run and it just blew up from there.'

The bad feeling came to a head when Hepi and the man had an argument over some property belonging to Murdoch, which Hepi tried to remove without permission. The row allegedly ended with Hepi shooting at his home and threatening to cut off his fingers.

At this time Murdoch was dividing his time between Swan Reach and Port Broughton on the South Australian coast where he was renting another property, a farmhouse which was used by his old mate, Darryl 'Dags' Cragan, with whom he went to school in Western Australia.

Cragan had also fallen out with Murdoch, who objected to his alleged injecting of amphetamines intravenously. (Even Murdoch had some standards.) But around the middle of 2002 it suited both men to work together again.

Murdoch bought him a car, an EA Ford Falcon sedan, and allegedly gave him a Glock 9mm semi-automatic pistol to protect himself. Cragan stayed at Port Broughton with Jack the Dalmatian while Murdoch returned to Swan Reach.

On 23 August the elderly former massage-parlour owner, whose partner and partner's daughter had allegedly been raped, telephoned Cragan and asked him to go to the Royal Adelaide Hospital.

'He just said something's happened and could I get down here.'

It was put to the court that Cragan agreed but before leaving allegedly removed $12,000 in cash and 1.8 kilograms of cannabis hidden on the Port Broughton property.

On reaching the hospital, he drove the man, the mother and her daughter to the Boliva Caravan Park near Adelaide, where they stayed for the next five or six days without contacting police.

In court Algie wondered whether there might have been a plan to frame his client so Cragan could steal his drugs and cash. 'It was all part of a pre-arranged little plan that you hatched with either [the stepfather] or [the mother] or both — do you agree with that?' he asked.

'No . . . don't you put words into my mouth,' Cragan snapped back.

As the trial continued, the case seemed to raise more questions than answers. Was the defendant being set up, as suggested by Algie? Or had the attack on the two women genuinely happened in the way they described?

In the final analysis the defence had raised too many doubts in the mind of the jury, who took four hours and 12 minutes to find Bradley John Murdoch not guilty on all counts.

'Make sure you write the truth,' Murdoch ordered journalists in the press bench.

Outside Algie said his client had been vindicated. 'As you know his defence has always been that he was falsely accused and set up with respect to these offences. He believes the verdict of the jury is a clear confirmation of that,' he added.

But Murdoch's acquittal did not mean he was a free man. As he walked out of court, he was rearrested inside the building on a Northern Territory warrant and two hours later bundled into a police car.

Soon he would be extradited to Darwin to see whether there was a prima facie case against him on the Falconio charges.

But the committal proceedings were still nearly six months away.

CHAPTER 19

....

THE STAGE IS SET

The pre-trial hearing of Bradley John Murdoch was eventually fixed for 17 May 2004 in Darwin. If the crime itself had caught the imagination of the public at large, the prospect of Joanne Lees coming face to face with the man accused of killing her boyfriend and attempting to abduct her was also eagerly anticipated by both the Australian and British media.

It clearly had the potential for high drama and those gathered in court number six were not to be disappointed.

Joanne was the first to arrive for the proceedings, flying into the Northern Territory more than a week before the case was due to open and promptly issuing a statement denying she was in hiding. Though the speedy nature of her departure from Darwin airport to a secret location in the company of officers from the Northern Territory's Tactical Response Group suggested otherwise.

She was also keen to put a stop to rumours that the young man she was accompanied by was her new boyfriend. In fact he was Mark Sanders, described by Joanne as 'one of Pete's best friends who studied with him at Brighton University'.

Joanne explained that she would be giving no interviews before or during the case on the advice of the Director of Public Prosecutions, Rex Wild QC. 'I'm in Darwin to prepare for the committal in which I will be giving evidence,' she explained in a statement to the media.

'I want Bradley Murdoch to receive a fair committal hearing as I believe this is the only way justice can prevail,' she added. 'I wish I was here under different circumstances as I still have many friends here and I have many happy memories of Australia. However, this is not a holiday and I am completely focused on the task ahead.'

Quite why she flew to Darwin more than a week before the case was due to begin was unclear. Joanne kept her head down and, despite the best efforts of photographers to snap her in public, the star witness remained frustratingly hidden away.

Defence lawyer Grant Algie and his right-hand man Mark Twiggs showed no such reluctance to face the media spotlight, taking the unusual step of calling a press conference at Darwin airport on the weekend before the committal opened.

It seemed both sides were making their positions clear early on in the proceedings, Algie keen to draw attention to the fact that his client did not enjoy the same level of back-up afforded Lees.

'I have called this press conference because Bradley Murdoch doesn't have a website and Brad Murdoch doesn't have a media liaison officer. What Brad Murdoch has is a presumption of innocence and an absolute right to a fair trial — a fair go — if he's to face trial,' he said.

'My concern is that we should not do anything to jeopardise or erode or destroy his chance of having a fair trial,' he added.

The defence lawyer pointed out that the manner of the pre-trial hearing would be vastly different from a trial.

'It's important to understand you will be unlikely to see a presentation of an active or positive defence — that is not part of the committal process. At the end [of the committal] you will, in all likelihood, have heard only one side of the story . . . It would be negligent for any defence counsel to put forward a defence in a committal,' he explained. 'A committal is the process which stands between someone being charged and someone standing trial. It's a filtering process.'

Algie's remarks suggested that there would be no intense grilling of the principal witness. He would not be 'exhaustively cross-examining' any witness, including Lees.

Nor would he be showing his hand by revealing the defence case in advance. That would not be presented until the trial, assuming magistrate Alasdair McGregor found that Bradley Murdoch had a prima facie case to answer at the end of the pre-trial hearing.

But this was not to suggest that the legal drama about to unfold in court number six would be anything less than gripping. The stage was set, only the key players had yet to emerge.

The authorities were proud of their new facility, trumpeted as the Northern Territory's first paperless courtroom and technologically transformed at a cost of $1m. Every page of evidence would be available electronically, each document or image could be accessed on a bank of 15 computer monitors and two large overhead screens.

Court six, with its partly wood panelled walls, red chairs and grey ceiling, combined state-of-the-art technology with an old-fashioned judicial look. At the far end sat the magistrate; towering over him were the two kangaroos of the Northern Territory coat of arms.

To the magistrate's left, the defendant was positioned behind a glass screen along with two Corrective Services officers.

Murdoch was dressed in a blue, long-sleeved, open-necked, denim shirt and wore metal-rimmed spectacles. His grey hair closely cropped, he shuffled nervously in the dock, revealing a habit of moving his shoulders up and down alternately while rubbing his chest at the same time.

The court was packed for the opening address by Rex Wild, who outlined the case for the prosecution. After detailing the facts of the crime, he declared bluntly: 'Peter Falconio is dead. He was unlawfully killed by the defendant. The circumstances of that killing, namely by gunshot, amount to murder.'

In three short sentences he had summarised the basis of the charge against Bradley Murdoch, before moving on to the second count of unlawfully depriving Joanne Lees of her liberty and the third of assaulting her.

He described how the young couple were waved down by a male Caucasian, aged between 40 and 45, with straight collar-length hair. How Joanne heard a 'distinct bang' followed by a man who appeared at the driver's side window of the Kombi brandishing a 'silver, western-looking' gun with a long barrel. How she was forced into the back of the gunman's four-wheel drive (though there was no reference to her manipulating her handcuffed body from the cab to the rear tray of the vehicle). And how she hid for 'many hours' in roadside bushland until she was rescued by two passing truck drivers.

While the body of Peter Falconio had not been found, the evidence that he was dead was compelling, Mr Wild stated.

'The blood found at the edge of the bitumen, which had been covered with earth, was the blood of Peter Falconio. It had the same DNA profile as the forensic biologist found on his asthma inhaler,' he said.

Then came the clincher. A tiny blood spot found on the back of Joanne's T-shirt had the same DNA profile as the blood of Bradley John Murdoch, he told the hushed court. The chances of the blood not being the defendant's were at least 640 billion to one, he declared.

While the DNA evidence was certainly compelling, it was also the sort of revelation that might unfairly influence potential members of the jury, and the defence was anxious to suppress this and other important disclosures made in the prosecution's opening statement.

The magistrate, also mindful of not wishing to prejudice Murdoch's right to a fair trial, accepted the need to suppress certain evidence from publication in the Northern Territory, but the move was not universally welcomed.

The Channel Nine television network opposed the suppression order and employed a barrister to argue its case, the main argument being about a magistrate's power to impose such an order in the first place. It was to delay the opening stages of the pre-trial hearing for several days as the matter was referred to the Supreme Court.

Before the case was adjourned on that first day there was only sufficient time to hear from Peter Falconio's brother Paul, 34, who was allowed to give his evidence early in the proceedings to enable him to sit in court with his 36-year-old brother Nick for the rest of the hearing.

His testimony was simply to reinforce the prosecution's view that Peter was dead.

Sitting in the witness box with his fists tightly clenched, Paul was asked if he had heard from his younger brother since 14 July 2001.

'Unfortunately no,' he replied.

Would he have expected to hear from Peter during that time if he had been alive and well, Mr Wild enquired.

'Without any doubt,' he responded emphatically. 'He always managed to get in contact with us at least every couple of weeks by phone or email.

'We continued to hear from him [while he was overseas] and he would let at least one member of the family know where he was and what he was doing. He kept us pretty well informed. The last time I spoke to him was approximately a month before he went missing,' Paul recalled.

The magistrate adjourned the first day's hearing until the following morning in the hope that the legal wrangling over the suppression order could be settled by then.

The next day offered the prospect of Joanne's first encounter with Murdoch since the night he allegedly killed her boyfriend. But once again the debate over the suppression order delayed proceedings and it was not until after lunch that Tuesday that the confrontation eventually took place.

'Call Joanne Lees,' requested the court assistant.

A long, uncomfortable silence followed as the message was relayed to the witness room where Joanne had been patiently waiting for the previous two days.

Murdoch shuffled his papers and looked down, apparently determined to treat the young woman with the disdain he thought she deserved.

At precisely 2.40 p.m. the double doors to court six opened and Joanne Lees swept through to complete what must have seemed like the longest walk of her life. As the young English woman made her way to the witness box, her lips pursed and her hair tied back in a short ponytail, all eyes except Murdoch's were on her.

If she was nervous then she didn't show it. Dressed in a newly pressed white, cotton blouse and a black skirt, she held her head high and briefly glanced across to the man in the dock. Murdoch avoided her gaze and defiantly tapped away with his ballpoint pen as he studied a sheaf of papers.

Rex Wild stood up and asked Joanne for her full name, age and occupation.

She replied clearly and calmly. Born September 25, 1973, in Huddersfield, West Yorkshire. Occupation — support worker for people with learning difficulties.

The questions continued for the next one hour 35 minutes as she spoke about the events leading up to the attack and its dramatic aftermath. Once in a while she made eye contact with Murdoch despite his best efforts to avoid her stare. Sometimes he would shake his head when he disagreed with a point.

Joanne's testimony became increasingly graphic as the afternoon wore on and the strain began to take its toll. The courtroom tension was palpable. Her voice sometimes trembling with emotion, she sipped from a glass of water to calm her nerves and clear her throat.

Rex Wild led her through every detail of the crime and how the couple had found themselves in Barrow Creek. 'Is that a picture of you and Peter?' he asked, holding a photograph of them together on her boyfriend's graduation day in Brighton.

Joanne nodded.

'And during your partnership with Peter, did you plan a trip to Australia?'

'Yes, we'd been planning it since 1998 but had to put it off because Peter got a very good job offer which he couldn't refuse.'

And so it continued, their friendship, their working life and their travels, every detail explored and examined to build an intimate picture of their time together. They appeared to be the perfect couple, enjoying the trip of a lifetime before settling down to marriage and having children.

She talked about the drive from Sydney to Alice Springs. 'We slept in the campervan, sometimes in laybys, sometimes in camp sites where there were toilets and showers.'

Ostensibly it was unimportant detail, but it underlined the simple nature of a journey that would be familiar to thousands of backpackers. This was the reality of life on the road, the trivia of travel.

As a couple they were happy in their own company and did not actively seek out others. But they were not antisocial and were happy to give other young travellers a lift.

There was the Canadian couple who had been hitch-hiking near Ayers Rock and with whom they spent a few days. 'While we were with the hitch-hikers we had some trouble with the Kombi, a problem with the steering wheel, I believe,' said Joanne. One of the Canadians named Mark may have fixed the steering rod using cable ties, the court was told.

In Alice they had gone to a tax accountant, to a library, to a VW repair shop to get their vehicle fixed and to a travel agency so that Peter could enquire about a flight to Papua New Guinea and Joanne could buy a return ticket from Brisbane to Sydney.

Reference to the travel arrangements was unexpected and provided the first hint that their relationship was not quite as it had been painted. Why was Peter going to PNG?

He was planning to fly to Cairns and PNG for a week before they met up again and left Australia together from Brisbane for New Zealand, Fiji and the US, Joanne explained.

Mr Wild did not pursue the matter and returned to the afternoon of 14 July 2001.

They had gone to the Camel Cup and left at 4 p.m.

'I was driving and Pete was in the rear reading,' Joanne told the hushed court. 'At one point I turned around and he was asleep. We had no plans. We were just heading north. I pulled up in a layby on the left-hand side of the road [at Ti Tree]. I rolled a joint and we smoked, just chatting, watching the sunset,' she recalled.

They stayed there for 20 minutes and watched the sun go down. 'Pete drove across to the service station and I went to the toilet while Peter went to buy some sweets and refreshments,' she added.

Ten minutes later they were continuing the journey north. Peter was at the wheel. It was at this point that something strange and inexplicable happened. A few kilometres out of Ti Tree they passed some grassfires by the side of the road.

'They looked as though they had been started deliberately,' Joanne replied to a prosecution question. 'Pete wanted to stop to put the fires out. I said it could be a trap or a trick and asked him to drive on.'

Joanne's boyfriend took her advice, but what had prompted her remarks? What or whom did they have reason to fear? Or could the fires have been a sign, a guiding light to indicate where they should stop to meet someone? Perhaps it had been a genuine bushfire started by a lightning bolt or a stray cigarette butt thrown by a passing truck driver.

Whatever the cause, the grassfires clearly indicated trouble so far as Joanne was concerned, but Mr Wild chose not to pursue the matter.

The sheer terror of the drama that followed left those who were listening to Joanne's account spellbound, her soft voice and the rustle of spiral notebooks the only sounds to emanate from courtroom six.

The bang, the struggle, the escape were all graphically recalled.

'The man had a gun in his right hand pointed towards me . . . I tried to struggle and fight . . . My head was down on my knees, my hands were behind my back and the man was tying them with electrical ties.'

Joanne was asked to stand and show the court how far apart her hands were tied — about 10 centimetres — before resuming her account.

'I was trying to kick him in the crutch with my hands behind my back . . . I asked him if he was going to rape me and if he had shot Pete . . . I started to slide from the back of the ute to the front and hung my legs over the tray and then I jumped down . . . It was difficult to run . . . so I chose to stop and finished under a bush . . . I could hear his footsteps crunching [and] he got very close to me . . . I thought he would shine his headlights into the bush to see me . . . I heard more driving. I thought the first vehicle headed north and the second vehicle headed south.'

'And then you passed your hands in front of you,' the prosecution prompted.

'I just lifted them from underneath my bottom and lifted my legs through. It was very easy,' she replied.

But the nightmare continued.

'I was too scared to get out of the bush I was hiding under. I didn't think it was very safe but I thought I'd have to be brave for Pete.'

Slowly she found her way in the pitch-black night through the undergrowth and back to the road.

'There was some long grass on the other side of the road and I lay down there. I was still very scared and then a road train came along — I ran towards the driver calling out — I was just so happy that somebody had stopped.'

Joanne was safe. She thought her outback ordeal was over, but in reality it was only just beginning.

....

CHAPTER 20

THE DOG THAT DIDN'T BARK IN THE NIGHT

With the legal row over the suppression order still unresolved, the pre-trial hearing of Bradley Murdoch stopped and started again with monotonous regularity. Witnesses and journalists alike expressed their impatience over the delays and, with little of substance to report from the courtroom, the media refocused its attention on Joanne, or rather her daily travel arrangements.

Her high-speed arrival and departure from court every day had already attracted the disapproval of newspaper photographers, some of whom had narrowly avoided being hit by the cavalcade of unmarked police cars.

There is nothing guaranteed to excite an army of snappers more than the reluctance of would-be subjects to co-operate with the press. They become a challenge.

And Joanne had already proved to be a formidable quarry.

The presence of civilian security personnel placed at the entrance to the court's underground garage and employed to keep cameramen and women at bay had further added to media disquiet, and a complaint had been made to court officials about their over-zealous behaviour.

So far nobody had obtained a clear picture of Joanne arriving or leaving court. Her minder, an attractive young woman who had accompanied her from Britain, had done all in her power to conceal her charge from nosey photographers, sometimes going so far as to cover Joanne with her own body as she lay on the floor of the car.

The resulting images in the newspapers gave the impression that Joanne was the accused and not the victim. They were the sort of snatched photographs normally associated with dangerous criminals arriving for sentence or departing for a long spell behind bars.

Why exactly Joanne was behaving in this manner — and more especially why the police were protecting her in this fashion when most witnesses have to make their own way to and from court in full public view — was a mystery.

It was left to Jane Munday, the Director of Public Prosecutions' spokesperson, to fend off mounting media anger and endeavour to resolve the problem. Efforts were made to persuade Joanne to make herself available for a photo opportunity, so that newspaper and television cameramen could satisfy their picture desks and leave her alone.

At one point it looked like the terms for a mutually acceptable truce had been agreed.

'The last thing we want is for someone to get hurt,' said Ms Munday. 'So Joanne has agreed that if you abide to the way she wants to do this, she's agreed to one photo of her. Our responsibility is to look after the witnesses. I can't order her to do anything. This is not a security issue. Joanne does not want to be photographed and our responsibility is to get her to court and make sure she gives evidence,' she explained to journalists.

'Please don't chase the police car, it's only going to make things worse,' she pointed out. 'Joanne has offered to have her photograph taken if it takes the pressure off. This is the best I'm going to be able to do.'

Warming to her theme — and anxious to keep reporters and cameramen onside — Ms Munday smiled, and said 'You are nice individually but collectively you are scary. We're really concerned someone is going to get hurt.'

It seemed the impasse was over and Joanne might agree to a deal with the media, but the early optimism proved unfounded. One still picture might have been acceptable to press photographers but it didn't satisfy the TV cameramen who needed moving images and wanted to see her walking.

However, Joanne refused to budge. Indeed it emerged she had further demands. She wanted the media to pay for the picture opportunity and donate the total amount raised to a charity of her choosing. There were urgent discussions between rival media camps but the idea was doomed to failure.

While some newspapers and television programs are occasionally prepared to pay for exclusive access, other news organisations have a policy of paying for nothing, especially if it smacks of chequebook journalism.

Their view is based on the premise that if they start paying witnesses every time they arrive at a hearing, such practices would strike at the very heart of the notion of an open court, where witnesses are expected to give freely of their time.

Inevitably the photo op was withdrawn and the ugly scenes at the back of the court continued.

The nearest Joanne came to providing an explanation for her behaviour emerged a few days later when she was cross-examined by Murdoch's defence lawyer Grant Algie about her reluctance to be photographed.

'You have been very guarded and protective of your image, particularly in Alice Springs,' he remarked.

She disputed the claim, replying with a firm, 'No.'

'There was a discussion about you allowing a picture to be taken on certain terms,' he reminded her.

'One donation to charity, yes. I thought the offer the media made was pitiful,' she explained.

The prosecution moved to object, querying the relevancy of the question.

'It's relevant because I want to explore from this witness that although she protects her image on certain terms, she has given a lengthy interview with Granada Television and been paid a large amount of money,' he replied.

'I want to ask her if that relationship with Granada is on-going. You entered a contract with Granada?' Algie enquired.

'Yes, that was before there was an accused and to raise publicity,' was her justification.

'Do you still have an arrangement with Granada?' he pressed.

'I get numerous offers from various media,' she responded.

But no exclusive deal with Granada, she insisted.

This still didn't explain her abhorrence of the media in general and photographers in particular.

It was left to the Director of Public Prosecutions, Rex Wild, to make Joanne's position plain when an application was made to release to the media some of the photographs of Joanne tendered to the court as part of the evidence.

The DPP made it clear that any such move would be opposed. 'My instructions are that Joanne Lees has been hunted throughout England for the past three years and that is the reason why she does not want her image regularly portrayed in the press. That is her prerogative and I would oppose her photo being released,' he stated.

While it was possible to sympathise with Joanne's plight, the cat and mouse game being played outside the court every day was a mere sideshow compared to what was to emerge the following week.

It was not until Wednesday 26 May that the pre-trial hearing resumed after the Supreme Court ruled against Channel Nine, thereby allowing the suppression order to stay in place.

Just after 10 a.m. and 10 days after the case began, Rex Wild rose to his feet and told the magistrate, 'We are now able to proceed. The order has been upheld by the full court so the suppression order stands.'

Eleven minutes later Joanne re-entered the court with a slight smile on her face and made her way to the witness box.

The prosecution continued where it had left off. Mr Wild took the witness through her arrival at the Barrow Creek Roadhouse, where she had been driven by the two truckies after the attack.

'Did you notice a dog?' he queried.

Yes, she had seen the puppy owned by Catherine Curley in the bar and they talked about the breed. 'I recognised it as the same breed of dog the man had. She told me it was a blue heeler,' she told the court.

Photographs appeared on screen of Joanne's injuries including grazes to the inside of her arm, which she said were caused by the electrical ties.

And what about the abrasions to her right elbow and left knee?

'They happened when I was pushed to the ground on the gravel.'

At this point a replica of the handcuffs she was forced to wear was produced in court. She agreed they were similar and had the same configuration as the ones used by the gunman during the assault.

The sight of the home-made handcuffs, intricately reproduced from black cable ties and electrical tape, was a stark reminder of the terror Joanne must have experienced that night.

A sketch of the man who attacked her was also shown to the witness.

'Is it an accurate representation?' asked Mr Wild.

'It's similar [but] the length of the hair was too long. The man I saw had his hair just past his ears. I never said he had shoulder-length hair but it was long and came beneath his hat,' she replied.

The sketch was followed by a photo of the man featured in the truck-stop surveillance video, which she was so uncertain about a few weeks after the attack. This was certainly the man she described at the time, she agreed, but the video was of much poorer quality then.

The pace was beginning to quicken.

She was reminded of a visit the police made to her in Britain in which she was asked about the gunman's dog and shown a selection of photographs from a book.

'Did you know in July 2001 what a blue heeler was?' the prosecution enquired.

Joanne: 'No.'

Wild: 'When you described the dog you saw, did you describe it as a blue heeler?'

Joanne: 'No. I was given the book and told to pick out a dog I thought looked similar. The size, width, build and shape of the dog's face and the ears of the dog were similar to the dog I saw that night.'

Wild: 'Was it the same colouring?'

Joanne: 'Not exactly. It was dark brown and white. It was half-and-half with patches of dark colour.'

The description of the dog, and how Joanne concluded that the animal which accompanied the gunman was the same breed as the one in the picture, was an important part of the prosecution's case.

Murdoch's pet dog, Jack, even though it was a mixed breed, looked more like a Dalmatian to the untrained eye. Yet Joanne had never mentioned spots in her original description, only a blue heeler.

Could a blue heeler with its speckled coat be mistaken for a Dalmatian? It was a crucial issue which had yet to be satisfactorily resolved.

So far Joanne's time in the witness box had not been unduly demanding. Certainly there were moments of emotion and high tension when she had to relive the most traumatic of memories, but Joanne had coped.

Now came the tough questions. If she hoped that Grant Algie, who had earlier indicated he would not be hard on the young woman, would be gentle with her in his cross-examination, she was in for a big shock.

The exchange began innocently enough.

GA: 'Did you enjoy the time you spent in Sydney?'

JL: 'Yes.'

GA: 'I assume your lifestyle was different?'

JL: 'Yes.'

GA: 'An extended holiday with your partner?'

JL: 'Yes.'

GA: 'Living at Bondi, not far from the beach?'

JL: 'Yes.'

GA: 'During the five months you were in Sydney did you develop a circle of friends?'

JL: 'Yes.'

Joanne might have suspected what he was leading up to and cleared her throat in anticipation.

GA: 'I need to ask you this, but you told us last week that you smoked cannabis at Ti Tree.'

JL: 'Yes.'

GA: 'Did you use cannabis in Sydney?'

JL: 'No.'

The answer had hardly been uttered when the magistrate reminded her that she was not obliged to reply to questions which might incriminate her.

GA: 'Did you use other drugs?'

JL: 'Yes. There was an occasion when I took half an ecstasy tablet.'

GA: 'Was that an occasion in a nightclub that was raided by the drug squad?'

JL: 'No.'

The cross-examination continued in the same vein as Algie expanded his area of questioning to the drive from Sydney to Alice Springs.

GA: 'On Friday, July 13, the day before you left Alice Springs, you and Peter were at Melanka Lodge [the backpacker hostel]. You didn't have an argument or fight at Melanka Lodge in Alice Springs?'

JL: 'No.'

GA: 'You were getting on fine?'

JL: 'Yes.'

GA: 'On Saturday July 14 you went to the Camel Cup.'

JL: 'I'd say we were there for approximately a couple of hours.'

GA: 'Did you meet anyone there?'

JL: 'We said "hi" to people, had a bit of a chat and exchanged names. People we just met.'

The defence lawyer's voice was getting louder and faster as he moved the clock forward to early evening at Ti Tree, when Joanne had earlier admitted smoking a joint with her boyfriend.

'Where did the cannabis come from?' he asked.

JL: 'Peter.'

GA: 'Who did he deal with? Where did he get it from?'

JL: 'I don't know for sure. I would be speculating.'

GA: 'Did Peter have a dealer in Sydney or was it obtained somewhere along the way?'

JL: 'Pete didn't have a dealer.'

GA: 'Did he get the cannabis in Sydney?'

JL: 'He obtained it in Sydney.'

GA: 'Was the cannabis stored or separated in one of the modifications on the Kombi?'

JL: 'I don't think so. He didn't hide it. It was just on the shelf.'

GA: 'You didn't say anything to the police about the cannabis?'

JL: 'I was not asked. I didn't see how it was relevant and there was still some cannabis in the Kombi which the police would have found, and if they wanted to ask me about it I would have told them the truth.'

This was a delicate issue because the couple's use of cannabis was essentially a criminal offence and Joanne had enough on her mind without having to face a charge of possessing illegal drugs.

Was Algie deliberately making life difficult for the witness or was he hinting at something else? Either way, he decided the court had heard enough of the couple's journey and their occasional use of drugs and decided to move on to what happened after the abduction when Joanne sought sanctuary at the Barrow Creek Roadhouse.

It was an opportunity to return to the question of the dog — the gunman's and a similar breed she saw in the Barrow Creek pub.

The attacker's pet, which remained so still and silent on the night of the murder, has drawn comparisons with the so-called 'dog that didn't bark in the night' story, much beloved of Sherlock Holmes fans.

In the short story, 'Silver Blaze', the ace detective is asked: 'Is there any point to which you would wish to draw my attention?'

'To the curious incident of the dog in the night time,' replies Holmes.

'The dog did nothing in the night time.'

'That was the curious incident,' Holmes points out.

Equally curious was the apparent reluctance of the killer's dog to bark at Joanne Lees when she was thrown into the front cab of the gunman's truck. Wouldn't it have been normal to expect a dog to react to a stranger? But according to Joanne not only did the dog remain quiet, it even refused to acknowledge her presence.

For whatever reason, Grant Algie decided not to pursue the animal's behaviour in the cab but concentrate on the apparent similarity between the gunman's pet and another dog she saw in the bar of the Barrow Creek pub.

GA: 'At the Barrow Creek Roadhouse you saw the same sort of dog as you did in the ute?'

JL: 'Yes.'

GA: 'And you'd never seen a dog like that before?'

JL: 'That's correct.'

GA: 'You said, that's the sort of dog in the ute?'

JL: 'Yes.'

GA: 'The next morning at the roadhouse did a similar thing happen with a four-wheel drive that you identified as the four-wheel drive [the gunman had]? Did you get in the four-wheel drive?'

JL (after sipping water): 'No. It belonged to someone else.'

GA: 'You saw it didn't have access from the cabin to the canopy and therefore you said "That's not the one."'

JL: 'It couldn't have been the one because the man driving it was not the one who stopped me that night.'

The ute Joanne referred to was one of many similar vehicles that attracted police attention in the weeks and months after the attack and was quickly ruled out of the enquiry. But it enabled Algie to move on to the investigation in Alice Springs following the crime.

And it was to lead to an embarrassing disclosure which shed an unexpected light on Joanne's love life.

GA: 'When you were in Alice Springs did a police officer drive you around car yards looking at four-wheel-drive vehicles?'

JL: 'Yes.'

GA: 'When you were accompanied by a chaperone . . .'

JL: 'I was very scared so I was happy to have somebody around.'

And then like a bombshell, the defence lawyer demanded to know: 'Did you have a secret email account?'

'It wasn't secret, it was a second account,' she replied defensively.

GA: 'Were you keen to protect that knowledge from your chaperone?'

JL: 'No. I said I would have to delete some emails because it was in danger of closing down because there were too many.'

GA: 'Were you concerned about police becoming aware of emails from someone called Steph? Who is Steph?'

JL: 'I don't know.'

GA: 'Is Steph a pseudonym for someone you write to called Nick?'

JL: 'Yes.'

GA: 'Who is Nick?'

JL: 'A friend from Sydney.'

GA: 'With whom you had a relationship?'

The cross-examination had reached a critical point and the Director of Public Prosecutions was anxious it did not go any further.

'I object!' declared Rex Wild as he rose to protest to the magistrate.

Algie had the bit between his teeth and was determined not to let the matter drop. Privy to the statements assembled by the prosecution, he knew this disclosure, if aired in open court, would provide a new perspective on Joanne's character. And he was keen to use it to his client's advantage.

'If there is another relationship it could be highly relevant to this case and I should be allowed to explore it,' he insisted.

'This material has been revealed by the prosecution and is not secret and I ask permission to explore it,' he added.

'The fact that we have provided material does not make it relevant,' Mr Wild interjected.

In court there was a stunned silence at what had just been revealed. The magistrate looked up at the clock. It was 4.57 p.m. 'At this stage I don't see it as relevant,' he observed before deciding to adjourn the court until 10 a.m. the next day.

Joanne Lees would have to endure another night before knowing whether she would be forced to divulge the nature of her relationship with the young man she had been emailing within days of Peter Falconio's death.

Her third day in the witness box began with a few questions from Grant Algie about the tailgate of the gunman's truck. She was shown an artist's impression of the vehicle, a progressive series of sketches culminating in a final version.

The cross-examination was slow and courteous. But if Joanne thought that the previous day's investigation into her personal affairs was closed, she was mistaken.

Suddenly the talk turned to the couple's last day together.

GA: 'Your driving plans changed when you were in Alice Springs.'

JL: 'Yes.'

GA: 'Because on July 14 you went and booked and paid for a single air fare for yourself from Brisbane to Sydney.'

JL: 'Peter and I went and booked it together. The

plan had not changed. It was just another holiday within a holiday.'

GA: 'You were not going to see Nick?'

JL: 'He wasn't even in Australia.'

GA: 'After Alice Springs you were communicating with Nick by email and you were making arrangements to meet up with Nick on the way home.'

JL: 'Not on the way home but at a later date.'

GA: 'Do you deny that by email in Alice Springs you made arrangements to meet Nick in Berlin?'

JL: 'I made a suggestion.'

GA: 'So you made a suggestion that it may happen.'

JL: 'Yes.'

The damage had been done. How could a young woman bring herself to discuss meeting up with another lover in Berlin when her boyfriend of more than five years had just been murdered?

Those gathered in court six could hardly believe their ears, but worse was to follow.

'In Sydney you were having a difficult sexual relationship,' said Algie.

Once again Mr Wild rose to his feet to object to the line of questioning. 'This is not relevant,' he claimed.

'It is relevant because of the relationship between this witness and Peter Falconio,' the defence pointed out. 'The picture painted by the prosecution is one of a harmonious and loving relationship and that is not the case and I should be entitled to explore it. I am entitled to demonstrate the relationship is not all as it appears. The fact that she has been having a sexual relationship with this man for a month in Sydney . . .'

Magistrate Alasdair McGregor motioned for Algie to continue, but added, 'I don't think it's going to get you very far.'

Grant Algie clearly didn't agree. Turning to the tense young woman in the witness box, he prepared to go in for the kill.

'During the time you were living with Peter you had an affair, a sexual relationship over a period of weeks with Nick. Yes or no?'

JL: 'I am going to answer yes but I would not classify it as an affair or a relationship.'

It was an odd response. What else could it have been? In one breath she had admitted to having a sexual relationship with Nick and in the next refused to describe it as such.

She might very well have been in denial about the affair, but the whole world now knew the truth. Joanne Lees' testimony would not only cast aspersions on her character but raise serious questions about her ability to tell the whole story.

Within hours of finishing her evidence she was on her way to Darwin airport, where she boarded Australian Airlines flight number 807881 to Singapore.

Throughout the flight she hid behind a curtain in seating normally reserved for cabin crew. At Singapore she refused to disembark until two photographers, who had also been on the plane, were ordered out of the transit area.

Eventually she was persuaded to leave the aircraft by security staff who escorted her to a connecting flight to Britain. Once again Joanne — just like at the news conference in Alice Springs nearly three years earlier — convinced the authorities that she deserved special treatment.

Back in Darwin, Jane Munday, the court's media liaison officer, had defended Joanne's behaviour by revealing that she was 'paranoid about her photo being taken'.

'She's fed up with people coming up to her in the street saying, "You are Joanne Lees." She had satellite dishes parked outside her home in England. She's had loads of offensive letters from people. She just wants closure.'

Be that as it may, Joanne's reputation had just taken an almighty tumble. From now on she wasn't just the victim, but the woman who cheated on her murdered boyfriend.

CHAPTER 21

....

HEPI AND THE REWARD

With the star witness gone, attention focused on those who had played more of a supporting role in the case against Bradley Murdoch. But there was one man in particular whose evidence had proved crucial to the defendant's arrest.

Without him the pre-trial hearing would not have taken place.

Had James Hepi not provided police with the incriminating evidence they required to link Murdoch with the Falconio murder, the odds are that no one would have been charged with the outback abduction.

Hepi had recognised the value of his information and traded the knowledge in exchange for a non-custodial sentence for the drug trafficking charge he had faced in Broome in 2002.

The question now was could he be regarded as a credible witness in view of the obvious inducement he had to tell the police what they wanted to hear? It was a point the defence was not slow to exploit when the well-built Maori took the stand during the committal proceedings.

Hepi talked at length about the defendant's love of guns and utes. How Murdoch modified his vehicle and how he reacted to suggestions that he might have been involved in the Falconio killings.

Murdoch's defence lawyer Grant Algie did not beat about the bush. 'Were you prepared to make statements to set up Murdoch in order to save your own skin?' he enquired bluntly.

'That's not correct,' the Kiwi replied indignantly.

'That's happened,' the defence suggested.

'No that's not,' said Hepi.

But hadn't he indicated to a Broome detective that he might be prepared to co-operate and ultimately make a formal statement about Murdoch, if some consideration or help was offered in return, Algie reminded him.

'That's correct,' he agreed.

GA: 'And at the end of the day when you appeared in court with respect to the serious criminal offence with which you were charged, did you plead guilty?'

JH: 'Yes I did.'

GA: 'And was the assistance that you might be able to provide conveyed to the judge?'

JH: 'Yes.'

GA: 'And what about the quarter of a million dollar reward, Mr Hepi? You'd have been in the running for that?'

JH: 'I have no idea. I haven't discussed it with anyone.'

GA: 'But if your evidence assists in securing a conviction of Mr Murdoch, you'd be proposing to make enquiries about the quarter of a million dollars?'

JH: 'I reckon I would.'

He may have been speaking the truth, but Murdoch's former business partner's candid admission was just what the defence had been waiting to hear.

'Because you see,' observed the defence lawyer, 'the combination of wanting to save your own skin with respect to the serious criminal offences that you faced, and the reward, is what led to you making false statements to set up Mr Murdoch.'

'That's not correct,' Hepi insisted.

The trap had been set and James Hepi had walked straight into it.

It was not the only evidence to place a question mark over the quality of the police case against Murdoch and the manner in which they found their suspect. Eyebrows were also raised about the standard of the early investigation and in particular the thoroughness of the search in the undergrowth at Barrow Creek where Joanne had hidden for several hours.

Superintendent Jeanette Kerr recounted how she stumbled across important evidence at the crime scene, three months after the area was supposed to have been examined in detail immediately following the incident.

She told the court how she had been on an orientation visit to the spot when she decided to inspect the tree under which Joanne had concealed herself.

As she bent down she saw two pieces of black tape on the ground which she concluded were the same strips of tape Joanne had described when she attempted to bite off the manacles that she had been restrained with.

Further discoveries were to follow. When crime scene examiner Ian Spilsbury, who was also nearby, looked under the tree he found a lip-balm stick, corroborating Joanne's earlier story that she used the balm to grease her wrists in an attempt to slide the handcuffs off.

This was an acutely embarrassing admission for the police. How could they have overlooked such crucial evidence when they combed the crime scene in July? What did it say about their search methods? And how did it reflect on the standard of the overall enquiry?

Other police forces in Australia were already joking about the investigative ability of their Northern Territory counterparts. Now it seemed the wisecracks might be well-founded.

In fairness, members of the Alice Springs task force assembled to investigate this most mysterious of murders were not the bumbling Mr Plods some suspected. Privately they had their own suspicions about Joanne's account of what happened and were eager to grill her more intensely.

Superintendent Kerr revealed how they were concerned about the number of apparent inconsistencies in Joanne's story, saying that there had been doubts about the gun and the vehicle allegedly involved in the attack, as well as Joanne's physical state and the lack of footprints at the scene of the crime.

She also admitted that no one could recall seeing a truck which allowed access to the rear tray from the front cab. 'Detectives made extensive enquiries with panel beaters and mechanics, but not a single vehicle matching that description could be located,' she said.

There was also concern about the gun that Joanne had described as a revolver with scrolling on the side of the barrel and which had been strikingly similar to the pattern on the door of the couple's campervan.

During cross-examination of Superintendent Kerr, Grant Algie asked, 'You are aware nobody could identify such a gun, and you put that to Ms Lees?'

'Yes,' the officer replied.

Then there was the apparent lack of injuries on Lees' body. Had these concerns been raised with the doctor who attended her at the time, the defence lawyer wanted to know. Then there was the question of frostbite. 'Did you raise with Ms Lees she had a lack of frostbite after being outside for hours?'

'Yes,' Superintendent Kerr replied to both questions.

Algie went on to ask about the electrical tape that was meant to have been around the victim's ankles and which turned out to be only 70 centimetres long, not enough to bind her lower legs.

Then he turned his attention to the length of time that Joanne had hidden in the bush. 'Did you tell her that police had obtained the opinion of Aboriginal trackers who said that nobody had stayed in that spot for anything like that length of time [on the night in question]?' he enquired.

'Yes,' she confirmed.

There were similar concerns over the lack of a pursuer's footprints and the absence of any marks on the roadside which might have indicated a body being dragged.

Then there were the doubts police had over Joanne's ability to see and hear what was taking place outside while she sat in the Kombi van when Peter was attacked. How could she have heard the conversation between her boyfriend and the gunman at the back of the campervan over the engine noise, and how could she have seen anything from her position, as she had suggested in her original statement?

'And was it of concern that the dog she described in the attacker's car was a dog of the same kind she'd seen at the Barrow Creek Hotel a few hours later?'

'Yes,' Superintendent Kerr again replied.

She also agreed the canvas bag which had reportedly been placed over the victim's head had raised suspicions too. The mail bag which hung inside the Barrow Creek Roadhouse appeared to be similar.

In all there were as many as 12 perceived inconsistencies in Joanne Lees' story, as well as the view of linguistic experts who had examined her earlier statement and concluded that 'vital information' was missing from her narrative.

However, there was also incontrovertible evidence which supported her account.

The court heard that a partial footprint from a rubber sports sandal she had been wearing at the time was found at the crime scene.

And the absence of bullet casings where Peter was shot was consistent with Joanne's claim that her attacker was armed with a revolver, a firearm that does not discharge a cartridge.

The court was also told that a black hair band identical to one Joanne had been wearing at the time had allegedly been found in a vehicle owned by Murdoch.

In an effort to clarify the inconsistencies, Joanne agreed to undergo hypnosis in Alice Springs but the results were not made public.

What did emerge during that day's evidence, however, was a reference to Joanne's response when her family and friends arrived in Alice Springs to offer their support. According to Superintendent Helen Braam, who acted as her police chaperone in those first few difficult days, Joanne was far from welcoming when her stepfather and the Falconios flew into the outback town.

Curiously she didn't want to see her family and friends, the officer told the court.

Why she appeared so anti-social was not revealed, but in some respects it reflected the manner she adopted at the Barrow Creek Roadhouse on the night of the attack, when she failed to telephone her family and Peter Falconio's parents in Yorkshire to tell them of her ordeal.

Maybe once again she couldn't face the grim reality of what had happened.

....

CHAPTER 22

HOW MANY SAW ELVIS?

Dressed in a green, long-sleeved shirt and wearing beige trousers, Bradley John Murdoch's appearance gave the impression that prison life was doing him good when he re-entered court on 9 August 2004, for the second stage of the committal proceedings.

Drug-free and with the benefit of three square meals a day, he seemed to have put on weight when he entered the dock that Monday morning. Certainly his stomach was bigger and he was fuller in the face.

In those first few days of part two of the pre-trial hearing, many of Murdoch's former friends and acquaintances took to the witness box in Darwin or gave evidence via video-link from Broome.

Most were tradesmen who had worked on the defendant's Landcruiser during the many occasions when he had requested modifications to the vehicle.

William Butterfield, a self-employed windscreen fitter, had tinted the screen.

Michael Somerville, who ran Karella Welding, had extended the rear tray and made a boat trailer for him. He had also supplied some of the material for a new canopy, which Murdoch planned to fit over the rear tray. It was going to be made out of aluminium, which had been ordered from a speciality shop in Perth.

Somerville was going to make it for him but in the end Murdoch took the work elsewhere.

Warren Minshull, who owned a mechanical repair shop in town, recalled how he had sold a bull bar to him.

Wayne Holmes had powder-coated his wheels a charcoal-metallic colour and later did the same to his bull bar.

Loi O'Dore, the Frenchman who ran Tropical Upholstery, explained how he had carried out several jobs for the defendant on various of his vehicles over the years, including the fitting of flywire windows to the canvas sides of the canopy.

He remembered working on the HJ75 which had a green, powder-coated aluminium frame with security mesh sides. It was some time after the Barrow Creek incident because he'd had that memorable conversation with Murdoch about the vehicle in the truck stop surveillance video.

'I mentioned that I had seen a photo of the vehicle and that it looked like the one we did for him. He said that he was up there at the time and it could have been him because he may have stayed at that truck stop,' O'Dore recalled.

Robin Knox, who worked at Broome Exhausts, fitted a new exhaust system to Murdoch's HJ75 Landcruiser. He told the court how he was surprised by the spotless condition of the vehicle — 'like it had been cleaned right up, which is unusual for a Broome car because you get a lot of red dust'.

'There was no dirt under the chassis. Everything seemed very clean like it had been rebuilt and tidied up,' he added.

The date was 22 August 2001, a month after the Falconio attack, and Murdoch's Landcruiser was virtually unrecognisable from the vehicle he had been driving a few weeks earlier.

One of the most eagerly anticipated witnesses was Brian Johnston, who was supposed to have given evidence during part one of the committal but could not be located.

This time the police were so determined he appear that they flew him to Darwin and put him up at the Crown Plaza, a five-star hotel, which was a marked improvement on his usual lodgings, a room in cheap, backpacker-style accommodation near Cable Beach.

Johnston, 51, slightly built with short, dark hair and an earring, had been close to the defendant for at least a year and was able to provide a detailed picture of his appearance and the sort of vehicles he had been driving from the summer of 2000 when they first met.

He was used to seeing Murdoch with a moustache, but he shaved it off around the middle of July 2001, said Johnston. His hair was also shorter.

Then there were the utes: the old HJ47 Landcruiser, the F100 which they had driven to South Australia and left there, and the newer HJ75 Landcruiser which had been bought in Adelaide and driven back to Broome.

The more recent model had a rectangular fuel tank which was bolted to the front of the rear tray just behind the cab. The tray itself was littered with plastic crates and fuel drums which covered most of the floor.

A couple of swags were usually rolled up on top and there was just enough space left for the dog to sit on top of the long-range fuel tank.

Brad Murdoch's truck was packed to the gunwales and left little room for anybody to climb inside, unless they lay horizontal. You could just about crawl from one end to the other but you couldn't sit up straight, Johnston made clear.

There was also a fire extinguisher attached to the back of the canopy with cable ties.

It had been bought, on Johnston's advice, for $120.

Murdoch would always carry cable ties. 'Mainly foot-long black ones,' the witness added.

'Did you ever see Murdoch with guns?' asked the prosecution.

'I did at Forrest Street when he was living in Broome,' Johnston replied.

'On one occasion I saw a Magnum .357. James Hepi was playing around with it in the lounge. Brad was there too. It was his. He told me it was a revolver.'

'Were there any other guns?' the prosecution enquired.

'There was one other similar one, which was apparently a .38 and smaller than the other one. It was a revolver as well, dark grey metal in colour.'

On the road Murdoch would hide it in a secret cavity in the long-range fuel tank or sometimes inside the driver's side door, Johnston went on.

During cross-examination, Grant Algie asked him if any of these guns had elaborate scrolling on the barrel.

'No,' he insisted.

And was there any way to climb directly from the cab into the rear tray?

'No,' he again replied.

'Was there a solid steel plate between the cab and the tray as part of the canopy?' Algie asked.

'Yes,' said Johnston.

There was little love lost between Murdoch and Johnston, who left the witness box with his head slightly bowed, seemingly unwilling to make eye contact with his old housemate. Johnston was aware how important his evidence was and knew that Murdoch would never forgive him for talking.

Clearly unnerved by the experience, he revealed to me afterwards that he would leave the country if Murdoch was found not guilty and freed.

'Do you think he did it then?' I asked.

'He's certainly capable of it,' Johnston muttered.

Murdoch's passion for firearms only added to his wild reputation. Most members of his immediate social circle were aware of his love of guns, including Rachel Maxwell, who knew the defendant through James Hepi in South Australia.

She remembers him cleaning them on the table and recalls one weapon in particular, a Wild West-style revolver with a silver barrel about 25 centimetres long and a brown grip.

'It was like an old gun John Wayne would have used,' she told the court.

While some of Murdoch's former friends might not have been the sort of people most respectable members of the community would mix with, it should be remembered they were giving evidence under duress and arguably at some risk to their personal long-term safety.

When Darryl Cragan, Murdoch's childhood friend and occasional buddy, appeared, it was obvious from the outset that he was a reluctant witness. While happy to answer simple questions about the defendant's appearance —

'always the same' — Cragan became angry when the prosecution seemed to be getting too curious.

'I am not answering any more questions,' he stated.

There was a stunned silence as all eyes turned to the magistrate, Alasdair McGregor, who asked: 'Have you got a reason for that before I think of how I deal with you for contempt?

'If something is going to come up which might incriminate you, then you are entitled to say, "I am not going to answer that question," and we will go no further,' the magistrate explained. '[But] if it is something else there has to be a good reason. I don't usually use the contempt laws but if I have to I will,' Mr McGregor added.

The warning had the desired effect and the questioning continued.

Although Cragan had little more of interest to relate, Murdoch's old mate was clearly a worried man who would sooner not be testifying against him.

The second stage of the pre-trial hearing was into its third day when Carmen Eckhoff took the stand. An experienced forensic scientist, she had worked on thousands of cases in the Northern Territory over a 14-year period and had been used as an expert witness on many occasions.

Eckhoff had visited the crime scene at Barrow Creek one night after the attack to carry out tests on the road and the campervan in the search for blood and evidence of gunfire residue. First she performed a Luminol test around the pool of blood at the roadside, which turned out to be from Peter Falconio.

'I was interested to see if there was a spatter of blood because the allegation was that a gunshot was heard,' she told the court.

Eckhoff stated that she was a veteran of crime scenes where people had been killed or injured. 'Often there is blood spatter on clothing and weapons,' she explained. 'But there was no blood spatter because dirt had been put on the wet road, which indicated the blood was restricted to that area.' She also pointed out that gunshot injuries did not always produce blood spatter. 'People exhibit different bleeding patterns,' she said.

The Luminol test did provide a positive result on a small area of rocks, but this turned out to be animal blood, most probably from roadkill.

She then repeated the procedure where the Kombi had been dumped. On this occasion there was no reaction to the Luminol, which suggested there was no blood present in the area, she explained.

Next she decided to examine the outside of the vehicle, which produced some positive reactions on the towbar and on the inside of the driver's side window.

But as already established, Luminol can also react to other agents and the tests on the campervan did not turn out to reveal human blood after all.

Surprisingly, there was no evidence of gunshot residue at the crime scene. Normally one would expect to have found residue on the back of the Kombi had Falconio been shot behind the vehicle, as described by his girlfriend. But there was none and neither was there any on the road where the body presumably fell.

The absence of gunshot residue was to raise concerns among investigating officers a few weeks later when Commander Col Hardman demanded the campervan and Joanne's clothes undergo further testing.

Meanwhile, Carmen Eckhoff was also keen to establish evidence of DNA and in particular identify the sources. First she examined the home-made handcuffs, which revealed Joanne's DNA and a small contribution from Vince Millar, the truckie who had cut them off. But interestingly there was no evidence of DNA that might have come from the defendant, who was alleged to have constructed the restraints.

Asked if she might have expected the person who made the handcuffs to leave genetic material, Eckhoff replied, 'I can't answer that because I don't know how they were made. He may have had gloves on.'

The prosecution wanted to know if it was possible to touch an article without leaving genetic material.

Yes it was, the court heard. 'Some surfaces are hard to leave traces behind while other people shed different amounts of skin cells, so it is possible to touch an item without leaving DNA,' she added.

Eckhoff did reveal that she found a short white hair that appeared to have come from an animal 'because it had a pointed shaft'.

But the most incriminating evidence was still to come.

What about Joanne's T-shirt, the prosecution enquired.

The forensic officer told how the light blue top was a French Connection T-shirt with red brown stains at the front and the back. There was also a sticker on the top left corner which carried the message, 'Try hugs, not drugs'.

The blood at the back of the shirt was 'like bleeding from a hangnail. Not very much at all,' she said.

In all, eight samples from the shirt were sent away for testing.

The results showed that the blood on the front of the garment was Joanne's, but the tiny spot near the back left sleeve was different.

The T-shirt had been examined on 17 July 2001 and at that stage the result merely indicated that the DNA came from a male person. It was not until 17 November 2003 that a controlled sample of Bradley Murdoch's blood was obtained from South Australia and it took another six weeks for it to be analysed in Darwin.

The delay, which was hard to understand given that so much was riding on the result, was never explained. But when the analysis came through on 31 December 2003, there was no doubt about the profile and the positive match it provided with the blood found on the back of Joanne's T-shirt.

As Carmen Eckhoff told the court, 'The likelihood is 640 billion to one that this blood came from Bradley Murdoch [rather] than any other person taken at random.'

There were also DNA tests on the gearstick and the steering wheel of the Kombi which revealed a mixed profile. The main contributors were Peter and Joanne but there was also evidence of a third. With only a partial DNA profile to work on it was impossible to say exactly who that third person was, but 'Bradley Murdoch is not to be excluded,' Eckhoff said pointedly.

Despite the positive DNA match, police did not close down Task Force Regulus. There were still other suspects to eliminate from their enquiries. From the beginning officers had identified over 2000 people of interest and 30 of them remained suspects.

Senior Sergeant Megan Rowe, who played a pivotal role in the early days of the investigation, was responsible for cross-checking information and confirming alibis.

The sheer scale of her work demonstrated the lengths to which police went to find the Barrow Creek killer.

People whose names were recorded at roadblocks were cross-checked with credit card and EFTPOS records throughout the Northern Territory.

A database of everybody who booked in to motels, pubs and lodges on the weekend in question was produced. It established that there were no fewer than 17,000 people staying in commercial accommodation on the night of 14 July 2001.

People who had made EFTPOS transactions in the Ti Tree area one hour either side of the time Joanne Lees and Peter Falconio were in the area were traced, though a similar effort at the Barrow Creek Roadhouse failed because the computer's hard drive had crashed during the period in question.

Generally speaking the only way to have evaded the police that night would have been to avoid the use of credit cards and mobile phones.

'If people don't use a credit card or EFTPOS, don't stay in hotels and only use the public phone, they can slip under the radar and not be recorded,' said Rowe.

She revealed that of the thousands of people who were in the area at the time 300 were considered hot prospects. At least half of them were happy to provide a DNA sample and if they had an alibi they were usually eliminated from the enquiry.

'Who could you not exclude?' the prosecution asked.

'The defendant. Mr Murdoch,' she replied emphatically.

Megan Rowe's evidence also covered the police investigation into the sort of vehicle and weapon described by Joanne as belonging to her attacker.

Curiously the officer's answers appeared to be at odds with earlier police testimony.

Asked if she had located any vehicles which offered access from the front cab to the back of the truck, she insisted she had found at least a dozen, including an F100 and an older model Landcruiser.

And then there was the revolver with the scrolling pattern on the barrel, the like of which police had earlier suggested they had never come across. Now Senior Sergeant Rowe was saying such revolvers did exist.

'There are western-style firearms which you can finding scrolling on,' she admitted, and produced a photograph of one such example to verify her claim.

It also emerged she was not particularly impressed by reported sightings of Peter Falconio alive. There had been about eight to 10 such sightings over the previous three years.

'Some people thought they'd seen him with Ms Lees, and a couple of other people claimed they saw Peter Falconio with a person similar to the man in the Comfit picture,' she said.

'And how many of them saw Elvis?' the prosecution asked jokingly.

'I don't know,' she said and smiled.

It was a rare moment of humour in an otherwise serious discourse.

While much of the pre-trial hearing concentrated on forensic evidence and statements from those close to the investigation, a different perspective was provided by David Stagg, the artist police used to transfer Joanne's memory to paper.

Stagg, who worked as an art teacher at the Charles Darwin secondary school in Alice Springs, had a diploma in fine art, painting and drawing, but little experience of working with the police. He had been asked to help because the artist whom police normally used was on holiday.

Stagg had no idea what the job would entail when the police commissioned his services and was surprised to see Joanne Lees walk through the door on 19 July 2001, when he turned up at Alice Springs police headquarters.

Maybe because he was a novice and unfamiliar with police routine, Stagg immediately struck up a rapport with Joanne and tried to help her visualise the gunman and his vehicle. 'There was a degree of empathy. Having a daughter myself I found myself not only as a police artist but also in a counselling situation,' he told the court.

The defence wondered whether the empathy might have got in the way of producing an accurate sketch.

'I tried to give alternatives,' the artist recounted.

Stagg's method was to ask Joanne questions and build up a series of sketches based on her answers. If something was not quite right he would remove it from the drawing. It was an exhaustive process which took up most of the day, but ultimately he created a picture which turned out to be remarkably similar to the vehicle revealed in the truck-stop surveillance video.

Joanne had glanced at the vehicle when it pulled up alongside the Kombi and also when she was being led from the campervan to the gunman's truck. From those briefest of glimpses she was able to confirm that it was a customised four-wheel drive.

The artist's questions also required Joanne to focus on the inside of the ute so that he could visualise the overall shape of the vehicle. His account of their conversation left no room for doubt about two aspects of Joanne's evidence which were to subsequently change.

First there was her description of the cab, which she originally claimed had an opening allowing her to crawl from the front to the rear tray but which was to disappear from later testimony.

Stagg said she definitely told him she was forced into the back from the front: 'She made it quite clear from the outset there was an opening at the back which she was trying to access from the passenger seat,' he recalled.

Realising this was an area that might later be the subject of dispute, Murdoch's lawyer pressed him further: 'She told you how she was pushed from the cabin into the canopy area?'

David Stagg: 'That's correct.'

Then came another revelation that contradicted earlier claims.

After spending the previous three years insisting that she had brought her manacled hands from behind her back to the front of her body while hiding in the bush, it emerged that Joanne had told the police artist this manoeuvre had happened sometime earlier while she lay in the back of the gunman's truck.

To ensure there was no confusion, Algie queried: 'And in the canopy she manoeuvred her hands from the back to the front?'

'Yes,' replied Stagg.

Algie pressed him further: 'She was able to use her hands above and in front of her to try to feel the contour of the vehicle and that information allowed you to produce a drawing?'

'Yes,' the artist said. 'She gave me the impression there were two parts of the canopy and she felt there was a circular area that could have been tied. That's what she was feeling for because she could not see anything,' he added.

David Stagg's recall of that conversation was based on an interview that lasted from 10.20 a.m. to 6.40 p.m. If there were areas of uncertainty during that period he would have been keen to clear them up in order to draw the best possible representation from Joanne's memory of the experience.

So why did she give one impression to him and another to the police? The meeting with the artist came just five days after the attack, so presumably she still had a clear picture of the sequence of events in her mind's eye.

How could she confuse the point at which she managed to get the handcuffs around to the front of her body? After all, this was a crucial stage of her attempted abduction and it would be reasonable to assume she would remember exactly when it happened.

This was not to suggest that Joanne was being deliberately misleading. Stagg made it clear that Joanne went out of her way to be helpful, describing her as 'absolutely co-operative'.

She appeared composed and gave 'clear and precise' answers, the artist said. But there were moments of tension too.

'At one stage when we asked her if she wanted a break, she rolled back her hair and covered her hands over her face and put her head back, but then offered more information, saying there might be something she missed that might be important,' he said.

She remembered the gunman as 'tall and stooped'.

And she was adamant that the dog was not a red or blue heeler, as previously described by the police.

'She couldn't explain what sort of dog it was. She just said it was lightish in colour and sat in the seat.'

Again Joanne's inability to identify the breed raised questions. If this was Murdoch's pet dog, Jack, most people would have immediately recognised it as a spotty dog. There is hardly a child in the western world who would not be familiar with Walt Disney's *101 Dalmatians*. So why didn't she describe it as such?

Did the interior light of the cab make the dog's coat appear darker than normal? Or was it another dog altogether?

It was the first time that David Stagg had been required to give evidence in court and he was anxious to be truthful and exact. He may have been a novice as a police artist and a witness but that only added to his credibility. He may not have realised it at the time, but he had shed more light on the inconsistencies of this case than most of the previous witnesses, though the hearing wasn't over yet.

When Pamela Namangardi Brown and her husband, Jasper, took to the stand on the penultimate day of the pre-trial hearing, their evidence seemed predictable enough.

This was the Aboriginal couple who had been driving south from Ali Curung on the night of the attack and passed two vehicles north of Barrow Creek on the Stuart Highway: an orange campervan was parked by the side of the road and another vehicle that had just driven onto the highway from the edge of the bitumen and was making its way north.

'It was different from other four-wheel drives. It was white and quite high,' Pamela told the court.

'There was a canopy on the back of the vehicle,' added Jasper.

What made their testimony so curious was that Joanne had never spoken of the gunman's vehicle being driven north. Certainly the campervan had been taken a few hundred metres up the road before being dumped in the bush, but the Kombi was stationary when the couple passed it.

The only recorded movement of the attacker's truck, according to Joanne, was when it did a U-turn and headed south after the killer returned from hiding the Kombi.

So which vehicle had Pamela and Jasper seen? And who was behind the steering wheel? Could there have been a third vehicle involved? If so, where was it heading and who was inside?

These were questions which would continue to loom large among those close to the case. Rarely has a crime thrown up so many different possibilities and created such intense debate, but these were not issues which the court had to deal with there and then. The Crown merely had to demonstrate that on the face of it the defendant had a case to answer.

'That concludes the evidence for the prosecution,' the Director of Public Prosecutions, Rex Wild QC, announced on the morning of 18 August 2004. 'We have had 53 witnesses and 146 exhibits and it is our submission that there is sufficient evidence at this stage for a prima facie case,' he advised the magistrate.

Alasdair McGregor concurred. 'Bradley John Murdoch, you stand charged before me that on or about July 14, 2001, near Barrow Creek, you murdered Peter Falconio and denied Joanne Lees of her liberty and assaulted her,' he said. 'These charges have been read to you. Having heard the evidence of the prosecution, do you wish to give evidence on your own account or say anything about the charges?'

As the defendant replied, 'I am not guilty of any of these allegations, Your Honour,' the telephone rang on the clerk's desk in the body of the court.

There had been a technical problem with the microphone, which had caused difficulties with the transcript of part of the evidence. Would it require the court to repeat certain aspects of the testimony?

If Murdoch thought he had been saved by the bell, it was not to be.

The magistrate, keen to get the matter over with, turned to the defendant again to ask, 'You said, "I am not guilty?"'

'That's correct,' said Murdoch.

The defence lawyer made it clear there would be no application for bail, and with that the court rose. As Murdoch gathered his papers together in the dock, he turned to the press bench and dismissed the assembled media with a wave of his arm while mouthing what appeared to be a phrase beginning with F and ending with F.

A few minutes later Grant Algie faced a media scrum outside on the front steps of the court. 'There is a limit to what I can say in the circumstances but there's been a committal. A committal is a step in the process, it is not the end,' he pointed out. 'The end result is a trial and that will be the important hearing and that's a while off.'

Indeed the trial was at least eight months away, providing ample time for the defence and prosecution teams to fine-tune their case.

This was to be no ordinary Supreme Court hearing. For the first time since the infamous Lindy Chamberlain case hit the headlines a quarter of a century earlier, Darwin was to have the international media spotlight shone on its judicial system once again.

Coincidentally some of the key names in that earlier case would be making a repeat appearance. While the identity of the defendant might have changed, many of the same kind of doubts that dominated the Chamberlain case would re-emerge.

As the incident at Ayers Rock went down in history as the Northern Territory's trial of the 20th century, so the events at Barrow Creek looked like becoming the trial of the 21st.

....
.

CHAPTER 23

MORE SURPRISES AS THE
TRIAL NEARS

As the countdown to the trial continued, I was asked to travel to Barrow Creek to film an interview with a British TV documentary crew. It provided a second opportunity to question Les Pilton and his partner Helen about the night of the attack. And I wanted to meet Pamela Brown and Jasper Haines, the Aboriginal couple who had passed the campervan and saw the truck drive out from behind it as they returned home to Ti Tree on that Saturday evening.

I needed to confirm how much further up the road the ute was by the time they had passed the Kombi — a few hundred metres, they believed.

They never saw how far it went, but it was travelling 'real slow', they observed.

If it was the gunman's car, perhaps he was looking for a place to dump the body. But this still didn't explain why Joanne never reported hearing or seeing the truck being driven north. Unless she was so confused and disoriented that it failed to register.

A local Aboriginal tracker, Dudley Hines, had also agreed to meet me at the scene of the crime. What he had to say was to raise further questions about the thoroughness of the police search.

Dudley had originally gone to the site a few days after the incident and was astonished to find a second pool of blood on the opposite side of the highway. The police had only ever said there was one pool, although they acknowledged that there was evidence of animal blood in the vicinity.

Was the blood on the other side of the road also animal blood? If so, where was the roadkill that it might have come from? Dudley certainly never saw a carcass nearby and remained convinced that it looked like human blood spill from a wound.

The pool was not as big as the quantity left by Peter Falconio but it was large enough to be noticed, so why hadn't the police mentioned it? A police sketch of the area made shortly after the incident revealed they found a cigarette butt in the middle of the south-bound carriageway, but there was no mention of a second blood spot.

Dudley said he assumed the police would have already noticed it so didn't say anything.

But he knew what he saw. 'The blood on the side of the road was smaller and in the grass,' he told me.

'Maybe the victim wasn't dead and staggered to the other side of the road, running away to try to escape,' he suggested.

But if that was the case, wouldn't there also have been a trail of blood from one side of the road to the other? The absence of blood, apart from the half litre or so found at the spot where it was assumed Peter Falconio was shot, was one of the enduring mysteries of this crime scene.

So was the lack of gunshot residue. Usually a shot from a revolver would leave a certain amount of residue on the gunman's hand and clothing, as well as the area around the victim's body.

Although it is extremely fine, residue should have been found from the propellent — which fires the bullet — on the back of the Kombi van and on the ground. Equally there would have been residue from the primer, the cap at the back of the cartridge case, which would have been left on the gunman's body.

In the absence of a killer and a body, forensic officers had to rely on a detailed examination of the campervan, Joanne's clothing and the home-made handcuffs, which had been produced from cable ties and duct tape.

Surprisingly no residue was found on the back of the Kombi, which would have felt the force of the blast, and none was detected on Joanne's clothing or the handcuffs, despite the fact that the attacker had had close contact with both during the struggle that ensued.

Detectives clearly believed there was a good possibility that any residue left behind on the gunman would have been transferred to Joanne or the manacles and that such a discovery would confirm her story.

Commander Hardman admitted as much in a memo written on 31 July 2001, demanding an additional examination of the Kombi, the clothing and the cable ties.

'The information provided by Lees suggests that the offender pushed her forward and may have touched the lower back of her shirt/blouse with his hands when applying the ties to her wrists,' he wrote.

'I know this is a long shot, but it may confirm in conjunction with the testing of the vehicle that a gunshot actually took place. It's worth a try, considering the firearm has been described as a revolver type, which one would think, having an open cylinder, may disperse a greater quality of GSR [gunshot residue] on the hands,' he added.

The results proved negative.

A similar examination was ordered on the back of the Kombi 'as the gunshot is alleged to have taken place in the vicinity of the rear of the vehicle, while Falconio was inspecting the exhaust area', Hardman explained.

Again nothing was found.

He also asked for the handcuffs to be completely dismantled. 'These manacles should/could hold the key as to who actually constructed them. The examination of this item and any forensic evidence obtained may redirect the investigation,' he suggested.

Nothing of consequence was found apart from the DNA left behind by Joanne and Vince Millar, the truck driver who had cut the handcuffs from her. The tiny spot of blood which contained the defendant's DNA, and which was found on the back of her T-shirt, had been discovered earlier.

Finally the police officer requested that the campervan be examined for blood by using the Luminol process. 'If we can confirm blood in the vehicle . . . it may discount some versions of events that are alleged to have taken place outside the vehicle and the disappearance of the body,' he pointed out.

Exactly what Hardman was suggesting was unclear, but the memo reinforced the view that police still had their doubts about Joanne's story and had not ruled out other possibilities.

Leaked documentation which also came into my possession revealed another startling claim about the blood that purportedly came from the body of Peter Falconio. DNA tests on the pool, which had been covered by gravel and scraped further to the side of the road before forensic officers were able to analyse it, confirmed that it wasn't only the dead man's blood, but also non-human blood. How the two came to be mixed was a mystery, unless one considered the possibility that the animal blood came from nearby roadkill. However, there was no indication of a fresh carcass by the side of the road although it is possible it could have been removed by another animal.

While dead kangaroos and other wildlife are extremely common along this stretch of the Stuart Highway, the police made no mention of roadkill in the immediate vicinity of Falconio's blood. And unless the animal had died around the same time or after the incident, its blood would have turned almost black in colour, making it easy for an experienced forensic officer to notice the difference between the two.

So if the animal blood didn't come from roadkill, how did it get mixed up in the pool from Falconio's gunshot wound? The police admitted there was partial evidence of animal blood on the bitumen, but it was so small that it was only visible to the naked eye by using Luminol spray.

On the other hand, did it suggest that Falconio's pool was mixed with blood from another source to increase the quantity left by the roadside?

If so, what sort of scenario would require additional blood? Here we begin to enter the realms of supposition, outlandish theory and fantasy, all of which, given the level of improbability and inconsistency associated with this case, could appear to be quite plausible.

Remember, there was no body and no gunshot residue, raising the possibility that a murder did not happen at all.

Alternatively, perhaps it did take place as the prosecution described, but the circumstances surrounding the attack were not quite as they seemed.

Assume that Falconio, for whatever reason, wanted to vanish and conspired to fake his own death, as previously alluded to. Maybe he had an accomplice who, unbeknown to Joanne, had agreed to help her boyfriend disappear.

The only way to suggest a killing would be to obtain a quantity of blood from the 'victim' earlier at another location and deposit it at the site of the so-called murder. To create more blood than he was able to provide without causing him discomfort, animal blood was added to the original sample.

As bizarre and unlikely as this scenario appeared, it was one of many equally improbable theories which those close to the case were forced to consider.

Les and Helen of the Barrow Creek Roadhouse had grown accustomed to the gossip and, like everyone else, agonised over the truth.

'Hardly a day goes past without someone asking us about the case, sometimes as many as 20 times a day,' Les told me.

But on one point he was sure: 'Something happened to Peter. Coming from his sort of family, he's not the type of young man who would just go missing and not contact any of his people. Something certainly happened, whether it was up the road from here or somewhere else.'

Helen also pointed out that Peter came from a loving family. 'Plus he had Jo. He would never leave his family in that sort of stew. Something happened to him, but what? That's the question, isn't it?'

Both agreed it was the absence of a body that continued to fuel the rumour mill, just like that other case a quarter of a century earlier.

'There are so many parallels with the Lindy Chamberlain affair, aren't there?' said Les. 'People will always be suspicious, and without a body there can never be closure.'

It was amazing how often the Chamberlain case was mentioned. While the circumstances were different, the Falconio crime also excited intense public debate about the woman at the centre of the story, Joanne Lees.

Unlike Lindy Chamberlain, who was initially (but wrongly) charged with the murder of her baby daughter, Joanne was never accused of such a crime, but there remained many who had doubts about her. Like baby Azaria, whose remains were never found, where was the body of Peter Falconio?

And, alleged the malicious gossips, you only had to look at both women to realise they were hiding something.

Lindy of course was subsequently pardoned, after the discovery of her child's matinee jacket in a dingo's lair at Ayers Rock. But by that time she had served three and a half years in prison and her marriage was heading for the rocks.

The Northern Territory government, desperate to prove its credentials after being granted self-government in 1978, was humiliated, its police and judicial system a laughing stock. This may partially explain why the Territory was so desperate to be seen to be doing the right thing in the Falconio case and why it was so keen to support the victim in every way.

A dastardly crime, which had attracted international media attention, had been committed in its jurisdiction and the authorities were anxious to remain above reproach. The Northern Territory legal system would bend over backwards to accommodate Joanne and its police force would find the killer at all costs. Here was an opportunity for the Territory to prove things had changed and it could now hold its own with the rest of Australia's police and judicial systems.

When Bradley John Murdoch was arrested and charged with the murder of Peter Falconio it seemed the Northern Territory could do no wrong. But had they really got their man or was the prosecution case built on a house of cards which might easily collapse under the close scrutiny of the defendant's eagle-eyed legal team?

With only a few months before the trial began, there was also a sense of déjà vu, as some of the key players in the Chamberlain case assembled in the wings in readiness for a second appearance in the media spotlight.

Joy Kuhl, whose damning claim of evidence of foetal blood in the Chamberlains' car had later been discredited, had risen to become head of police forensic biology in Darwin. Though now retired, her more recent findings relating to the forensic examination of the Kombi would be used in the Falconio case.

Ian Barker QC, who had prosecuted Lindy Chamberlain in the 1980s, now found himself acting for the man accused of killing Peter Falconio during legal discussion before the trial opened.

Coincidentally there was also another Brian Martin, who in the 1980s as the Northern Territory's Solicitor-General had played a major role in bringing murder charges against Mrs Chamberlain.

Now his namesake — no relation — would preside over the trial of Bradley John Murdoch, as Chief Justice of the Northern Territory Supreme Court.

CHAPTER 24

NEW DNA BOMBSHELL DELAYS TRIAL

After covering the Falconio case for more than four years I had become accustomed to expecting the unexpected. With little more than a week to go before the trial of Bradley John Murdoch, the case was thrown into disarray by revelations from the prosecution that tests on mixed DNA samples taken from the steering wheel and gearstick of the couple's campervan had produced a positive match with the defendant.

Previously only Peter Falconio's DNA had been detected; examination of the rest of the mixed sample could not positively identify another contributor.

But according to a leading British laboratory which pioneered the use of a revolutionary scientific method called Low Copy Number (LCN), forensic experts had now been able to identify the tiny quantities of mixed DNA from the swabs taken from the campervan by amplifying the contents.

What's more, the prosecution were now intending to send the manacles worn by Joanne Lees to England to undergo the same examination.

If Murdoch's DNA was found in the mixed sample taken from the home-made handcuffs, it would clearly place him at the scene of the crime. The evidence would be damning and the defence knew it.

The bombshell was dropped shortly after 10 a.m. on Thursday 21 April in the Northern Territory Supreme Court in Darwin. The defence had got wind of the new claim the night before but this was the first time it had been disclosed in court.

Officially it was a hearing to discuss legal restrictions during the trial, part of a so-called voir dire where the judge rules on the inadmissibility or otherwise of evidence to be put before a jury.

The defence team had engaged the services of one of Australia's most experienced lawyers, Ian Barker QC, to argue their case. And the illustrious silk had plenty to get his teeth into that morning.

He branded the new interpretation of the DNA evidence as of 'tremendous prejudice' to the defendant.

'We can't be expected to proceed with this case one moment more unless we have seen what is going to come from England and until we have the time to consider the enormous significance of it all and time to engage our own expert,' he said.

Unfortunately there was another problem. While carrying out the tests on the swabs taken from the steering wheel and the gearstick, the British lab had destroyed the remaining DNA sample.

This meant that the defence would be unable to carry out their own independent analysis, placing them at a severe disadvantage. Understandably they did not want to see the sample from the manacles disappear in the same way.

The tests on the mixed DNA had been performed by Dr Jonathan Whitaker, a top British scientist who works at the Forensic Service Science Laboratory in Wetherby, Yorkshire.

The technique pioneered by Dr Whitaker and his colleagues has been so successful since it was introduced in 1999 that it has been accepted by courts in Britain and other parts of the world, including high-profile cases such as the controversy surrounding the murder conviction of James Hanratty in England and the assassination of the Swedish Foreign Minister Anna Lindt.

But while the method has won the respect of courts as far apart as New Zealand and Sweden, it is not used by other forensic laboratories of international repute. Even the FBI has not adopted the procedure.

Its critics argue that the amplification of tiny samples of DNA cannot be relied upon to give an accurate identification.

The other question pertinent to the Murdoch case was why it had taken the Northern Territory so long to have the DNA samples tested by the British laboratory. After all, the Darwin forensic officers had had them since July 2001 when their laboratory was housed in a much older building.

The original DNA tests, which were unable to produce a positive match with the defendant's, had been carried out in what was known as 'the cupboard', a facility which was not strictly accredited for DNA work. That changed later when the Northern Territory forensic team moved into smart new premises which had been fully accredited for DNA use.

But this still did not explain why over four years had elapsed between the time the DNA had been obtained from the Kombi and the decision to send it to the United Kingdom lab, which had been operational for several years.

Had the prosecution deliberately left it to the last minute so that the defence could do little to carry out their own independent examination in the time available?

There was only one course of action in the circumstances and it would result in the case being delayed for up to six months. Chief Justice Brian Martin agreed that the swab samples from the manacles, which were still in Darwin, should be flown to Britain that afternoon by Dr Whitaker, who had only arrived in Australia a few days earlier.

At precisely 4 p.m. on Friday 22 April he boarded an Australian Airlines flight to Singapore where he would connect to London. By coincidence it was the same service which Joanne Lees had used to fly out of Australia after she had finished being cross-examined during the committal proceedings nearly a year earlier.

Dr Whitaker said he could complete the necessary tests on the cable ties and electrical tape, out of which the manacles had been fashioned, within a few weeks. But because the defence would also want to have their own independent examination it might take double that time for the exercise to be completed.

By then Darwin would be well into the 'dry', the peak tourist season when it is difficult to get a bed in the city unless it is booked several months before. With nearly 80 witnesses being called from all over Australia and some from Britain, it would be almost impossible to accommodate them.

After discussion between the prosecution and defence, and following advice to the judge from the court sheriff, it was agreed to delay the trial for up to six months.

Justice Martin ordered that the suppression order should be temporarily lifted so that he could explain the position to the public.

'I have previously, and this week, heard legal argument, evidence and submissions concerning a number of legal issues which must be resolved before a jury is empanelled,' he explained.

'It has become apparent that in fairness to both the Crown and the accused, the trial before the jury cannot commence as planned. Further investigations concerning possible evidentiary material must be conducted. It is inappropriate to give any details of the material or the investigations. It is sufficient to observe that the trial cannot proceed until the investigations by both the Crown and the accused are completed.

'I urge the media and the public at large not to speculate as to the nature of the investigations or the material under consideration. I have reluctantly concluded that the trial date on May 3 must be vacated and I order accordingly.'

Indicating that it might be delayed until October, the judge pointed out that even that month could not be guaranteed. 'It may be that a different date from October is ultimately determined as the trial date,' he conceded.

Once again the Falconio case was up in the air. Travel plans would have to be postponed. Witnesses stood down for several months. And, more crucially, further tests had to be performed on DNA swabs which had the potential to provide incriminating evidence against the accused.

There was no application to free Bradley Murdoch on bail, though he must have been equally frustrated by the decision as he sat in his prison cell at Darwin's Berrimah jail. After all, he remained innocent until proven guilty and he had already spent nearly two years behind bars in the Northern Territory while waiting for the wheels of justice to turn.

If he was upset about the delay, he wasn't showing it. Those who had had contact with him said he was philosophical about the postponement and continued to be upbeat about his chances of an acquittal.

Yet the prospects were not looking good for Murdoch. If the DNA on the handcuffs matched his own and the judge permitted the evidence to be put before the jury at the trial, the chances of a not guilty verdict would be slim.

It wasn't the only incriminating testimony to emerge during the legal wrangling: on the third day of the pre-trial hearing, Rex Wild, the Director of Public Prosecutions, let slip a further juicy morsel which had hitherto remained out of public view. The defendant, he said, had been working as a drug courier at the time of the Falconio attack, moving large quantities of marijuana around the country.

He had been in business with a friend known as James Hepi.

'It is the intention of the Crown . . . to lead evidence that the business undertaken between Mr Murdoch and Mr Hepi was to transport marijuana from South Australia to Broome,' he told the court. 'It is an important part of the explanation for the trips conducted by Mr Murdoch.'

This was the first specific reference made to the defendant's drug trafficking activities in court. It had been alluded to during the cross-examination of Hepi during the committal proceedings, but now it was in the public domain. Outside the Northern Territory, where the Supreme Court legal hearing was not subject to a suppression order, the drugs claim could now be published.

On Wednesday 27 April 2005, *The Australian* headlined the revelation of Murdoch's involvement with narcotics with the words: 'Falconio accused "a drug courier"'.

For the first time in the reporting of the mystery surrounding the disappearance of Peter Falconio and the attempted abduction of Joanne Lees, a drugs link had been revealed.

While those close to the case were already well aware of Murdoch's illegal activities, the public were not. The prosecution's disclosure, which hinted at another side to the mystery, would have surprised and intrigued readers.

What else did they not know? What was being suggested? Where would it all lead?

They would have to be patient. Another six months would elapse before the full picture began to emerge.

....

CHAPTER 25

JOHN DAULBY AND THE UNANSWERED QUESTIONS

2̶0 May 2005. Once again I am dumbstruck by the degree of coincidence that runs parallel to the Falconio case and my own enquiries.

The week starts with a trip to Swan Hill in northern Victoria on an unrelated story, and continues by way of a circuitous route via Kylie Minogue's family home in Melbourne, where the singer is awaiting tests for breast cancer.

On Thursday I am asked to fly to Darwin to follow up a tip about the whereabouts of the girlfriend of a man regarded as the prime suspect in a savage attack on British woman Abigail Witchells, who was left paralysed near her home in Surrey.

It is a needle-in-a-haystack job and one which bears no fruit, but on the way back to my hotel I stumble across a key figure in the Falconio case, former Assistant

Police Commissioner John Daulby, whom I have been trying to contact for months.

This one-in-a-million encounter is all the more improbable given that he works as an adviser to the police in East Timor and only returns to Darwin four times a year.

He is talking to a friend so I wait for the conversation to end before introducing myself. Unsure how he will respond, I prepare for a polite no comment. Much to my surprise he invites me for a coffee and a quick chat before agreeing to meet again the next day.

There is much I want to ask Daulby, if only to put to rest some of the rumours surrounding the disappearance of Peter Falconio.

He acknowledges he has some regrets about the way part of the investigation was handled, including the initial search of the crime scene and the failure to find Joanne Lees' lip-balm tube, which was eventually discovered about three months later.

He also believes Joanne's reluctance to speak to the media in the early days of the murder hunt created an unnecessary climate of animosity towards her. 'If she had been persuaded to talk earlier there would have been a much friendlier and less sceptical media,' he now accepts.

It was not through lack of trying. Daulby says the police did all in their power to convince her that it would be for the best, but alternately the final decision was up to her. By the time she did agree to a press conference the damage had been done and Joanne's image risked being irrevocably tarnished.

I move on to the perceived inconsistencies in Joanne's evidence, including the gap in the back of the cab of the gunman's truck. We know now that none of Murdoch's vehicles had such access to the rear tray, yet Joanne had told police she manoeuvred her way through the hole before making good her escape.

And then there was the description of the attacker's hair — shoulder length, according to Joanne to begin with, but short according to the picture of the man in the truck-stop surveillance video.

'I can't explain the inconsistencies,' Daulby admits, but points out that shock and stress can sometimes play tricks on a person's memory. 'I think you have to reflect on the trauma she was under — some things you remember quite clearly and others you don't.'

After all, she had been through a terrible experience and it was easy to understand if her mind was muddled.

Daulby has always had the utmost sympathy for Joanne and is certain she is telling the truth. Equally he has never doubted that Bradley Murdoch is the man responsible for the death of her boyfriend.

But what was the motive, I ask. How did it happen? What provoked the attack?

Although he cannot be sure about the events which led to the shooting and Joanne's attempted abduction, he is certain that Murdoch was out of his mind with drugs and capable of anything on that night.

'He was paranoid and may have thought the couple's VW Kombi was after him,' suggests the retired police chief. 'But who knows? Murdoch's certainly not going to say.'

And what about the rumours that Falconio had met Murdoch earlier and may even have done some kind of drug deal with him, a transaction that may have somehow gone wrong?

Once again the former Northern Territory Assistant Police Commissioner is adamant.

'There is no evidence to say that Peter Falconio met Murdoch. The theory that Peter or Joanne had entered an agreement to do something illegal with Murdoch just doesn't fathom.

'They were simply on an el-cheapo holiday minding their own business, just like thousands of other young travellers.'

To suggest otherwise would be unfair to both of them, he argues.

Likewise, contrary to prevailing scuttlebutt at the time, the campervan did not contain a large amount of cannabis when it was found, merely a small quantity for personal use.

And there was certainly no proof that Joanne Lees' boyfriend had made two trips to Thailand while living in Sydney, as some sources had suggested.

I have no reason to disbelieve Daulby who has always been regarded as a man of truth and integrity throughout his unblemished career as a policeman. Yet he is clearly troubled by some aspects of this case, especially the search of the crime scene which 'could have been handled better', he admits.

'It's easy to be wise in hindsight, but overall I believe the police response was as good as possible under the circumstances,' he says.

But would they have caught Murdoch without the assistance of James Hepi whose evidence was crucial?

'Even if Hepi hadn't talked, Murdoch would eventually have been found by process of elimination,' claims Daulby.

Murdoch's days were numbered, partly because of the company he kept. They were a motley crew whom

Daulby refers to as a 'bowl of fleas'. Even the bikies didn't want anything to do with him, he says.

'He had become uncontrollable.'

What also concerns John Daulby is the absence of a body. Not because he wonders whether Peter is still alive, but because without the human remains being found there will never be complete closure, especially for the Falconio family.

'There will be a lot of debate about this case and a lot of finger pointing about the handling of the case, but there's no closure without Peter,' he points out.

Somewhere in the outback he is buried, but where?

Daulby thinks the body lies within 50 kilometres of the scene of the crime, or possibly within a similar range to Alice Springs.

'Maybe he had the body in the back of the ute at the truck stop,' he ponders.

By that time the drugs would have started wearing off and he would be thinking more clearly so he wouldn't dump the body near where Peter was shot, he reasons.

In the final analysis we can theorise and speculate forever. There is no real logic to the gunman's actions, which were most likely the result of a series of random choices made under the influence of narcotics.

I fire a few final questions before my time runs out. It is 12.20 p.m. and my plane to Sydney departs at 1 p.m. I am anxious to gauge his response to one or two other puzzling points.

What was Murdoch doing so far north of the start of the Tanami Track which he usually chose for his long drive back to Broome?

Daulby doesn't know.

Then there were the Aborigines who saw the truck pull out from behind the Kombi and head north on the night in question, when Joanne only recalled the gunman's vehicle doing a U-turn and driving south.

Again the ex-police chief has no explanation.

Neither is he aware of the second pool of blood reportedly found by the Aboriginal tracker, Dudley Hines, on the other side of the road.

Nor does he know that the blood from Peter Falconio's body also contained animal DNA.

In fairness Daulby left his job as the man with executive responsibility for the murder investigation in August 2003, so it is understandable that he would not remember everything and would not be privy to more recent forensic findings.

This is a highly complex case which requires intense study to maintain a full and detailed grasp of all the evidence. Yet obviously many questions remain unanswered. These gaps in the story might play into the hands of the defence team who could be expected to exploit them to maximum advantage.

When I bid my farewell the former police chief is in reflective mood. Our conversation has reminded both of us what this prosecution is really all about — the cold-blooded murder of a young man in the prime of life and the conviction of whoever was responsible.

'Whatever happens my feelings are for the Falconio family who will always ask, "Where's Peter?"' he remarks.

It is a poignant moment.

The week had ended in a most unexpected fashion, the happenstance of the previous couple of days reinforced by yet another uncanny confluence of timing.

Twenty-four hours earlier the Northern Territory Supreme Court Chief Justice, Brian Martin, had set a new date for the trial of Bradley John Murdoch.

The case would open on 17 October and last for up to two months.

I had not intended to be in Darwin when the announcement was made, but it was a curious coincidence. What other unseen forces might be at play between now and the end of the year?

CHAPTER 26

....

LET BATTLE COMMENCE

Sunday, 16 October. The weekend before the start of the trial had an almost surreal atmosphere to it. So many people had waited so long for the case to resume that it was hard to believe the time had come.

The key players were already in Darwin. Members of the Falconio family were among the first to fly in to the Northern Territory. Peter's parents, Joan and Luciano, and his brother Nick, had arrived on 11 October.

Joan, on her first visit to Australia, felt it her duty to be there for the duration of the trial.

Nick admitted that his parents were 'apprehensive' about being in the Northern Territory but he hoped the experience would provide a degree of closure. 'We just want to do justice for Peter,' he explained. 'It's been a long time now and we just want a conclusion.'

His brother Paul, who would be one of the first witnesses to be called, arrived in the early hours of Sunday morning.

Significantly, the Department of Justice appeared to have learned some lessons from the committal proceedings, which became something of a media circus when Joanne arrived to give evidence 17 months earlier.

Clearly anxious not to repeat the scenes, officials organised a pooled picture opportunity at Darwin airport when the star witness arrived on a Qantas flight from Singapore early on Friday morning. A few cameramen were allowed to be there on the understanding they would share their pictures with other media.

As Joanne disembarked from flight QF082 at 4.10 a.m. she walked some 40 metres from Gate 7 in front of a small group of cameramen and journalists to an unmarked police vehicle.

The new media-friendly approach to the case even extended to a detailed press release about Joanne's appearance, from the Department of Justice. 'She has long, straight, dark brown hair and wore a beige sleeveless knit top, jeans and gold sandals,' the statement cooed.

It had shades of the oily prose more commonly associated with a member of the royal family than a major witness in a criminal trial. And as if to underline the importance of the occasion, the announcement revealed that her welcoming party included members of the Northern Territory's Response Section, a senior detective and a representative of the Department of Justice.

The theory behind this carefully orchestrated picture opportunity was that once Joanne's image had been filmed, the media would lose interest and leave her alone for the rest of her stay. It was also revealed that she would walk through the front entrance of Darwin's Supreme Court on the first few days of the trial, unlike the unseemly cat-and-mouse game that was played out behind the building during the committal as Joanne was driven in and out of the rear entrance at breakneck speed.

It has to be said that Joanne looked in pretty good shape when she flew in to Australia, despite the fact that she had been travelling for the best part of 24 hours. Although media reports of her arrival claimed she looked tired and nervous, she appeared to be in good health.

Her hair was much longer than before and her piercing, grey-blue eyes stared resolutely ahead as she ignored reporters' questions. She was also accompanied by a family liaison officer from the Sussex Police Force and a male friend (though not Mark Sanders who'd supported her during the pre-trial hearing).

Her companion was named simply as Martin, a friend from Huddersfield. She had known him for the past 16 years and the relationship was purely platonic.

While the media-friendly approach was largely welcomed by the gathering army of newsmen and women, the Department of Justice was also anxious not to send the wrong signals about coverage of the case. In a stern reminder to journalists, Director of Public Prosecutions Rex Wild issued his own warning:

'It is important that jury deliberations are not tainted by media coverage (before or during a trial) of any issue that may arise outside court hearings, or legal discussions held in the absence of the jury. I ask for your co-operation again with particular emphasis on internet publications, which have the inherent power to cross jurisdictional borders, unlike print, radio or television reports, which can be stopped.

'You should also be aware that there are severe penalties, by way of fine and/or imprisonment, for failure to observe some of the matters that I have outlined, but in keeping with the spirit of this letter I do no more than point this out,' he added.

Point taken. Though in reality it was becoming harder and harder to stop discussion of the trial appearing on the internet. While the news media could remove coverage of the case from their websites, there was no way of preventing bloggers from having their say.

I was reminded of the legal ramifications while writing a preview story for London. While most newspaper websites had abided by the Northern Territory's laws, the same did not apply to the printed version produced by overseas outlets and I was constantly fearful that suppressed detail mentioned in my own reports might accidentally find its way onto the newspaper's on-line coverage. I did not want to get evicted from the court at this late stage, yet some extremely interesting information had come my way and I was not sure whether to reveal it.

A few months ago a source told me that Joanne and Peter had stopped somewhere else on the Stuart Highway before they got to Ti Tree. He claimed they were seen at the Aileron Roadhouse about 90 minutes' drive north of Alice Springs.

This was never disclosed by police or referred to at the pre-trial hearing and it represented a fascinating new line of enquiry. If true, the roadhouse owner, Greg Dick, might have been one of the last people to see Peter Falconio alive.

I rang Greg, who confirmed the sighting and claimed that several of his staff saw the couple too. 'The only reason I remember them is because of their vehicle. I saw their orange campervan outside,' he recalled.

'I was sitting at the table next to them. They had a toasted cheese and tomato sandwich and were going through their travel maps, talking and laughing.'

More intriguing was the time of their arrival. They walked into the Aileron Roadhouse about 3.15 p.m. and left just before 4 p.m, he revealed. If the time frame was correct it was completely at odds with the pre-trial testimony from Joanne, who told the court that they did not leave Alice Springs until about 4 p.m.

Why had Joanne not revealed their earlier departure? And why would they have stopped at Aileron in the first place, if they had enough petrol to get to Ti Tree where they eventually filled up? Were they early for a rendezvous? Were they waiting for someone? Were they killing time?

I asked Greg whether he had told the police about the couple's visit. He said officers had spoken to him after the Barrow Creek incident but never followed it up.

'They weren't interested and brushed it aside,' he claimed.

Then, unprompted, the roadhouse owner volunteered another curious snippet. Before Joanne and Peter arrived another man came into the café.

'He was an odd fella who looked like a real bushie and who could obviously look after himself. He was about 35, had sunken cheeks, was clean shaven and said he came from Port Augusta. He told me he was going to live in the bush for a bit, in the Davenport Ranges near Wauchope.'

It was not only the bush-like character who made an impression on Dick, but also his dog. 'He bought a pie for the dog and a bottle of Coke for himself. I offered to put sauce on it but he said the dog didn't like sauce.'

Who was this man and why was so little known about him? Could he have played a role in the drama that was about to unfold between Ti Tree and Barrow Creek?

More crucially, would Greg Dick be called to give evidence at the trial? On 13 October I telephoned him again to see whether he had been contacted by anyone. He recalled someone ringing a few weeks earlier and saying he might be subpoenaed to attend. But he had heard nothing since.

I was aware the defence knew about the Aileron connection but it remained to be seen whether it was in their interests to bring it up during the trial. Though clearly it would raise further questions about the accuracy of Joanne's evidence.

The Aileron link was fascinating and reinforced Greg's belief that someone else was responsible for Peter Falconio's murder.

The bushie who bought a pie and a Coke in his cafe that Saturday afternoon in 2001 was not Murdoch, he insisted. He knew what the defendant looked like and the man he served was not him.

I was also aware of rumours that two men might have been involved in the attack on Peter and Joanne. Darwin was awash with gossip on the weekend before the trial and I had learned from experience to take all the stories with a pinch of salt. But this one was intriguing, partly because it came from a reliable source.

According to the latest story Peter Falconio had been recruited in South Australia to deliver a stash of drugs to someone in the Northern Territory. It is a common practice for backpackers to be used as so-called mules because they provide the perfect cover. As young travellers, they are unlikely to attract attention or suspicion from the authorities and are always interested in earning extra cash. They are therefore easy prey for unscrupulous traffickers who need to transfer their narcotics from one part of Australia to another.

While there was no suggestion that Joanne was in on the rumoured deal, was it possible that she suspected her boyfriend's intentions? Could this explain the unease she felt when they passed the grassfires on that Saturday evening north of Ti Tree? Was this why she didn't want to stop to put them out?

When the supposed delivery took place — and the fanciful story goes that it happened somewhere off-road in the vicinity of Ti Tree, which could explain the additional six kilometres on the odometer — Falconio apparently retained some of the drugs for himself. The story has it that, after the recipients discovered they had been short-changed, one of them flew into a rage and chased the two young Britons up the Stuart Highway, where he stopped their campervan and killed Peter in an act of cold-blooded revenge.

Meanwhile, his accomplice, who was in another vehicle following up behind, was so aghast when he came across the roadside mayhem perpetrated by his partner in crime that he realised urgent action was required, if they were not to be discovered.

Loading the body into his own truck, he might have driven north to find a suitable place to bury the corpse. Was this the vehicle noticed by the southbound Aboriginal couple who saw a truck pull out from behind the campervan as they passed the scene of the crime and drove up the Highway? By this time the killer could also have been on his way, heading south.

Who pulled a gun on Peter Falconio was not clear.

Such a scenario was never publicly raised by the police. Nor would it fit comfortably with the charges they would eventually prepare against Murdoch. They already had their man for the outback ambush and this line of enquiry, if it was true, would only dirty the case for the prosecution.

Was this the real story behind the killing of Peter Falconio or just another piece of scuttlebutt?

From Monday, it was up to the jury to separate fact from fiction.

....

CHAPTER 27

ONLY THE RED CARPET IS MISSING

'The Queen against Bradley John Murdoch.' The sentence echoed loud and clear around the court as Chief Justice Brian Martin took his seat at 10.12 a.m. on 17 October 2005. To sit in the Northern Territory Supreme Court that Monday morning was to see the judicial process in its ultimate ceremonial form. The judge, bewigged and red-robed, cast a sobering stare across the floor towards the batteries of legal teams, media and members of the public who had gathered to witness the selection of the jury.

Fifteen were to be chosen from a pool of 59 men and women good and true, three more than usual because of the likely length of the trial. The extra three, all of whom would sit in the jury box, would act as reserves in case anybody had to withdraw because of ill health or any other unforeseen circumstances.

Chief Justice Martin told them that he realised it might be the first time some of them had been in a criminal court and acknowledged that they might be feeling apprehensive.

'I appreciate you are in unfamiliar surroundings but please relax,' he urged them.

It is hard to say how the defendant felt as he stood to hear the charges against him but he looked composed enough. Wearing his usual blue denim shirt and beige trousers, Murdoch replied 'Not guilty' to each of the three accusations against him — that he murdered Peter Falconio, assaulted Joanne Lees and deprived her of her liberty.

Then, with his lawyer Grant Algie standing by his side, he inspected the prospective jurors as they were selected by means of what appeared to be an old tombola drum, the sort of receptacle more commonly associated with church raffles or fairground lotteries.

Each of the 59 had been given a number, and every time the drum was turned, a court official put his hand inside and withdrew a small numbered disc. Whoever possessed the corresponding numerical symbol was asked to present him- or herself to the judge. During those few seconds the defence and the prosecution had to decide whether they were the sort of people who might help or hinder their case.

Algie challenged 11 of the potential jurors, all of them women. Crown prosecutor Rex Wild objected to two of the men.

Chief Justice Martin advised the chosen 15 to approach the trial with an open mind. He accepted the situation they faced was not easy. 'You have been brought together for a particularly important task,' he emphasised. 'Everything that happens in this trial is designed to help you carry out your task. Do not be afraid of what lies ahead of you. Your role is to listen to the evidence and decide whether the Crown has proved the accused guilty. It's absolutely critical to give your attention to the evidence. You must ignore anything you have seen outside the court as the trial progresses.

'There's been an enormous amount of publicity about this matter and about the accused, resulting in much discussion in the community. Whatever you have seen or heard in the past or hear in the future outside the court must be put aside and ignored,' he added.

The judge recognised that jurors might have read about a previous case involving the accused, though he did not mention the nature of the prosecution, the South Australian rape charges on which Murdoch was acquitted.

'Whatever you have heard must be put aside and ignored, otherwise it would be totally unfair to the accused,' he made clear.

He also warned them against accessing the internet to read about the case or the defendant. And the same applied to discussion of the trial with those they knew outside the jury room.

'The importance of your role carries through to the requirement that you must not speak to anyone about the case except a fellow juror. When you go home tonight no doubt your family will want to know how you got on, and what it's like to be on the jury and what the case is all about. You must not talk about the case. You must tell them firmly you can't talk about anything concerning the trial.'

The assembled media was also given the benefit of the judge's view on overzealous photographers. Making his position clear from the outset, he ordered them not to enter the driveway at the back of the building to film the comings and goings of the defendant or any of the witnesses. Nor to harass those who used the front entrance.

'I appreciate there is great media attention in one or two witnesses but they are entitled to enter without being distressed by the crush of media. I hope you will enjoy your time in the Northern Territory. I am sure you will understand my concern to conduct this trial fairly and properly.'

As it was, the decision by Joanne Lees to walk through a roped-off path up to the front entrance worked to everybody's advantage. There was no unseemly crush, although the arrival of the star witness, who usually alighted from a sleek, black sedan with tinted windows into an explosion of flash guns, did seem to have more in common with a Hollywood movie premiere than a murder trial. Only the red carpet was missing.

It was shortly after midday that the trial proper got underway in court six, the same room where the pre-trial hearing was staged a year earlier. Rex Wild QC, dressed in the traditional black top, winged collar and wig, stood to outline the case for the prosecution.

His delivery, quietly spoken and perhaps deliberately understated so as to reinforce the dramatic impact of his words, was to continue, allowing for the lunch break, until 2.55 p.m.

Turning to the jury, he recounted in graphic detail what occurred leading up to the Stuart Highway attack, elaborating on the intricate series of events surrounding the killing of Peter Falconio, and explaining the prosecution's interpretation of the evidence it had amassed and why it believed the man responsible was Bradley John Murdoch.

After describing the outback drama of 14 July 2001, the Crown prosecutor moved on to other aspects of the case.

He explained a little of Murdoch's working life in the transport of cannabis before outlining the evidence against him. It could be proved that the accused was in the vicinity of the crime scene on the day in question, he said. Then there was the defendant's change of appearance after the incident, his four-wheel drive's change of appearance, his alleged description of the best place to bury a body, the truck-stop video surveillance footage, DNA results: all of which would be discussed in detail later in the trial.

Rex Wild also had another card up his sleeve. He explained that as well as DNA matching Murdoch's profile having been found on Joanne's T-shirt, as was revealed in the committal proceedings, English DNA expert Dr Jonathon Whitaker had recently conducted tests on the cable ties used to handcuff Joanne and found DNA on them belonging to Murdoch. Mr Wild produced a mock-up of the manacles to demonstrate the location of the sample. The prosecutor added that Dr Whitaker had also found DNA matching Murdoch on the gearstick of the campervan.

Reaching the end of his speech, he conceded that this was a circumstantial case — 'We rarely have an eyewitness to a murder: usually the witness is the person who is killed,' he observed — but declared that circumstances cried out for the jury to decide that Murdoch had fired a shot that had killed the British tourist. It was his belief, he said, 'that the evidence and the facts ... will lead you inevitably to the conclusion that Joanne Lees was attacked, and Peter Falconio murdered, by Mr Bradley Murdoch at a dark and lonely spot on the Stuart Highway.' With that, the Director of Public Prosecutions sat down.

The first witnesses called by the prosecution were Paul and Luciano Falconio. For an hour the court listened intently to their testimony, as they impressed on the jury how Peter had been part of a close and loving family back home in Yorkshire. How he always kept in touch and how the last time they had heard from him was on 12 July 2001.

Luciano, fighting back tears, recalled how his son had earlier phoned to say they were leaving Sydney because 'it was starting to get cool'. He remembered the cottage Peter had bought, back home in New Mill, which he had purchased in his own name.

'He had a mortgage. It's still in his own name,' he pointed out, as if the tiny property was still waiting for its owner to return.

'If Peter was still alive would you have expected to have heard from him?' asked Rex Wild.

'I would more than expect him. He would definitely ring,' Luciano insisted.

'Do you know anyone who has heard from him?'

'No.'

Few could have doubted the sincerity of Luciano's words. He had travelled halfway around the world to testify on behalf of his lost son. His duty done, he wiped his eyes and left the witness box to take his seat in the front row of the public gallery alongside Joan, Paul and Nicholas.

A hush had fallen on the court, the type of quietness one might experience just before the curtain rises at the theatre.

Then at precisely 3.48 p.m. the sepulchral silence was broken by a simple order which rang out loud and clear: 'Call Joanne Lees.'

It took at least a minute for Joanne to walk along the first floor gallery to the entrance of court six. As she strode through the wooden doors and made her way to the witness box, past the press, the public, the banks of lawyers and the man in the glass-panelled dock, she stared resolutely ahead.

The lack of acknowledgment was mutual. Bradley John Murdoch looked down at his papers and shook his head, feigning boredom in the presence of his nemesis. Who would cast the first glance?

Joanne, dressed in a charcoal skirt, white, open-necked blouse, and with her hair tied into a ponytail, looked like a secretary waiting to take dictation. Her straight back and determined look gave her an air of confidence which had been missing from her earlier appearances at the pre-trial hearing. Here was a woman who had steeled herself for this moment over several years and she had no intention of cracking.

Wild went through the opening pleasantries, asking for her place of residence, date of birth and occupation. She was a support worker for people with learning disabilities, Joanne explained.

For several minutes she recalled her life and times with Peter. Their holidays together in Italy and Greece. His graduation from Brighton University. His work for John Laing, the building company where he was able to put his degree in construction to such good effect.

And then their long-planned odyssey to Asia and Australia, which had been delayed because of Peter's work commitments. They had arrived in Sydney on 16 January 2001, the court was told, and had shared

© Newspix

Forensic scientist Carmen Eckhoff (left) holds up the T-shirt worn by Joanne the night of the attack, while Northern Territory Assistant Police Commissioner John Daulby (right) shows a copy of the review into the police investigation.

© Newspix

Murdoch's much-modified Landcruiser. Months after the attack on Peter and Joanne, the vehicle was almost unrecognisable.

© Newspix

Joanne Lees, with Commander Max Pope (left) and Paul Falconio, at her press conference in Alice Springs 11 days after the incident. She agreed only to read out a statement and answer three of 13 questions previously submitted by journalists. If Joanne thought her appearance before the media would dampen speculation about the case, she was quickly proved wrong.

Emeritus Professor Barry Boettcher, a retired head of biological sciences at Newcastle University, believed that a mark left on the driver's side window of the Kombi could be a handprint. It was potential evidence that was ignored, he believed. Here Professor Boettcher poses with a video image of the mark.

Joanne arrives at the Darwin Supreme Court on the floor of a car during the committal proceedings in May 2004. Her attempts to keep the media at bay sometimes created the impression of her being the person on trial.

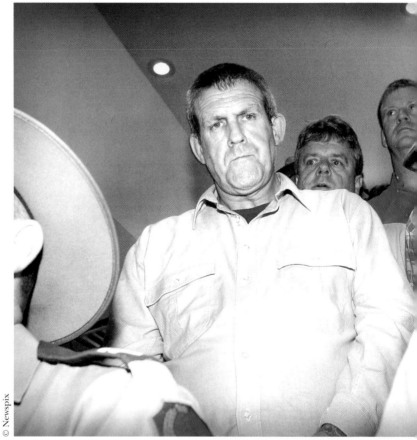

Murdoch under police escort at Darwin airport in November 2003. He'd been arrested immediately after his acquittal on charges of rape, false imprisonment and assault in South Australia.

Bradley Murdoch's lawyer Grant Algie
arrives at the pre-trial hearing.

© Newspix

Crown Prosecutor Rex Wild QC. Mr Wild sparked a minor controversy when he was allegedly heard calling Supreme Court Chief Justice Brian Martin by his Christian name during the trial, a report both men vehemently denied.

© Newspix

© Newspix

Jan Pittman, Murdoch's girlfriend. During the trial, she would gesture to him to calm down when he appeared to be getting agitated.

Joan, Luciano and Nick Falconio arrive at the Darwin Supreme
Court during the trial.

Joanne during the trial. She'd steeled herself for this moment for
several years and had no intention of cracking.

Flanked by Nick Falconio (left) and his brother Paul, Joanne delivers a statement to the media after the guilty verdict was announced. 'We are pleased with the verdict,' said Nick, grateful for the end of their four-year ordeal, 'but this will not bring Pete back.'

accommodation with a father and his daughter in North Bondi. As they found their feet, friendships developed.

Rex Wild saw this as an appropriate time to address the ongoing issue of Joanne's relationship with fellow backpacker Nick Riley. Anxious not to allow the defence to take further advantage of Joanne's illicit love affair, which had so undermined her credibility when it was aired during the committal proceedings, the prosecution invited her to put the record straight.

She had met Nick through some friends while working at Dymocks bookshop, she told the jury.

'He was a friend, a good friend, and we became close,' she admitted.

Was Peter Falconio aware of their relationship, Mr Wild enquired.

'No, we were just friends and we overstepped the boundary of friendship,' she replied.

In a few short sentences Joanne had put the controversy to rest. She agreed they had gone too far and the affair was over.

Changing tack, the prosecution moved on to the journey from Sydney to Alice Springs. They had stopped in a caravan park in Adelaide, though Joanne could not recall the name of it. As they made their way north they had slept in the Kombi, parking in lay-bys and occasionally camping sites.

The journey via Ayers Rock, Kings Canyon and on to Alice Springs was fun but largely uneventful. Then on Friday the 13th of July came the first indication that Peter's luck might be changing for the worse.

It came in the form of an appointment with a local accountancy firm where he learned that, far from being entitled to a rebate on his tax, he owed the government money. Peter wasn't pleased but it didn't stop him from visiting a travel agency and enquiring about the cost of a flight to Papua New Guinea. He intended to go with a mate from Sydney.

'They were both keen on adventure holidays but I didn't share their enthusiasm so I was going back to Sydney and spend the week with his [mate's] girlfriend,' Joanne said.

On Saturday they went to the Camel Cup but she wasn't sure when they left. In the afternoon they went to a caravan park where they had a shower and, according to Joanne, finally drove out of Alice Springs between 4 and 4.30 p.m. This was to prove a crucial time in view of what the defence team had up its sleeve. But for now she was more than happy to answer questions about her memory of their journey up the Stuart Highway, a drive which averaged 88.5 kilometres an hour.

Joanne was driving and Pete was lying in the back reading *Catcher in the Rye* and listening to his favourite band, Texas.

'Did you stop anywhere along the way?' Mr Wild asked.

'No,' she responded.

'Did you pass a service station at Aileron?'

It was the first time the remote outback community had been mentioned in the case and the prosecution had clearly got wind of Grant Algie's intention to raise it later.

Better to get in first, the prosecution must have reasoned, if only to quell the rumours that were circulating about the young couple's visit to the roadhouse.

Joanne seemed unfazed by the question, agreeing that she might have driven past but didn't know for sure.

However, she did remember stopping at Ti Tree. It was here that Peter woke up from his afternoon nap when Joanne braked heavily. They stayed there for about 20 minutes, buying water, stretching their legs and watching the sun go down while sharing a joint, Joanne recalled.

Once again she emphasised that the cannabis had come from a friend in Sydney and had been stored on a shelf under the dashboard.

And what sort of effect had the drug produced, the Crown prosecutor enquired innocently.

It made them sightly relaxed, Joanne admitted.

'Was it a happy time for you?'

'Yes.'

Rex Wild and his star witness had brought the curtain down on day one of the trial by leaving the jury with the image of a loving couple, sitting back, listening to music and smoking a joint, as the golden rays of a setting sun emblazoned the outback sky. It might have come straight from the pages of a romantic novel.

Next day Mr Wild returned to the journey from Alice Springs. There was mention of a visit to the Red Rooster restaurant on the outskirts of town, the first occasion there had been any reference to the fast-food takeaway. Joanne, dressed in a smart navy-blue suit, said Pete had ordered a meal while she had some pizza. It was shortly after 4 p.m.

It took over two hours to get to Ti Tree. Peter filled the tank while Joanne got out to go to the toilet. Peter paid for the fuel and, as usual, asked for a receipt so he could scrawl the odometer reading in ink across the top. The current mileage was 89,272, though it had probably gone around the clock more than once, since the

Kombi was built 30 years earlier. The receipt also confirmed the time of the purchase — 6.21 p.m. Cashier Robert Lake's name was printed on the bottom.

As Peter returned to the campervan Joanne moved across to the passenger seat to let her boyfriend take over at the wheel.

'The sun had set and it was beginning to get dark,' she recalled.

As they drove off up the highway Pete selected a track from The Stone Roses. It was his choice not hers. Whoever was driving got to play their favourite music. That was the deal they'd struck and while Joanne didn't like the British rock band, she was resigned to listening to them.

Wild asked her if they'd discussed where they would spend the night. Joanne said they hadn't decided. Pete was refreshed after spending the previous few hours dozing in the back, so they were going to see how far they could get.

They continued chatting, at one stage wondering where they'd be when they celebrated their birthdays a few months hence. Pete thought they'd be in New Zealand come 20 September. Joanne hoped to be in Fiji for her birthday a few weeks after his. As the small talk continued the crimson sky began to fade to black.

'It got darker and darker,' Joanne told the court.

The dusk doesn't hang around in this part of Australia. Suddenly it was pitch black, she added.

Did she see anything unusual, the Director of Public Prosecutions prompted her.

'Yes, a fire burning,' she replied.

The flames had spread onto the road itself and Joanne was worried. It looked as though it had been deliberately lit.

'I felt afraid and uneasy,' she remarked.

Once again she recounted how her boyfriend wanted to stop to put the fire out but she persuaded him to continue driving, although she said that part of her felt they should have pulled over and extinguished the flames.

What caused the roadside blaze remained unclear. But how could the flames have spread onto the bitumen without the encouragement of some form of accelerant? If the fire had been started deliberately, as Joanne suggested, what was the reason? Was it a signal placed by someone to mark a drop-off point? Or was it merely an accidental blaze sparked by a stray cigarette?

The conspiracy theorists among those following the case had even raised the possibility of the flames being used as landing lights to guide a small aircraft down on to the Stuart Highway. Interestingly, this is not such a crazy idea as it sounds. Burning oil drums and makeshift flares are often used to help light planes land in the outback and a long straight road provides the perfect runway.

But for now such speculation fell into the realms of fantasy. There was to be no further examination of the curious fires. The prosecution had put the matter to rest with a few throwaway questions in readiness for the most dramatic stage of Joanne's testimony.

'Were you aware of another vehicle?' Mr Wild enquired.

In court there was an air of expectation, all eyes focused on Joanne as she sat apprehensively in the witness box. She was centre stage and she knew that her every word would be recorded and reported in gruesome detail.

She took a gulp of air and swallowed nervously, a habit she was to repeat frequently in the coming days.

'Yes, Pete said he wished the vehicle would just overtake us,' she told the Crown prosecutor.

Suddenly a white four-wheel drive appeared alongside them. The interior light was on. There was a dog sitting on the passenger seat. The driver was gesturing to them to pull over.

Joanne's memory of the detail that night was quite extraordinary. She recalled the bullbar on the front of the other vehicle — 'it was very bright and could have been silver or chrome.'

She remembered the baseball cap the man was wearing and the motif on the front. He had a shirt with long sleeves and a T-shirt underneath. He looked like a local man, an 'older gentleman', she observed, with a Mexican-style moustache which grew down each side of his mouth.

The vehicle stayed parallel with the campervan for about a minute, she said, until Pete stopped the Kombi on the left-hand side of the road and the four-wheel drive parked just behind.

Joanne urged her boyfriend to continue driving. Maybe it was a woman's intuition of imminent danger, but by now Pete had ignored his girlfriend's pleas. There was no going back.

Peter opened the door and walked to the back of the campervan, where the man was standing. Joanne moved across to the driver's seat. She didn't want to get out but she had a proprietorial interest in knowing what was wrong with the Kombi.

'It was my vehicle as well and I didn't want to think that we had broken down in the middle of nowhere,' she advised the jury.

She saw Pete talking to the man at the back. They were illuminated by the four-wheel drive's headlights which Joanne confirmed remained switched on. This was an important detail given that she did not see her boyfriend's body as she walked past the gap between the two vehicles a few minutes later.

She listened out for snippets of conversation. There was mention of sparks coming out of the exhaust. She noticed Pete, who was 180 centimetres tall, was shorter than the other man, who 'looked down' on her boyfriend. The other driver's posture also stood out. He was 'hunched and stooping'.

Joanne heard Pete say, 'Cheers mate, thanks for stopping,' before he returned to the front door, collected his cigarettes and asked her to rev the engine.

'I didn't really know what I was supposed to be doing. I just kept revving the engine and then I heard a bang, like a car backfiring but also like a gunshot.'

Joanne's reference to the sound of a gun was surprising given that a few days after the attack, in the interview she gave to the *Centralian Advocate*, she denied thinking it was the noise of a gunshot.

The apparent contradiction was allowed to pass. Though the judge did interrupt the exchange for further clarification: was she actually revving the engine when she heard the bang?

'I can't remember. First I thought it was the vehicle backfiring and it was because of what I had been doing,' she explained to Chief Justice Brian Martin.

So when did she think it was a gunshot, he asked.

'It was afterwards,' she told him.

Wild wanted to know if the Kombi had been backfiring.

'Yes,' she said, but not on that particular night.

The prosecution lawyer paused for a moment, as if to allow the witness time to prepare for the horror she was about to relive. He reminded the court that the window on the driver's side of the campervan was wound up when a man's face appeared in the glass.

Joanne swallowed nervously and uttered the simple phrase, 'He stared at me.'

For a split second, she said, their eyes met — hers in fear, his perhaps in anticipation of what was to follow. He wrenched open the door and produced a silver revolver in his right hand. Until that point he had remained silent. Now he was ordering her to turn the engine off. She couldn't. She was 'shaking too much'. So he did it for her.

'He's moving into the car and coming towards me . . . I back away into the passenger seat . . . He asks me to put my head down and my hands behind my back.'

Joanne said that he pointed the gun towards her right temple, close enough for her to see its design in every intriguing detail. Joanne had never seen a real gun before. It was a Western-style revolver similar to those used in old cowboy movies. And some kind of scrolling pattern had been engraved in a rectangular box along the side of the barrel.

Terrified by the sight of the firearm, Joanne began to obey the gunman's commands, but then thought otherwise. Summoning all her inner strength, she decided to fight back.

'I thought, no, I'm going to try to escape and get out of the side of the vehicle.'

She placed her feet against the dashboard to give herself enough leverage to swing her body around and somehow push herself out of the passenger door.

But the move proved unsuccessful. Her attacker bound her wrists with the home-made manacles he had manufactured from plastic cable ties and tape. They were extremely tight but there was a three-inch (7.5 centimetre) gap between each cuff, allowing her a certain degree of movement.

Joanne had seen the gunman close-up for only several seconds but she would not forget his face.

'Do you see that man here today?' Mr Wild asked.

The reply came without hesitation.

'Yes, I am looking at him,' Joanne declared as she stared across the court and nodded to the man in the dock.

Murdoch shook his head. Someone close to him thought they heard him mutter under his breath, 'It wasn't fucking me,' as he lifted his head towards Joanne.

She in turn appeared to mouth the words, 'Oh yes, it was.'

For a moment there was a hint of the terrified gaze from four years earlier, as her eyes fixed on the man she believed was responsible for her boyfriend's brutal killing. For his part, Murdoch sat resignedly behind the glass partition and rustled his papers. Joanne had the upper hand in the unfolding courtroom drama and he was powerless to act. It was the ultimate in frustration for a man whose quick temper usually demanded swift retribution.

At such times he would glance across to his girlfriend, Jan Pittman, who had a specially reserved seat in the front of the public gallery. She knew Murdoch well enough to recognise his explosive tendencies, and on such occasions would motion to him with her flattened hands above her lap to calm down. The unspoken communication was enough to have effect. With Murdoch settled, Joanne continued with every graphic detail of her nightmare experience.

Suddenly she found herself lying face down on the gravel beneath the passenger door of the campervan. Her attacker was straddling the back of her body, trying to tie her legs together and place tape around her mouth. She remembered grazing her knees and elbows, in fact she still bore the scars. The judge suggested she turn her arms to the jury so they could see the marks. She raised her elbows accordingly.

Then, recalling the salty taste of blood in her mouth, she told how she lifted her head to protect her face from being scratched by the roadside grit. With her hands tied behind her back, she also attempted, unsuccessfully, to reach out and grab her attacker's testicles. He was so furious that he delivered a vicious punch to her right temple, momentarily stunning her. (Significantly, she had forgotten the blow when she was examined by a doctor in Alice Springs the following night, as his testimony a few days later would confirm.)

Meanwhile, still unaware of her boyfriend's fate, she started screaming out for Peter to come and help her. Tellingly there was no response. Inevitably Joanne was forced to give in to her attacker's overwhelming strength.

Pulling her to her feet, he marched her towards his own vehicle, his hands guiding her shoulders and her eyes looking straight ahead. He reached into the canopy which covered the rear of his four-wheel drive and produced a sack which he placed over her head.

Already shocked and traumatised, Joanne was now disoriented by the lack of sight. Afraid of being smothered, she gasped for air.

'I was screaming, "I can't breathe,"' she told the jury, who, like the rest of the court, were transfixed by her vivid and chillingly graphic account.

Thankfully the hood fell off as she was pushed into the cab of the gunman's four-wheel drive, offering her a glimpse of the dog which she had seen earlier. It was 'broad and chunky' with pointed ears and a 'black or dark brown' coat with white patches. Was this Jack, Murdoch's Dalmatian-like cross-breed? Certainly it wasn't aggressive, which fitted Jack's character. But it didn't seem to have the look of a spotty dog either, although perhaps the dim light was playing tricks with her eyes.

Joanne's recollection of what happened next produced even more questions. She was about to recall the crucial stage of her transition from the front cab to the rear tray of the gunman's vehicle, a process which had originally aroused such doubts about her story. None of Murdoch's trucks had access points from the front to the rear, according to those who knew him or others who had worked on his vehicles, so there was intense interest in the detail of her account. As it transpired, those who had hoped the trial would clear up any lingering uncertainty about her earlier testimony were to end up more confused than ever.

Joanne's account of how she found herself in the back of the four-wheel drive has varied since the attack happened. The police artist in Alice Springs, David Stagg, said she definitely told him she was pushed from the cabin into the canopy area and that there had been an opening behind the passenger seat.

This time she was less clear, as would emerge under cross-examination. Initially, she told Rex Wild that the man 'somehow pushed me into the rear of his vehicle . . . maybe over some seats into the back'. There could also have been a fire extinguisher below the passenger seat 'where the seat belt came out', she added.

While this account was similar to her earlier recollections, it was to subtly shift by the time Grant Algie raised the matter under cross-examination.

Knowing that the opening was a feature of some dispute, Joanne had to rethink her testimony for her questioning by the defence later in the week. Could there have been another entry point into the back? We would have to wait another few days for the answer.

Until then there was plenty to listen to. Joanne's story was only just beginning.

CHAPTER 28

··

JOANNE MOVES THE GOALPOSTS

As Joanne Lees lay on her stomach in the back of her temporary prison, a thousand thoughts flashed through her mind. Immobilised by the manacles and consumed by fear, she pondered Peter's fate and what the gunman had in store for her. How had it gone so wrong? Was her boyfriend dead? Would she be next? Or did her assailant have other plans before despatching her?

'I was almost more scared of being raped than shot by the man. Then the realisation hit me that he might have killed Pete . . . I thought, I'm going to die if I don't get out of this situation,' she explained in court.

Beneath the canopy it was dark but not without the hint of illumination. The interior bulb from the cab cast a weak light. And at the back of the tray she noticed what appeared to be a gap. The inside wasn't uncomfortable either. It was flat and smooth, as though a mattress had been rolled out.

Slowly twisting her torso, Joanne just about managed to sit upright. As she did so she heard the ominous sound of scraping gravel. Was her attacker dragging Peter's body or removing other evidence of his foul deeds? Her imagination had become a personal hell. She could hear the man only a few feet away. What was he up to?

It was pointless lying there speechless, so she shouted out.

Repeating her story for the benefit of the jury, she said, 'I asked him why he was doing this. Did he want money? Did he want to rape me?'

We'd heard it before but the account never lost its spine-tingling drama.

'He came back and told me to shut up or he would shoot me. [Then] he went away and did something which he was doing before and I just thought about Pete and wondered what he had done to Pete.'

Summoning up the courage to confront the unthinkable, Joanne asked him if he'd shot her boyfriend.

'No, I haven't,' he replied.

Had Peter escaped? Was he hiding in the bush waiting to flag down a passing vehicle to raise the alarm? Or was he dead or lying mortally wounded on the roadside? More crucially, was he hatching a plan to save her?

Joanne's emotions ebbed and flowed between hope and desperation. If Peter had been murdered she would almost certainly be next. She knew she had to get away from the beast outside. But how?

With her eyes towards the back of the vehicle, she noticed once again the vague outline of an opening

280

etched against the natural light outside. Slowly she edged her body forward. Thanks to the mattress, the floor of the truck was higher than normal. She found she was able to hang her legs over the side and within seconds had dropped onto the ground.

It wasn't a silent exit. There was the noise of crunching gravel as her feet hit the roadside. Where was he? Had he heard her? Joanne didn't stay around to find out. She just ran, she told the court. But he wasn't far behind.

'I knew there was no way I could run far or outrun the man who was following me,' she admitted. So she had to find a place to hide.

With her hands still tied behind her back and the tape half-wrapped around her legs, she stumbled through the bush in a southwesterly direction, ending up about 30 metres from the highway.

'Still had your shoes on?' Rex Wild queried.

'Yes.'

'Hands behind your back?'

Mr Wild was keen to reinforce the point about her manacled hands. He knew that David Stagg had told the committal proceedings that Joanne had said she was able to feel the curved contour of the canvas canopy because she had already brought her hands round to the front of her body. The lawyer wanted to put the record straight in case the defence returned to the issue later in the trial. While the apparent contradiction might be viewed as relatively insignificant, why would Joanne confuse the timing of such an important stage of her abduction? Wouldn't she have remembered precisely when it happened?

Joanne nodded in agreement as Mr Wild continued.

'You're a good runner?'

'Yes.'

But it wasn't easy to move fast in the dark, surrounded by such thick vegetation.

'It was rough, there were shrubs and long grass and the bushes were getting bigger,' she said.

She didn't look over her shoulder, though she heard her assailant in pursuit.

'I was conscious of him just behind.'

Eventually Joanne came across a small tree which helped to conceal her. She tried to roll herself up into a ball underneath the foliage.

'I hid my face in my knees and covered myself up.'

All the time she knew he was hunting her. She heard crunching noises as he scoured the bush with his torch, though fortunately his dog remained in the truck. Quite why he didn't use the animal in his search remains a mystery. Surely any normal dog would have discovered the cowering young woman within minutes? But perhaps the gunman was worried that his pet would be more interested in the body or the pool of blood at the side of the road.

Whatever the reason Joanne stayed motionless under the tree, hardly daring to breathe for fear of drawing attention to herself and exposing her hideout.

Did she see the man?

'No, I just kept my head down.'

How long did she stay like that?

'A very long time,' she sobbed.

The court was spellbound as Joanne paused for a moment before continuing her story. She heard the man return to one of the vehicles and turn the engine on. Had he given up the search or was he simply biding his time? Now the headlights were on. She thought he was going to use the extra light to aid his search, but then the vehicle moved off.

If Joanne believed he had gone for good she was mistaken. Shortly afterwards she again heard the sound of crunching undergrowth and gravel. Her dreams of escape were dashed.

'I thought he had come back to look for me.'

In the still of an outback night every noise is magnified. Joanne could hear the cracking twigs and rustling leaves with the gunman's every step. And then came the noise she'd heard before as she lay in his truck. He was dragging something. She almost certainly recognised the sound for what it was.

'I thought it could be Pete.'

This time her assailant did not continue his search. He opened the door of his truck, started the engine and headed south. It was between 8 and 8.30 p.m. For the first time since her ordeal had begun Joanne allowed herself the luxury of movement. She started to relax and fiddle with the cable ties around her wrists.

Feeling the loops which linked the handcuffs, she realised it might be possible to bring the contraption round to the front of her body. It turned out to be much easier than she thought. The procedure took all of half a minute.

Joanne stood up in the witness box to show how far her hands had been apart when she brought her arms underneath her body. Next day she would give a personal demonstration of the manoeuvre in front of the judge.

Now that her wrists were in front of her she attempted to free herself from the manacles which were so tight they were in danger of cutting off her circulation. At first she tried to bite them off, but without success. Then in a moment of inspiration she reached into the pocket of her board shorts for a tube of lip balm which she kept there.

Joanne removed the cap and rubbed the waxy substance over her hands, hoping that she might be able to slide the cable ties off her wrists. Sadly it didn't work. The lip balm and its lid disappeared into the undergrowth, though the plastic tube was to play a significant role in the subsequent police investigation, raising key questions about the thoroughness of the search.

Still severely traumatised by what she had just been through, Joanne waited and listened. She wasn't exactly sure how long she stayed there, but it must have been nearly five hours. Finally satisfied that her attacker had gone for good, she stood up and felt her way through the bush towards the road. It was dark, but the stars gave just enough light to help her find the right direction. On reaching the highway, she shuffled across the bitumen and collapsed in the grass on the other side of the road.

There was very little passing traffic that night and Joanne waited patiently for the distant sound of an engine. Her plan was to stop a road train because she knew the crew would be genuine truckies, professional drivers who would recognise her plight. But in the back of her mind was the fear that the gunman might come back.

'I was paranoid that if I jumped out in front of a car it could be the man who attacked me,' she explained to the jury, who could understand her trepidation.

The story of her eventual rescue by Vince Millar and Rodney Adams has already been well-documented.

How Vince thought he'd skittled a sheila and was amazed to find her still alive when he brought his road train to a halt just north of Barrow Creek. How the two men cut the cable ties, hoisted her into their cab and drove off in search of her boyfriend before discovering that the man who attacked her had a gun. Understandably Vince and Rodney thought it safer to head to the Barrow Creek roadhouse and telephone the police rather than risk coming face-to-face with an outback madman.

The two truckies would have their day in court again as the trial progressed, but the judge was more interested in Joanne's emotional state during the attack.

'What was running through your mind?' he asked her.

The young witness seized the invitation.

'I just kept thinking, "This isn't happening to me." I felt alone. I kept shouting for Pete. I thought I was going to die,' she sobbed. 'It all happened quite quickly from being tied up. I was screaming out for Pete to come and help me because I was fighting so much. Once he put me into the back of the vehicle I thought, "I'm going to die." [Then] I got some inner strength and I concentrated on just getting out of there.'

If the jury had any doubt about Joanne's account of that night, her tearful performance in court six that Tuesday afternoon would almost certainly have persuaded them otherwise. Through his timely questioning, Chief Justice Martin had reminded everybody what this case was all about. A woman frozen by fear, trapped in the most horrendous of circumstances, fights off her assailant and escapes against all odds. Now it was up to the jury to decide if the defendant was guilty. They could be under no illusion as to the grave responsibility they shouldered.

Rex Wild, who for a brief moment might have wondered if the judge was intending to take over as Crown prosecutor, stood up to resume his role. He wanted to clarify Joanne's description of her attacker and his vehicle.

A tall man, aged 45-ish with an oval, lined face, drooped eyes, straggly hair coming from underneath his cap, grey flecks in his eyebrows and a Mexican-style moustache, she recalled. Then there was the checked shirt and heavy-duty blue jeans. The detail remained much the same as before, though the shorter hair was in stark contrast to the shoulder-length variety depicted by police in the Photofit image produced a few days after the attack.

Had the police wrongly interpreted her description or was her memory too vague? Perhaps it was time for Joanne to put the record straight.

'I was never sure about the hair and about the length of the hair,' she admitted in court.

Later she revealed that she felt under pressure from the police to release a picture of her attacker as soon as possible so that the public had something to go on.

Was she confident the long-haired man in the Photofit was the person?

'No,' she admitted.

'I said the hair was not quite right.'

Who was responsible for the confusion is still unclear. Perhaps it was due to the limitations of the Photofit technique, which did not provide enough options. Whatever the reason, the mystery over the length of the gunman's locks would remain unsolved.

As would the puzzling manner in which Joanne gained access to the rear of the truck. For the benefit of the jury, David Stagg's sketch of the gunman's four-wheel drive appeared on the courtroom screen. It showed what appeared to be a gap at the back of the cabin allowing entry to the rear tray.

Returning to the issue for the second time, Rex Wild was determined to settle the matter once and for all.

'How did you get from the front to the back?' he asked.

'I don't know exactly because I didn't put myself in the back. I was put [there] by the man. He grabbed me and put me in the back. I am not sure whether from the front cabin into the back or around the side.'

If the prosecuting lawyer had hoped to resolve the ongoing uncertainty he was to be disappointed. Once again Joanne Lees appeared to have moved the goalposts. Not once over the previous four and a half years had she alluded to the possibility that she might have accessed the back of the truck from the side. So what had happened to change her mind?

The ever-perceptive judge, mindful of the subtle change in testimony, endeavoured to get to the bottom of it.

'Did you tell the artist you had gone from the front to the rear [of the vehicle] inside?'

'Yes,' she confirmed.

'[But] now you are not sure whether you came around from the outside. Has anything happened to cause you to doubt the reliability of your initial recollection?'

While those in court might have thought she was cornered, Joanne had her explanation at the ready.

She told the judge how she might have somehow got confused with the front-to-rear access in the Kombi van.

'As I have had time to reflect on my initial statement and I remember landing in the rear of the vehicle on my stomach, it's possible he may have pushed me through the side of the canvas,' she explained.

It was enough to satisfy Chief Justice Martin, who let the matter rest as the clock approached 4.30 p.m. It remained to be seen whether Grant Algie would be so accommodating.

CHAPTER 29

....

CABLE TIES, NECKTIES AND FAMILY TIES

For the moment the question of how Joanne gained access to the rear of the gunman's truck was put on hold. It was day three of the trial and Rex Wild still hadn't completed his examination of the witness. There were several other loose ends to tie up, not to mention the occasional red herring to address.

First there was the question of the hair band similar to one worn by Joanne and later found in Murdoch's possession. The brand was Lady Jane and was widely available in most pharmacy shops.

Joanne confirmed the hair tie on the screen was hers. What the prosecution failed to mention was that the defendant also bought them regularly because he used them to secure the leather strap on his shoulder holster. The fact they were identical to Joanne's hair band was purely coincidental and had little or no bearing on the case.

Wild moved on to his next question which concerned the area between the rear of the campervan and the bonnet of the four-wheel drive. Where had the man been situated as he marched her from one vehicle to the other?

'Slightly to the left and behind me,' she explained.

And did she attempt to look for Peter as she walked past the gap?

'No, because he [the gunman] was blocking my view.'

The prosecution was also keen to clear up any misunderstanding about the truck-stop security video and why Joanne had initially failed to identify the man on the tape as the same person who attacked her.

This time when a still frame was shown on the court screen she confirmed 'that's the man' without hesitation.

So what had changed her original view?

'The police were able to show me a better-quality picture.'

Joanne seemed to have an answer for everything. Such was her confidence and the plausibility of her explanations that it was almost as though she had been coached beforehand.

Matters of identification continued to dominate the questions. There was the photograph of the accused that she saw on a BBC website on 10 October 2002, which might have played a part in her identification of Murdoch when she was shown a mugshot of the defendant a month later.

Joanne had been working in Sicily when a friend told her there was something of interest she should look at.

It was a news story about the police investigation going on in Australia.

'Did it indicate there was a suspect for the murder?' Wild asked.

'Yes,' she confirmed.

And when she saw the picture on the second page, what did she think?

'That's the man,' she replied.

'When you went to the website did you expect to see the suspect's photo?'

'No,' she insisted. 'I just knew that it was him. I didn't really study it for long.'

About five weeks later on 18 November, Australian police flew to Britain to show Joanne a selection of mugshots. By this time she had returned from Italy, a country she clearly enjoyed visiting, perhaps because of the young Mediterranean men with dark hair and olive skin who might have reminded her of Peter.

Back in Hove she was invited to meet two Australian detectives who wanted to show her a photoboard which 'might or might not' contain a picture of the man who attacked her, they said.

There were about a dozen images to choose from and Joanne's eyes were instantly drawn to number 10. There was no doubt about it.

'I was very positive,' she said.

Her finger pointed to a photograph of a bearded Bradley John Murdoch. However, given that she had seen a similar image of the man linking him to the murder of her boyfriend on the BBC website the previous month, could she have been influenced in her decision? It was yet another question for the jury to ponder.

Much the same might have applied to her description of Jack, the attacker's pet, and Tex, the dog she saw at the Barrow Creek roadhouse after her rescue. She'd been told it was a blue heeler.

Was it similar to the gunman's dog, Wild pressed her.

Yes, the colouring, the head and the width of the animal was much the same, though Tex was younger.

Strangely, she insisted there was no way she would confuse either animal with a Dalmatian, even though Murdoch's Jack was covered in spots. After all, she remembered the Walt Disney film and she had never thought of *101 Dalmatians* being about an Australian breed.

'The dog the man had that night was clearly an Australian dog, a blue heeler breed that I had never seen before,' she assured the jury.

And it was similar to Tex because the eyes, the ears, the colouring and the width of each animal were much the same. Certainly Tex had a patchy black and white coat, but it was nothing like Jack which, though cross-bred, looked more like a Dalmatian than any other dog. How could she get the two breeds confused? Again it was a matter for the jury.

Grant Algie began his cross-examination with quiet determination. He had no wish to harangue the witness, which would have risked getting the jury offside. But he was keen to expose any inconsistencies with Joanne's previous accounts of what happened that night.

He took her back to the scene 10 kilometres north of Barrow Creek as the four-wheel drive approached and drew parallel with the Kombi. She'd told police at the time that the driver's vehicle had a chunky, chrome or silver-looking bullbar at the front, but now she wasn't quite so sure.

Had she seen it as the gunman marched her to his truck?

'No.'

Why?

'Because I wasn't looking at the bullbar and the man was blocking my view. He was guiding my vision.'

Yet she claimed to have seen some kind of roo bar because 'it was set against such a dark night and everything seemed white and shiny', she told the court.

So when had she gained that impression? If she hadn't noticed the metal bars when she passed the gap between the two parked vehicles, was it possible she saw them as her attacker's vehicle was being driven adjacent to the Kombi earlier?

Joanne admitted that the only time she had seen the bullbar was when the truck came alongside them, but Algie wasn't satisfied.

'Has it ever been mentioned to you that Mr Murdoch does not have a chrome bullbar?' he queried.

Joanne was adamant that it had not.

Algie put it to her bluntly: 'How is it that your recollection no longer accords with that [earlier] description and you don't feel able to express an opinion?'

'There's a possibility that it was not a chrome bullbar and the reason may be the brightness of the light against the darkness of the night,' she responded.

Was she really sure the truck's lights were on at the time? Joanne was pretty certain they were because 'she could see the man clearly'.

But on further questioning about why she had not spotted Peter's body she expressed some doubt.

'Now I think about it, I don't think the lights were on because all I could see was darkness. I'm sure if there had been light I would have struggled to look,' she agreed.

If the jury were not confused already they soon would be. First the lights were on, then they weren't. First she'd seen a shiny bullbar, now she wasn't sure. If it was part of the defence team's strategy to undermine Joanne's recall of the night in question, they were succeeding.

Grant Algie moved on to her memory of the gunman's revolver when he pointed the weapon at her temple in the campervan. Given that the firearm was so close to her head, had she felt the heat from the barrel?

'No.'

And given that it might just have been used to shoot her boyfriend, did she smell any gunpowder?

Again the answer was negative. How odd that she sensed no heat or odour from a gun which had just been fired. Or was she simply too traumatised to remember? Maybe it would have been easy to overlook such detail in the mental turmoil of the moment, but could the same apply to the infamous hole in the back of the gunman's cab?

Algie knew that Joanne's account of how she was pushed into the vehicle's rear tray presented a serious weakness in her evidence. If she could be so uncertain about how she got there, how could the court accept other parts of her story?

The defence lawyer didn't beat about the bush. Once again Joanne knew she had to provide a reasonable explanation to convince the jury or risk having her testimony called further into question.

Algie advanced on several fronts in an effort to elicit the truth, asking her to outline the sequence of events. She couldn't recollect them in detail but she knew she was forced into the back by the man and not under 'my own steam'.

He reminded her that the police had at first expressed surprise about the so-called hole behind the seats, telling her on 7 August 2001 that it was 'hard for us to find' such a vehicle.

'There's no other possible way you got into the back? Can you think hard about that?' asked Algie.

Under pressure, Joanne conceded, 'That is what I believed at the time. Consequently after that [police] interview I began to doubt myself.'

The defence asked if the police had spoken to her about the rear access when they visited her in England. She couldn't remember. Though she agreed she'd said in her statement that it was 'my belief' she was pushed through a gap behind the seats.

Then, perhaps remembering what she'd told the judge earlier, Joanne volunteered, 'It's possible I came out of the vehicle and back into the vehicle by some other means.' Maybe she was thrown in where the driver had previously raised the canopy to obtain the canvas hood, she said. 'That's possibly where I got in. I don't believe I walked around the vehicle but it's possible.'

Was this a satisfactory explanation or did it merely create further doubt? Once so sure that she was pushed through a gap behind the seat — and even saw a red fire extinguisher — Joanne was now openly canvassing the possibility that she was thrown into the rear tray from the side of the vehicle. Was it again a measure of the sheer horror and confusion of that night or indicative of a story that would not stand up without further shifting of the goalposts?

Under further cross-examination Joanne faced new claims about the final few hours before she and Peter were attacked. There were unexpected questions. Could she have left Alice Springs as much as two hours earlier than she had told the police? And might she have brushed against Murdoch while having a meal in the Red Rooster? Joanne seemed taken by surprise, especially by the questions about a phone call she made to a female friend in Sydney about 1.30 p.m. She'd rung the friend while waiting for Peter to finish his shower at the caravan park and then they'd gone to the Red Rooster.

'Do you recall seeing Mr Murdoch there?' asked Algie.

'No.'

'If you passed by Mr Murdoch is that something you would remember now?' he continued.

'I don't recall seeing him and I don't recall bumping into anybody or coming close to him or anyone speaking to me,' she insisted.

'I'm not suggesting you spoke to him, but if he was in the vicinity would you remember it?' he pressed her.

'No, why would I?' she said.

Was Algie preparing the ground for new claims later in the trial? Was he going to suggest that accidental contact between the two in the Red Rooster might have led to the transfer of his DNA onto Joanne's T-shirt?

And what was the significance of Repco, the auto shop opposite the fast-food takeaway? Why had the defence made mention of it? Again the court would have to remain patient.

The defence was also curious about the apparent uncertainty about the time the couple left Alice Springs. Asked if she agreed she might have left town as early as 2.30 p.m. she said she didn't believe so.

'I thought it was later. I didn't recall the time. I wasn't paying attention to the time. I was on holidays and had no reason to know what the time was. I thought it was later.'

Algie reminded her that she'd told the police they left Alice between 4 and 4.30 p.m. bound for Ti Tree, 197 kilometres further north.

'You certainly wouldn't have been able to travel that distance if you left between 4 and 4.30 p.m.,' he suggested.

'All right, okay,' she conceded.

And had they stopped off on the way at the Aileron Roadhouse?

No, they hadn't stopped anywhere until they reached Ti Tree.

It was an apparently insignificant response to an innocent question, but the court had yet to hear from Greg Dick and his staff, who would refocus attention on the isolated service station and snack bar a few days hence.

If the jury had cause to disbelieve any of Joanne's evidence so far, they could have had no such doubts about her version of how she contorted her body to bring the manacles around to her front. While in the early days of the investigation some had questioned whether such a feat was possible, she was about to demonstrate that it did not require the flexibility of a ballet dancer to perform the manoeuvre and even offered to give the judge and jury a personal demonstration.

At 2.45 p.m. on the fourth day of the trial, Joanne walked from the witness box and sat on the carpeted floor in the body of the court only a few metres from the defendant.

This time her hands were bound by a man's necktie instead of a replica of the handcuffs, in recognition of the emotional toll the experience might have on her. Dressed in grey tracksuit pants and top, she succeeded in bringing her tethered hands underneath her body and around to the front so quickly that many people in the court that day missed the movement. In fact, the action was so quick that Chief Justice Martin thought it appropriate to record the time it had taken.

'Something in the order of one to two seconds,' he announced.

It was the climax to an extraordinary and clearly exhausting three-and-a-half days for Joanne. Shortly after the demonstration she completed her testimony and left the witness box. She had been giving evidence since late Monday afternoon. Clearly relieved that the experience was over, she strode to the public gallery and sat next to Peter's parents, Joan and Luciano. Brothers Nick and Paul Falconio were also nearby and when the court rose the two young men made a point of escorting their murdered brother's girlfriend to her waiting car.

It was a show of unity after more than four years of adversity, a defining moment in a tragedy that had befallen two families on 14 July 2001. With the memory of Joanne's fling with Nick Riley still fresh in the family's mind, it was time to heal old wounds.

....

CHAPTER 30

ROUND UP THE POSSE

Joanne Lees arrived at the Supreme Court on the fifth day visibly relieved that her time in the witness box was over. Wearing a black-and-white striped skirt, a short-sleeved top, dark glasses and an orange carrier bag over her shoulder, she could have been just another young professional on her way to work. Or maybe a tourist taking in the local sights. But this was no time to relax her guard. The trial had still only heard from five of the expected 70 or more witnesses and, as the days turned into weeks, many of those called to give evidence would raise further questions about the accuracy of Joanne's memory and doubts about the prosecution's case.

The jury did not have to wait long to hear further testimony which appeared to contradict, or differ from, earlier statements and evidence. While the perceived inconsistencies might have seemed relatively insignificant on their own, they would carry much more weight when added together. And this was clearly the defence team's ultimate objective.

It was Doctor Matthew Wright who set the tone for much of what was to follow. On Sunday evening, 15 July 2001, he was on duty in the emergency department of Alice Springs hospital when Joanne arrived accompanied by two police officers.

First he asked her what had happened to prompt her visit to the hospital, though he probably already had a good idea.

'She was fairly quiet and subdued,' he recalled.

He remembered how she had multiple abrasions to her knees and elbows, as well as a small cut over her left knee and scratches to her lower back. Curiously he did not notice any bruising on her face, an observation that Mark Wilton had also made when he interviewed her for the *Centralian Advocate* a few days later.

The lack of bruising did not make Dr Wright suspicious because such marks could often take two to three days to appear. But there was another important reason why her head seemed injury-free. Joanne had told him that she had not been hit about the head during the attack. This contradicted her statement to the police, who were left in no doubt that the young backpacker had been punched on her right temple, a claim she was to repeat on several occasions both in and out of court.

Had Dr Wright been mistaken? Not so. Standing in court six that Friday morning, the defence questioned him about a statement he had given to the police on 31 July 2001, in which he described asking Joanne if she'd been hit in the head during the attack.

'And she said she had not?' Grant Algie asked him.

'That's right. I would certainly hope my statement is correct,' he replied. Dr Wright admitted he could not find any reference to the punch in the medical notes he had taken at the time. 'But I guess the statement [to the police] was made at a time far closer to the incident than today,' he pointed out.

How could Joanne have forgotten to tell the doctor about the blow? Especially as it remained clear in her mind more than four years later. Indeed, she had recalled the punch in graphic detail only a few days before when she described the struggle with her attacker after she fell out of the Kombi. Yet just 24 hours after the attack she had no memory of being beaten about her head. Was she still in shock and simply unable to recount every detail? Or was the blow a figment of her imagination? She remembered not losing consciousness and made that plain to the doctor. So how could she have forgotten being hit?

The mystery over what might or might not have happened on that day deepened further when Greg Dick and his staff from the Aileron Roadhouse took the stand the following Monday morning. Apart from Grant Algie's question to Joanne the previous Thursday, the roadside cafe and service station 132 kilometres north of Alice Springs had barely rated a mention in the case. But in view of what Mr Dick had told me on three separate occasions over the past year, I was keen to see how his story would stand up in court.

Here was a man who was convinced Joanne Lees and Peter Falconio had dropped in for a toasted sandwich on their way north that Saturday afternoon. He remembered their orange campervan and even two of his employees saw them. Yet Joanne had no recollection of stopping at Aileron. Why would she when the couple had eaten at the Red Rooster just over an hour earlier and they didn't need any petrol?

Greg Dick, a knockabout Aussie with a larrikin sense of humour but no reason to joke about what he saw that day, was adamant. Dressed in shorts and with a packet of Winfields in his top pocket, he took his seat in the witness box with the air of a man who couldn't quite believe anybody doubted him.

He was working that Saturday afternoon mowing the lawn when he decided to take a smoko. 'I was in a bludging mood — like those government workers,' he smiled, knowing outback types would understand his dig at the wage slaves who lived off the public purse.

Then he saw what he wrongly assumed were a couple of hippies. 'I thought it was a load of ferals and I was going to have a mouthful to them,' he informed the jury. The woman, who had a pommy accent, looked 'pretty all right', he said. Though, momentarily aware of the sexist overtones, he also made it clear, 'I wasn't perving that hard.'

Warming to his more respectable theme and perhaps conscious of his surroundings, Mr Dick told the court that the couple were well-dressed.

'The girl was very neat and tidy and had fairly long hair. And she had this fellow with short, cropped hair, like Italian, Greek or something,' he explained.

'You can pick they are foreigners,' he advised the jury with the cosmopolitan confidence of a man who had served many nationalities over the years. 'I would say it was definitely them, otherwise they would have a good set of twins in Australia.'

Michael Oakley, the roadhouse manager, also saw them and their orange campervan with its distinctive pop-up top. The young man had an 'ethnic' look but he was not sure of his accent. However, shown a photograph of the pair at a later stage by police, he was '90 per cent sure it was the couple who were there that day'.

And assistant manageress Anne Mary Floyd, who made them the toasted sandwiches, was similarly convinced. She said the young woman had straight, brown, shoulder-length hair and a blue top. 'They were laughing and talking about where they were going,' she observed.

If this wasn't Joanne and Peter, who was it? What were the chances of another young English woman in a blue top and her short-haired Mediterranean-looking boyfriend driving an orange Kombi with a pop-up top on that remote stretch of road that Saturday afternoon? Particularly as no similar travellers or vehicle came forward after the incident.

If this case was beginning to look increasingly bizarre given the number of contradictions, reported sightings and subtle changes of testimony, the trial itself was also in danger of becoming a little odd. At the beginning of the second week, Northern Territory judicial sensibilities were exposed by an article which had been written for the London *Guardian* but which was subsequently republished in the Melbourne *Age* and the *Sydney Morning Herald*.

British journalist Andrew Clark, who was on secondment to the *Herald*, had penned a light-hearted account of his first week in Darwin, a week, he pointed out, in which the second-biggest story in the *Northern Territory News* after the Falconio case was a study concluding that most victims of attacks by saltwater crocodiles were drunk.

'The locals dislike their image in Australia as slow-speaking eccentrics with a taste for grog,' he noted.

However, it wasn't so much the facetious tone of the article that aroused the judge's ire as a far more serious allegation that struck at the very heart of the justice system. After describing the state-of-the-art electronic screens and the barristers and judge dressed in all their finery — 'despite soaring humidity' — Clark claimed that 'every so often, the impressive facade slips'.

'Rex Wild QC usually remembers to address the judge as "your honour" but occasionally calls him "Brian",' he alleged.

To suggest that the Director of Public Prosecutions and the Chief Justice were on first-name terms in court did not reflect well on the Northern Territory Supreme Court and the judge was quick to make his feelings known.

'Not only does it reflect unfairly and inaccurately on Mr Wild, it also reflects upon me, the court and the system of criminal justice in the Territory,' he said.

Chief Justice Martin vehemently rejected any suggestion that the Crown Prosecutor had called him Brian and complimented him on the fact that the DPP always afforded him 'proper respect'.

He also criticised the article for alleging that occasionally the 'impressive facade slips', a claim which he branded as 'highly objectionable . . . not truly reflected in reality' and 'utterly incorrect'.

He demanded an immediate retraction and apology from the offending publications.

What made Clark's position worse was that the article appeared on the Melbourne *Age*'s website, a clear breach of the judge's order that there should be no discussion of the case within the Northern Territory. While most media organisations had made every effort to keep any stories which might cause legal problems out of their on-line editions, this one had clearly slipped through.

The judge's fierce denunciation of what had been alleged prompted reporters covering the case to scurry to their notebooks. Something was not quite right. At least 10 journalists sitting in a jury room being used to accommodate those who could not find space in the court or the official media room also thought they had heard the name Brian mentioned. Unfortunately, nobody had taken a note of the dialogue because the jury had not been present. In the time-honoured tradition of court reporting the golden rule is that if the jury's not there, nothing of what's said can be published so journalists usually drop their pens.

Jane Munday, the judge's media consultant, promised to obtain the transcript for the day in question to quash any rumours. Certainly there was no use of the Chief Justice's first name there.

Lawyers representing Fairfax, publishers of the *Herald* and *The Age*, also wanted to be sure before agreeing to a retraction or apology and asked to hear the audio recording of the case for themselves. Once again, no reference to the name Brian could be found.

Could 10 print and broadcasting journalists representing Australian and British media outlets all have been mistaken? Had the sound system on the television monitor in the overflow press room somehow distorted the exchange? I was in the overflow room that morning and I know what I heard.

The trouble was I had no proof. The evidence, like so much else in this trial, was a little shaky.

By this time Clark had left town, not in fear of the judicial consequences, but because his office had recalled him to Sydney a few days earlier. Though in retrospect he was probably wise to get out when he did, just in case the judge was tempted to send out a posse.

When Chief Justice Martin learned the reporter was no longer in the Northern Territory, he assumed he had done a runner.

'Seeing that his article portrayed Darwin as somewhat of a hick town, how did he get out? Presumably by horse and carriage,' the judge sniffed.

Ouch! Clearly civic pride was at stake as well as judicial honour.

'Nobody in the Territory minds being sent up in a fair way. We all have a sense of humour,' he told the court.

'Cities around the world are sent up by journalists. But there is a right way and a wrong way of doing things. People who blow in for a short time to send us up unfairly and then scarper are not appreciated,' he said.

Retractions were duly published and the Supreme Court's honour was restored.

But it was, perhaps, a measure of the Northern Territory's sensitivity about the case that a fun-poking background article should have been taken so seriously in the first place. Clearly the specific allegation about the DPP using the judge's first name overstepped the mark, but by taking such umbrage, the Chief Justice exposed the very inferiority complex which the Territory had been struggling to overcome since the Chamberlain trial 20 years previously.

Darwin might be able to boast a new multimillion-dollar Supreme Court building with all the modern bells and whistles, but had anything else really changed?

CHAPTER 31

....

MISCOMMUNICATION AND THE MISSING LIP GLOSS

If the first week of the trial had raised serious questions about the reliability of Joanne's memory, the second week posed a similar level of concern over the way the police had carried out their investigation.

Given the stuff-ups that had emerged in the early days of the search, it was inevitable that specific areas of evidence would come under even closer scrutiny in court.

To begin with, there was the mystery of the missing lip balm tube and why it was not discovered at the scene of the crime until three months after the attack. It was Senior Constable Ian Spilsbury who had the unenviable task of explaining why the police search hadn't uncovered such a crucial piece of evidence sooner.

As an experienced crime scene examiner he was summoned to Barrow Creek on Sunday, 15 July 2001.

Initially he had been involved in metal detecting. He knew the ignition keys to the campervan were missing and he was anxious to find them in the hope they might produce the attacker's fingerprints or DNA.

He was also aware of the possible presence of the lip balm because Joanne had told investigating officers that she used the waxy substance to grease her wrists in the hope of slipping off the manacles. It wasn't long before the cap to the lip balm tube was found close to the spot where Joanne had been hiding, confirming the essence of her story. But somehow the tube itself was overlooked.

Asked why the rest of the tube had not been found at the time, Senior Constable Spilsbury put it down to miscommunication.

'When we were at Ti Tree we were advised that a lip gloss may have been used and then shortly thereafter I received a call from Detective Lenny Turner, who advised me that a lip gloss lid had been found,' he said.

After the lid was located, it was photographed and taken away.

Anthony Elliot for the prosecution wanted to know why he hadn't spent more time searching the area, but instead returned to the metal detecting.

Spilsbury explained that he was under the mistaken impression that other officers had already completed a thorough search of the area.

'I believed they had looked further under there. There was a miscommunication. They probably thought we had, and unfortunately it wasn't found,' he added.

Grant Algie was less polite with his questioning and went straight for the jugular.

'Surely you would have had a look around to make sure there was nothing else around?' he asked.

'Certainly we looked under the tree [and] if we'd seen the lip gloss we would have collected it,' he assured the defence lawyer.

'Is it because there wasn't a lip gloss there?' he demanded.

'I don't know,' replied Spilsbury.

The inference was clear. Had the rest of the tube and the black tape, which was found at the crime scene three months later on 15 October 2001, been planted?

The jury had the advantage of seeing before and after photographs on their electronic screens. One, taken on 16 July 2001, showed a picture of the lid in the grass.

Algie went in for the kill, pointing out that neither the container nor the tape could be seen in the shot. If the items had been there, surely they would have been noticed, he remarked.

'Certainly in the photo I can't see them,' the officer agreed.

All of which begged the question as to why they could be so readily observed in a later photograph of exactly the same position taken on 15 October.

Algie: 'You were quite thorough in taking detailed photographs of the area. If the tape or lip balm were there, you would have seen it?'

Spilsbury: 'I don't know.'

Algie: 'Did somebody put the lip balm and the tape in the area where you photographed it in October before you were asked to photograph it?'

'No,' Spilsbury insisted.

Was the lid found first because it was in a more obvious position? Were the tube and the black tape obscured by vegetation? Certainly photographs of the position suggested there were twigs and grass in the area, although not as much in the picture taken in July, which was the middle of winter.

Was it possible the tube and the tape had been exposed by a native animal which might have disturbed the spot? Or was it simply a case of police oversight?

While the stuff-up theory was probably the most likely, the evidence presented to the court could not exclude a more sinister explanation. Such suspicions would also emerge later in the week when exhibits containing crucial DNA would be brought into question.

Of all the advances in forensic science in recent years, the acceptance of DNA as a foolproof method of confirming the identity of a suspect has revolutionised police investigations. Now that detectives are able to establish who was there by the unique profile that everybody carries within their cells, any speck of blood, sweat or skin tissue left behind can be examined for its DNA in the hope of producing a positive match with the perpetrator of the crime.

This assumes that the right techniques and protocols for obtaining, analysing and storing DNA samples are also rigidly followed. For just as DNA is an exact science, it also requires an exact and highly disciplined approach by those who work within this highly specialised field. The danger of cross-contamination is one of the greatest risks scientists face when dealing with police exhibits which are removed from the scene and kept in a secure environment until the investigation is complete.

In the Falconio case it wasn't long before serious doubts emerged about the way crucial pieces of evidence containing the accused's DNA had been handled. Fundamental to the police case were the cable ties which bound Joanne's wrists. While scientists had been unable to identify Murdoch's DNA on the manacles to begin with, it was important that they not be contaminated by any of his belongings, just in case they were re-examined at a later date.

The cable ties spent most of the time in a padlocked freezer in Darwin's newly built forensic biology unit. Only a few people were allowed access to the container, including the Director, Dr Peter Thatcher, who made sure they were kept in a paper bag within a paper bag to reduce the possibility of contamination.

Police who needed to inspect exhibits were required to complete the appropriate documentation before being allowed to remove them.

Among the officers was Senior Constable Timothy Sandry, a crime scene examiner who investigated the construction of the cable ties when they were sent to Darwin after being retrieved from the tool box in the road train driven by Vince Millar and Rodney Adams.

The officer examined the manacles for clues about their origin for several days during August 2001. As always he was meticulous about the way he handled them, wearing surgical gloves and using bleach to ensure the tabletop was clean.

The defence wanted to know why he hadn't been equally meticulous with the log book used to keep details of the movement of exhibits in and out of the laboratory.

'They didn't leave the biology section so they didn't appear in my name,' he explained.

Algie also asked what he was doing with the manacles between 25 and 27 February 2002.

Sandry said he couldn't recall seeing them at that time.

'Surely you made notes about who released them?' the lawyer suggested.

'If I'd taken them, yes … during the whole investigation I was busy, not busy, I was instructed to do other investigations on a lot of other cases. And it may be that over that time when I was going to go down and grab them, I became … involved in another investigation and I said, "Look, I'm not going to touch the cable ties, I'm just going to put them back into the custody of the biology section,"' he told the court.

'So you or others may have had dealings with the ties and it's not in the log,' Algie commented.

'That's correct,' Sandry accepted. Though he was also certain that he would not have forgotten about any actual work he did on the manacles because they were 'such an important piece of evidence'.

Certainly he had a clear recollection of removing the cable ties on 8 October 2002 in preparation for a trip to Adelaide. He was due to hand the manacles to Superintendent Colleen Gwynne, another Northern Territory officer, who was also going to Adelaide. She intended to visit Murdoch, who was by now incarcerated in South Australia's Yatala jail. Sandry had to inspect a few of the accused's old haunts, including a property in Fern Gully where Jack the Dalmatian was living. He needed to take a photograph of the dog and obtain a DNA swab from its mouth, as well as a hair from its coat.

Before travelling to Fern Gully he took the precaution of storing the cable ties in the exhibit room of the South Australia Police headquarters, which also contained other items connected to Murdoch.

Sandry was aware of the cross-contamination risks

and was at pains to store the manacles as far away from the other items as possible.

'How far away?' he was asked by the prosecution.

'About 10 feet,' he said, adding, 'in hindsight maybe I should have paid more attention to the objects near it.'

The next day at precisely 1.10 p.m. he officially handed the cable ties over to Superintendent Gwynne. He knew where she was going but was not aware she intended to take the manacles with her. The chances of cross-contamination if they were taken from their paper bag and placed anywhere near Murdoch in his prison cell were obvious.

Algie: 'Did you impress on her the need to avoid contamination?'

Sandry: 'I made her aware to be careful of contamination issues.'

Algie: 'Did you ask anyone at the lab in Darwin, until the time you handed the ties to Superintendent Gwynne, why you had been asked to bring the ties to Adelaide?'

Sandry: 'No, it wasn't until later that I realised what she had intended to do with them.'

Algie: 'Were you not aware that she was preparing to go into prison and take the ties with her to see Mr Murdoch?'

Sandry: 'I knew she was going to the prison. I didn't know she was going to take the ties with her.'

Algie: 'What do you think she was going to do with the cable ties?'

'It doesn't matter, Mr Algie,' the judge interjected.

Later it was to emerge that Superintendent Gwynne had not removed the manacles from the paper bag while talking to Murdoch in jail. But why had she taken them there in the first place?

Sandry retrieved the cable ties from Superintendent Gwynne and flew back to Darwin with them on 14 October 2002. The next day they were again locked in a freezer, separate from any other Murdoch exhibits.

'I knew a lot of the property in South Australia belonging to Mr Murdoch was going to be brought back to Darwin. I wanted to keep it completely separate from anything Mr Murdoch owned just in case of cross-contamination,' he emphasised.

If Senior Constable Sandry had hoped the worst of the questioning was over, he was mistaken. In a final thrust Algie enquired about the absence of paperwork documenting the return of the cable ties.

'In fact there is nothing after October 8, 2002,' the defence lawyer pointed out.

'That's correct,' the officer confirmed.

'Is that because the cable ties were no longer seen as reliable because they had been released to Ms Gwynne?' he enquired.

Once again Chief Justice Martin intervened, preventing the police officer from responding.

While it is easy to appreciate the level of demands placed on a busy police forensic laboratory, it is equally important to understand the need for the correct procedures to be followed. In the highly complex world of DNA, where the tiniest of samples can be accidentally transferred from one exhibit to another, the handling and movement of evidence should be treated with the same paramount concern.

No one proved that any of the exhibits or samples were cross-contaminated in Darwin or Adelaide but there was clearly the potential for such an eventuality, as a later witness was to reveal.

....

CHAPTER 32

DNA MATCH PUTS MURDOCH AT THE SCENE

B ack in July 2001, forensic scientists in Darwin were still operating out of the old laboratory on the first floor of the Berrimah police centre. It was not an ideal situation. Facilities were basic to say the least. In fact, the lab was not even accredited by the National Association of Testing Authorities because it was not deemed to be up to the proper standard.

The freezer where exhibits and DNA samples were kept was situated in a hallway. While not officially a public thoroughfare it meant that those who worked there had to be doubly careful when carrying samples backwards and forwards.

It was in this substandard environment that exhibits and DNA samples from Peter Falconio and Joanne Lees were stored for the first few months of the police investigation. The team leader of the biology section was Joy Kuhl, whose handling of the forensic examination of the couple's campervan — not to mention her mistaken identification of foetal blood in Lindy Chamberlain's car two decades earlier — had raised so many questions.

Carmen Eckhoff, who has been a forensic biologist with the Northern Territory police since 1992, worked alongside Kuhl during the early days of the Falconio inquiry. She told the trial that Kuhl left the service in 2002 after the department had moved into smart new premises, which were fully accredited, in December 2003. The freezer was now housed in a proper examination room and two special benches were used for the extraction of DNA.

The protocols that were followed emphasised the need for extreme care in an environment where cross-contamination from other people or samples was an ever-present risk if the correct procedures were not put in place.

The benches were always wiped down with bleach, gowns were donned and surgical gloves replaced every time they came into contact with a foreign object. Even picking up a pen to make a note required a change of gloves afterwards.

While one assumes similar handling standards would have been in place in the old laboratory, the inferior facilities clearly posed risks, especially when transporting exhibits or samples to the freezer in the hallway. Even more worrying was the human factor.

Incredibly, it emerged during the trial that the head of the Northern Territory's forensic science unit himself had left his own DNA on the cable ties. Dr Peter Thatcher was said to have come into contact with the manacles on five separate occasions — four times in July 2001 and once in October 2002.

Not unnaturally, the defence demanded an explanation.

'You'll have to ask him. I wasn't there when he was handling it,' Eckhoff replied.

She admitted Dr Thatcher had handled the cable ties several times and conceded he may not have been wearing gloves.

'My staff are well trained. What the director does I can't be responsible for, and as I said previously you need to speak to him,' she remarked pointedly.

It was understandable that Eckhoff was not going to carry the can for her boss's mistakes. Nor was she prepared to remain silent over what subsequently happened to the cable ties.

Asked about the decision to take the manacles to Adelaide, she told the court that she was uneasy about the request.

'I was unhappy about them leaving my possession, especially if the forensic examination was not complete,' she added.

Had she expressed her reservations to Colleen Gwynne who was planning to take the cable ties to Murdoch in prison?

'I believe she was aware of my feelings,' Eckhoff said.

If the handling of the cable ties raised concerns about the validity of the DNA results, could the same apply to the other key piece of prosecution evidence, Joanne's T-shirt, which had the tiny blood spot on the back? This had also been stored and analysed in the old laboratory in the early days of the investigation, though there was no suggestion it had been tampered with.

The stain was important not just because of the DNA it provided but because of what it told Eckhoff about how it got there. On close examination she concluded that the smudge was the result of close physical contact with the attacker and not random flicking from someone Joanne might have passed in the street or a more enclosed area.

It wasn't until the end of December 2003 that the DNA from that spot of blood was positively matched to the defendant. The chances of it not being Murdoch's DNA were put at 150 quadrillion to one. For those not of a mathematical bent that meant it was 150,000,000,000,000,000 times more likely to have come from the man in the dock than a random member of the Northern Territory's population of about 200,000, the court was told. If the statistic was correct the evidence was compelling.

Eckhoff also revealed that she found DNA within the tape used to wrap around the ties to create the manacles. The samples came from Joanne, Vince Millar, the truckie who had helped release her, and a third person whose partial profile was deemed to be 'uncallable'.

When small quantities of DNA are mixed with other people's DNA it is often difficult to produce a recognisable profile. This was why Dr Jonathan Whitaker's Low Copy Number technique was so valuable to the prosecution case. After he took a loop from the manacles back to his laboratory in Yorkshire in May 2005, he had identified beyond doubt that the DNA on the inside of the tape belonged to Murdoch. While not going so far as Eckhoff's quadrillion statistic, he claimed that the likelihood of it not coming from the defendant was 100 million to one.

As if addressing a class of children — and if the truth were known most of those in court that day would have struggled to understand every detail of Dr Whitaker's complex subject — the British boffin spelt it out in lay terms:

'If the DNA profile had originated from an unknown person unrelated to Mr Murdoch, a fair and reasonable estimate would be one in 100 million. That means it is 100 million times more likely to get that DNA profile if it came from Mr Murdoch than someone else.'

He also revealed that a band of mixed DNA from the campervan's gearstick could also have come from the defendant. The chances of that were a more modest 19,000 to one, he said.

Dr Whitaker, who had been forced to kick his heels for four or five days in Darwin before being called to give evidence, appeared to grow impatient in the witness box as the defence dared to question the scientific basis for LCN.

'That's why I am the expert!' he reminded the defence at one stage under cross-examination, as Algie tried to get his head around one of the scientist's increasingly complex explanations.

Occasionally Dr Whitaker would make minor concessions to the defence lawyer's negative line of questioning. When Algie asked if one of the major concerns of LCN was the issue of contamination, he agreed, 'I think that's fair.'

But when the defence suggested that the amplification of minuscule amounts of DNA also amplified any contamination and thereby affected the reliability of the result, the forensic expert dismissed the assertion with a brusque 'Not really'.

Dr Whitaker acknowledged that the Low Copy Number technique was not recognised universally, but pointed out that it had been used successfully in court cases in many countries, including Britain, Ireland and the Netherlands.

As an expert witness he was impressive, but whether the jury was much the wiser after listening to several hours of scientific theory and sometimes incomprehensible jargon was debatable.

Dr Whitaker had a plane to catch. He had served his purpose and undoubtedly strengthened the prosecution's case. If Murdoch's DNA profile had been positively identified on the inside of the tape which formed part of the manacles, then it clearly put him at the scene of the crime.

But the defence were far from satisfied with the prosecution's assertions. There was still the issue of cross-contamination, as well as the accuracy and reliability of the LCN technique which other DNA specialists continued to question. While the positive DNA match would be hard to rebut, Grant Algie had already succeeded in raising doubts about many aspects of the case.

Questions also remained about Dr Thatcher's DNA on the cable ties. Under pressure from the defence, the prosecution was forced to call the forensic science section director, who was on sick leave. Despite his ill health, he agreed to take the stand in an effort to dispel rumours of lax practices in the laboratory.

Dr Thatcher agreed he was first given the manacles on 17 July 2001 when they were required as an exhibit in a police teleconference. He took them out of the paper bag and placed them on a coffee table.

Asked if it had been normal protocol to wear gloves

at the time, he replied that he saw no reason why it wouldn't.

'I can't specifically remember four years ago putting on a pair of gloves, but it was the protocol to do so,' he said.

Using gloves he examined the cable ties again on 30 July before putting them back in the biology section.

They remained there until 8 October 2002, when they were requested by Senior Constable Sandry, who needed to take them to Adelaide, where they were to be handed over to Superintendent Gwynne.

Dr Thatcher was not happy about this arrangement, as he made clear in court. Questioned by the defence about the risk of cross-contamination he admitted that he advised the police strongly against taking the manacles to South Australia.

'Did you tell them why?' Grant Algie pressed.

'Yes,' replied Dr Thatcher.

And with good reason, given the ease with which DNA could be accidentally transferred.

Dr Thatcher did not know at the time, but his own profile was to be identified on the handcuffs in early 2004, reinforcing the notion that exhibits could be contaminated even under the most stringent of protocols.

So how did it happen?

'I would have thought that my DNA probably got on the manacles in one of the first two times I examined them,' he admitted.

Once again Algie went for the jugular.

'Are you acknowledging there's a possibility you may have examined these items on an occasion without wearing gloves?' he asked.

'I don't think so, but as I said, I can't stand here and swear that I can remember pulling on the gloves. It's my belief I was wearing gloves.'

Algie: 'Do you acknowledge a possibility that you weren't?'

Thatcher: 'I have to, under those circumstances, of course.'

And if he was wearing gloves? What might be the explanation for the presence of his DNA?

'It would be through a primary transfer like a sneeze or dandruff . . . or it could be a secondary transfer. For instance, wearing gloves, but writing with a pen that had my DNA on it and then handling them [the manacles] again,' Dr Thatcher explained.

If such a transfer were possible even in the most controlled of environments such as a laboratory, how much greater the risk in a police exhibit room? Yet this is exactly what happened in South Australia when the cable ties were taken there.

It was Senior Constable Sandry who revealed the possibility of accidental exposure when he was recalled to the witness box on 28 November. Sandry admitted he had allowed another officer, Sergeant Paul Sheldon from the South Australian force, to examine the manacles for tool markings — the edges left by a cutting implement when used to slice a piece of tape. These could then be compared with other exhibits which belonged to Murdoch.

Sandry said he took the cable ties out of the paper bag and gave them to Sheldon, who looked at them under a microscope. Asked if he had been wearing gloves, Sandry said the correct procedures were followed and that Sheldon would have done likewise.

Even so, the NT officer failed to mention the incident in the examination room during his earlier testimony and the defence wanted to know why.

'You didn't tell us on the last occasion about it [the handcuffs] being informally examined, did you?' Algie reminded him.

'No I didn't,' confirmed the officer.

Algie: 'You'd forgotten about that?'

Sandry: 'Yes.'

Algie: 'And were the handcuffs in the brown paper bag actually placed on a shelf underneath shelves that contained various items to have been possessed or owned by Mr Murdoch?'

Sandry: 'No, not that I can recall. I believe it was done in a separate area. Separate from those items.'

While there was no reason to disbelieve the officer, the damage had been done. By forgetting to mention the examination of the cable ties by the South Australian police during his earlier appearance in the witness box, Sandry had raised questions about the reliability of his memory.

Had he forgotten 'any other times'? the defence demanded. 'No,' he insisted.

But the seeds of doubt may have been planted in the jury's mind. Could they be absolutely certain that there had been no cross-contamination of the manacles with DNA from Murdoch's other property in the Adelaide police exhibit room?

These were important considerations when the jury came to deliberate on their verdict. Apart from the DNA found on Joanne's T-shirt, the inside of the cable ties and the Kombi's gearstick, the rest of the prosecution's case was purely circumstantial. There was no body, no motive and no other incontrovertible evidence that linked Bradley John Murdoch with the murder of Peter Falconio.

And while the jury might decide the positive DNA match was enough to convince them of the defendant's guilt, the question of cross-contamination in the lab or accidental contamination in the Red Rooster might be just enough to persuade them otherwise.

The more the defence could undermine the police and forensic scientists involved in the investigation, the greater the chance of acquittal.

CHAPTER 33

....

THE MAN ON THE CCTV

While the DNA evidence played a critical role in the prosecution's case, it is worth reflecting that the police might never have established a positive match with Murdoch had it not been for the co-operation of his partner-in-crime James Hepi. So it was inevitable that the two men would be daggers drawn when the 39-year-old Maori gave testimony during the fourth week of the trial. His appearance did not disappoint.

Tempers flared as Hepi recalled Murdoch's return from his outback drugs·run on 16 July 2001 and how he'd had trouble getting across the West Australian border because they were looking for the gunman who attacked two backpackers.

Murdoch volunteered, 'It wasn't me,' and insisted that the Landcruiser in the truck-stop video wasn't his either. But Hepi became suspicious when his fellow drugs trafficker started talking about spoon drains being 'fairly good' for hiding a body.

'The digging was easy because they regularly get turned over by machinery and the ground is soft,' Hepi claimed Murdoch told him.

'I said, "Well, I run drugs, not kill people,"' he added.

In the dock Murdoch was quietly fuming. He knew that Hepi was responsible for his current plight and could listen to him no longer.

'You're a fucking liar!' the defendant exclaimed.

'Fuck you,' the witness sneered.

'Alright, thank you,' the judge interrupted as the two adversaries glared at each other. 'That's enough.'

Back in July 2001, relations between the two men were already strained because each believed the other wasn't pulling his weight. Later, 9 kilograms of cannabis and $125,000 in cash went missing and Hepi wanted to know where the money and the drugs were. It culminated in a blistering row in a pub car park and the two men went their separate ways.

While there might be honour among thieves no such loyalty existed between Murdoch and Hepi. It was clearly only a matter of time before one would betray the other. It happened in 2002 when Murdoch admitted to a family friend that he had 'dobbed in his Kiwi mate'.

Benjamin Kotz, who had known the defendant since he was a child and called him Uncle Brad, revealed Murdoch was 'pretty distraught' and confided to him, 'I've done something wrong'.

Murdoch said he had tipped off the police about Hepi's drug smuggling and advised them how and where to catch him.

The New Zealander had no doubt where the information had come from as only Murdoch was aware of his travelling arrangements. He also appreciated that what he knew about his former business partner could provide him with a 'get out of jail free' card.

Hepi certainly had a strong incentive to co-operate with the police and was quick to implicate Murdoch in the Falconio case. But how could the court be sure that Hepi hadn't made up the story to save his own neck? It was a theme that the defence were eager to pursue.

'Would it be wrong to suggest to you, Mr Hepi, that you are lying, fabricating, exaggerating your evidence in implicating Mr Murdoch?' asked Grant Algie.

'Yes it would be wrong,' he replied.

'And would it be wrong to suggest that you might be doing that in order to save your own skin?' the defence pressed him.

'My skin's already saved, mate. I'm sitting here. He's sitting there,' Hepi observed as he motioned to the man in the dock.

The response was fair enough in the circumstances, but Algie wasn't satisfied.

Algie: 'In May 2002 you were looking for a long term of imprisonment, weren't you?'

Hepi: 'Yes.'

Algie: 'And that's your motivation, I suggest, for fabricating your evidence against Mr Murdoch.'

Hepi: 'That's your suggestion.'

Perhaps the possibility of a $250,000 reward might have also played a part, the defence lawyer enquired.

'If Mr Murdoch is convicted you'll be making an application for it, won't you?' Algie suggested.

'I haven't yet. I don't know how to do it yet, but yeah, if he's convicted I will,' he confirmed.

Algie: 'It's a big motivation for you to give false evidence, isn't it, Mr Hepi?'

Hepi: 'Yes.'

The defence had got the answer they wanted but how much difference it would make to their case depended on their success with other witnesses. It was the end of week four and several other key players were yet to take the stand. Among them was Peter Jamieson, Murdoch's friend who ran the Fitzroy Crossing roadhouse and servo.

Jamieson's testimony was crucial because he was the only person to confirm that the defendant was towing a camping trailer when he arrived there on the Sunday evening, 15 July 2001. This was a critical piece of evidence because the trailer, which the defendant claimed he purchased in South Australia just prior to his journey north the week before, was not captured on the truck stop security camera.

The roadhouse operator admitted in court that he was unsure about Murdoch's involvement in the Falconio case at the time, because he had commented on his likeness with the man in the video. Indeed, Jamieson even asked him if 'he did it'.

'No,' Murdoch assured him.

'Why did you ask him that question?' the prosecution wanted to know.

'To clarify and make sure my family were happy,' he explained.

Jamieson was aware of Murdoch's love of guns and understandably did not want to get mixed up in any trouble which might threaten the safety of his loved ones. But Murdoch, whom he had known for several years, satisfied his old mate and they remained on friendly terms.

Jamieson said he remembered Murdoch driving his Landcruiser into a parking area behind the premises in the early evening of that Sunday. 'It had a canopy on the back and he was towing a camper trailer,' he told the jury.

So where was the trailer if it was Murdoch's vehicle in the CCTV footage? Had he left it somewhere and reattached it prior to his departure from Alice Springs? Or was it simply not his vehicle?

Murdoch was to make it plain later in the trial that his own Landcruiser had another style of bullbar to the one in the video. The vehicle shown in the security footage also had a different exhaust pipe, mudguards and a side fuel tank, he said. Though the differences were so slight that only an expert eye would detect them.

Could the position of the truck stop camera have excluded the camper trailer? This was most unlikely as there were several CCTV cameras focused on the garage forecourt and the Landcruiser was clearly not towing anything. Indeed, the court had the benefit of hearing from a security specialist, Shane Ride, who installed the system at the Alice Springs service station.

Ride was also able to shed further light on the quality of the image and why the police had not been able to identify the registration plate on the vehicle. Although the garage had supplied a VHS recording of the footage, the pictures were also stored on a hard drive for several days.

This conflicted with service station manager Val Prior's memory of the situation. She told me that she was under the impression there was no hard drive, whereas in fact the Shell truck stop had an extremely sophisticated Dallmeier surveillance unit from which the rego number might have been retrieved.

Unfortunately the police never seized it.

Grant Algie wanted to know if the pictures from the hard drive could have been digitally enhanced.

Ride admitted, 'It could be possible. The technology of the Dallmeier unit back in 2001 was quite advanced for Australia. To be able to extract the data on the hard drive would be very expensive [however] and it wouldn't have been an easy task to do. We wouldn't have been able to do it locally.'

But if they had and if the police had managed to identify the registration plate, a long and expensive investigation might have been avoided. As it was, they relied on the VHS cassette and cameras which were not set up to focus on number plates.

When the presence of the recording was finally acknowledged at a press conference three weeks later it was too late to go back to the hard drive, which had been erased nearly a fortnight earlier. It was not the Northern Territory police force's finest hour.

While the quality of the truck-stop video was poor, it was still possible to make out the essential features of the vehicle and its driver. One of the expert witnesses called during the trial argued that there was enough information in the image to prove that the man in the footage was almost certainly Murdoch.

Meiya Sutisno, a consultant forensic anatomist who specialises in body mapping, demonstrated how the size of the body, its facial appearance and its gait all matched the defendant. By subdividing the head into individual parts and analysing the features — including a depression over the upper lip, which suggested the absence of upper teeth — she was able to establish a strong likeness with Murdoch.

There were also similar characteristics in the way the two men moved. She showed how the suspect's body, walking mannerisms, shoulders and the way he swung his hands were similar to the defendant's.

'In terms of gait there is that side bending . . . the sway of the hand in the opposite direction to the step and the feet pointing out,' she said.

By overlaying the outline of Murdoch's body on top of the man in the CCTV footage 'you'll see an alignment of features', she told the jury. It was an impressive performance, but was it an accurate interpretation of the facts?

Certainly not, according to Professor Maciej Henneberg, a human anatomy expert called by the defence, who poured scorn on Meiya Sutisno's expert evaluation. The academic, who holds the Wood Jones chair of Anthropological and Comparative Anatomy at Adelaide University, said he was able to determine very little from such a 'poor quality' video.

'All I can say from those images is that they show a man of a particular body build, which I assessed as lean, and of a body size that is medium to large, but not excessively large,' he advised the court. 'I also concluded there's nothing peculiar or unusual in the walking or other movements.'

As for the face, he claimed there was not enough detail to make an accurate anatomical assessment.

'What about the cheekbones or the jawbones?' the defence asked.

'There is a complete whiteness in the area of the cheek so it is impossible to tell,' he answered.

'The only thing I can tell you is that this man has a face. It's light in colour and there is some form of moustache. That I would be happy to say,' he concluded.

The trouble with expert witnesses called by the prosecution and defence is that they rarely agree. Both sides had made their point when it came to the identity of the man in the truck-stop video, but who would the jury favour? They would face a similar quandary over the interpretation of the mixed DNA profile and the Low Copy Number technique employed by Dr Whitaker.

Dr Katrine Both, a forensic scientist who gave evidence in the Snowtown murder trials in South Australia, told the court she had 'a large number of concerns' about LCN and the reliability of the results generated.

'My concern is that it is such a sensitive process that it can pick up the DNA that may have got into a sample at the crime scene, in transport to the lab, in the lab, even from just, say, glassware,' she explained.

Dr Both, who specialises in DNA analysis, claimed that the LCN technique was 'pushing science to the limit' and should not be relied upon in criminal cases.

When scientists and other specialists could not agree on the interpretation of evidence, what hope the men and women of the jury? They had been bombarded by complex data and conflicting testimony for weeks. Soon they would be asked to make sense of it all. The way things were going it would require the wisdom of Solomon to make a fair and accurate judgement.

CHAPTER 34

....

MURDOCH IN THE WITNESS BOX

'Mr Murdoch, where did you bury Peter Falconio?' The question could not have been put more bluntly. The court had just completed the afternoon tea break when Rex Wild fired his opening salvo in his cross-examination of the defendant.

Murdoch had entered the witness box earlier in the day. The defence team had given no indication of calling him until that morning, a move that was regarded as a high-risk strategy.

Few of those in court had heard the defendant speak, apart from his not guilty plea and some tape-recorded telephone conversations he had had with friends and relatives. Would he blow it? Would his voice and manner damage his case? While he had every right to maintain his silence, the defence concluded there was little to lose and possibly everything to gain.

Murdoch walked confidently across the body of the court after being released from his glass-panelled cage, though prison staff were taking no chances. Two security guards flanked the defendant as he took his seat in the witness box.

Grant Algie allowed him time to feel his way. Despite his height and build, Murdoch's voice was several decibels less than had been expected. While not soft in tone, it was certainly calm and measured. Often he would turn to the jury while expressing himself with his hands. On some occasions it sounded like blokey chat over a pub bar, particularly when he got on to his favourite subject of cars and engines.

Murdoch loved nothing more than dismantling his motors and doing them up.

'Some people call it an obsession. I've always mucked around with my vehicles. I love doing that sort of thing,' he said.

He was proud of his work and the admiring glances he'd win for his mechanical prowess. The defendant turned knowingly to the men in the jury whom he might have seen as fellow car enthusiasts.

'I was one of the first persons to take an 18Z motor with an overhead cam and fit it into a 47 series,' he recalled with obvious satisfaction.

'So every time that bonnet was lifted up it was a bit of a talking point — nobody had ever sort of done that before.'

For a moment it could have been one car bore trying to impress another in the local club, but Algie steered it back to the matter in hand. He asked about the drug runs and where he hid the cannabis. (In a specially designed aluminium capsule built into the long-range fuel tank, as it turned out.)

Murdoch talked about the route he took from Sedan in South Australia to Alice Springs, driving slowly along the limestone tracks and always leaving after dark so that his neighbours would not know his property was unattended. Once on the open road, and with his camping trailer on the back, he tried to give the impression he was just another 'Tommy tourist' travelling the outback.

When he stopped on the night of Friday, 13 July 2001, he was 160 kilometres south of Alice Springs but decided against continuing his journey for fear of being stopped by the police. Fridays are favourite times for random breath tests and Murdoch did not want to risk being pulled over and his vehicle searched.

Instead he made camp for the night 40 kilometres north of Erldunda near the Finke River crossing. Murdoch, who was a creature of habit, rose early the next day, had a cup of tea and a couple of Weetbix and continued his journey to Alice, where he arrived about 10.30 a.m. His timetable for the rest of the day was to play a crucial part in his defence and was examined in detail by Mr Wild.

First he went to the Red Rooster to buy chicken for himself and his dog. Then he went to Kittles garage, where he washed the limestone mud off his Landcruiser. (Driving into WA with white mud stains on his vehicle would reveal where he'd come from.) After that he went to Barbecues Galore to check out the prices, the BP garage to refuel, and Repco, the automotive spares outlet, where he purchased a couple of plastic petrol drums. The timing of the Repco visit was confirmed by the manager, David Pierson, who produced a computerised record of the sale which was made at 1.15 p.m. Finally he stopped to buy provisions at the Bi-Lo shop, which he claimed to have left about 2 p.m.

Murdoch said he eventually left town at 3 p.m. and by the time of the attack he was close to the Aboriginal settlement of Yuendumu about 600 kilometres by road from Barrow Creek. But his movement around Alice Springs raised as many questions as it answered. Did it really take him about four-and-a-half hours to complete his varied tasks? And if he was worried about being stopped by the police, why did he hang around town for so long?

Had he spent an hour at Bi-Lo just to buy a few items of food and drink, the prosecution queried. 'Are you serious about that?' asked Wild.

'Very serious,' replied the defendant, who was becoming increasingly irritated by the tone of the lawyer's questioning.

'You're pinpointing this time, Mr Wild, I wasn't looking at the clock . . . You're fine lining this, you know, you're coming with these time slots. I leave, I drive around, I park, I wait, I get in, wash the vehicle, takes a while to wash all the dirt off . . . This is roughly how I've gone along and done a few things. It's my rough estimate of how and when I left Alice Springs.'

There was also the coincidence of his visit to the Red Rooster on the same day that Joanne and Peter had gone there. Did he brush against her inside the cafe? Could his DNA have been transferred to the back of her T-shirt as they passed each other? This seemed unlikely, given that the restaurant was fairly quiet when the couple had gone there and Murdoch could not recall seeing an orange VW Kombi in the car park. Yet the fact remained that Falconio and his girlfriend could easily have crossed paths with the defendant on that day.

If he did leave Alice at 3 p.m. and turned left on to the Tanami at 3.30 p.m., why had it taken him nearly 27 hours to get to Fitzroy Crossing in Western Australia and just over 36 hours to reach Broome, journeys which, according to some witnesses, could be completed in half the time? Indeed it was Hepi who had told the court that it was possible to drive the approximately 1800 kilometres from Alice Springs to Broome in as little as 16 to 20 hours.

Why had Murdoch taken so much longer, or had he left later than he said — in the early hours of the following morning?

Wild: 'I'm suggesting that you could have done this trip from Alice Springs to Broome on your ear . . . easily?'

Murdoch: 'On the ear?'

Wild: 'Yes, [it] means easily, Mr Murdoch.'

Murdoch: 'Yes? In what time?'

Wild: 'I suggest to you in the time that was available to you to leave the truck stop crossing at 1 a.m. and get to Fitzroy by 1800 hours or thereabouts the next night?'

Murdoch: 'I wouldn't like to have tried it.'

The defendant justified the time he'd taken on the grounds that he drove slowly and stopped frequently.

'It takes you around a day and a half from Alice Springs to Broome, depending on road conditions, depending on whether you're in a hurry or not. That's what it's all about. It's not how quick you want to do the trip,' he explained.

The prosecution left the question of the travelling time and moved on to the vehicle he was driving, and in particular the canopy which covered the rear tray. In March 2001 Murdoch moved the green canopy from his F100 to his 75 series Landcruiser. Underneath the canvas was security mesh, which could be padlocked. Murdoch needed to be confident that his cannabis and other valuables were well protected on long journeys.

However, the prosecution accused him of removing the mesh some time before July. This might explain how the gunman was able to reach into the side of his vehicle on the night of the attack and produce a canvas hood which he placed over Joanne's head. It might also indicate how she was able to escape from the rear tray by slipping over the side. And it could shine fresh light on her theory that she might have been pushed into the vehicle from the side, as opposed to a hole in the back of the cab.

'I suggest to you that all you had to do to put things inside was lift the flap and throw things in,' the lawyer remarked.

'No,' he snapped.

Murdoch was also shown pictures from the truck-stop video and invited to point out the differences between the vehicle in the CCTV footage and his own. He tried, but it was hardly a convincing performance. He agreed the canopy appeared similar to his own and when it came to specific details the discrepancies were minor.

'The little tie-down lugs that I had running all the way alongside of it — don't really show too well in this photograph — I'd say that would be one difference,' he commented.

But he agreed it was a similar height and shape and the windows cut into the side of the canvas were much the same, though they might have 'come down a little bit longer . . . and the canvas that was on my side of the vehicle had a distinct straightness to it', he pointed out.

And what about the man in the truck-stop video and the defendant's appearance at the time? Hadn't most of his mates and even his father drawn his attention to the similarity, the prosecution asked.

Murdoch admitted that many people had asked him if it was him and he agreed there was a likeness.

'It looks similar to a lot of people,' he said he'd told them. 'I know it's not me there and I know it's not my vehicle. So that was basically the end of the conversation.'

Yet he had changed his look within days of the Barrow Creek incident, shaving off his moustache and cutting his hair. Not that there was anything unusual in that. Murdoch often altered his facial appearance.

'Sometimes I'd have a beard, sometimes I'd have a mo, sometimes I'd have it clean shaven,' he told the jury.

But it wasn't looking good for Murdoch. The prosecution challenged him at every turn. By day two in the witness box the defendant's initially avuncular style was marred by flashes of anger and barely contained fury. Bradley John Murdoch was running out of excuses.

Like a frightened animal in the glare of a spotlight, the man at the centre of this epic legal battle knew that time was running out. The Crown prosecutor went in for the kill.

Wild: 'Mr Murdoch, I suggest that on 14 July 2001 you were following a Kombi up the Stuart Highway?'

Murdoch: 'No.'

Wild: 'And you saw a woman driving along in that Kombi, somewhere between Alice Springs and Ti Tree?'

Murdoch: 'No.'

Wild: 'I suggest you were travelling with your dog in the front of the vehicle up the Stuart Highway?'

Murdoch: 'Not at Barrow Creek I wasn't, no.'

Wild: 'I suggest you pulled over the Kombi and met the driver at the back of the vehicle.'

Murdoch: 'No.'

Wild: 'And shot him dead!'

Murdoch: 'No.'

Wild: 'You threatened and assaulted Joanne Lees at that time?'

Murdoch: 'I did not.'

Wild: 'Forced her out onto the gravel on the side of the road through the passenger door.'

Murdoch: 'No.'

The lawyer produced a mock-up of the cable ties.

Wild: 'Having tied her up with handcuffs — manacles. I suggest you made handcuffs out of cable ties in that form, Mr Murdoch.'

Murdoch: 'No, I didn't.'

Wild: 'You had them available with you at the time.'

Murdoch: 'No, I did not.'

Wild: 'I suggest that you were making them at your property, at Mr Hepi's property at Sedan — in front of Mr Hepi.'

Murdoch: 'No I didn't.'

Wild: 'Your DNA is found deep inside those handcuffs.'

Murdoch: 'I understand that. And no.'

Wild: 'Have you ever made such handcuffs?'

Murdoch: 'No, I have not.'

Wild: 'I suggest to you that despite forcing her into your vehicle she managed to escape.'

Murdoch: 'No.'

Wild: 'You had to move the body that was on the roadway.'

Murdoch: 'No.'

Wild: 'That you fled to Alice Springs.'

Murdoch: 'No, I did not.'

Wild: 'When you got home you shaved your moustache, you cut your hair short.'

Murdoch: 'A couple of days after, yes.'

Wild: 'That morning, I suggest to you.'

Murdoch: 'No.'

Wild: 'You set about with some urgency to change your vehicle.'

Murdoch: 'No.'

Wild: 'You stopped your drugs run for the rest of the year.'

Murdoch: 'Drug runs were stopped not because of that reason. It was time . . . for Hepi to take over.'

Wild: 'I suggest that it was so that you wouldn't be caught roaming around Australia.'

Murdoch: 'No.'

Wild: 'You had to, on the night, move the Kombi from the place it was.'

Murdoch: 'No.'

Wild: 'And as a result of doing that you left your DNA on the gear stick of the Kombi.'

Murdoch: 'No.'

Wild: 'You had to dispose of clothing and the keys.'

Murdoch: 'No.'

Wild: 'You had to dispose of Peter Falconio.'

Murdoch: 'No.'

Wild: 'You're a fastidious man, aren't you, Mr Murdoch?'

Murdoch: 'I am a bit meticulous.'

Wild: 'You didn't want any blood in your vehicle, did you?'

Murdoch: 'I never had Mr Falconio in my vehicle and I did not commit this, so . . .'

Wild: 'You used the denim jacket to wrap his head in.'

Murdoch: 'No, I did not.'

Wild: 'You ended up with a hair tie as a souvenir.'

Murdoch: 'No, I did not.'

Wild: 'Mr Murdoch, you've denied that you were at the truck stop that night. Is that because you think that puts you in the frame for the murder?'

Murdoch: 'No, I wasn't at that truck stop.'

Wild: 'How do you explain, Mr Murdoch, your DNA on Ms Lees' shirt?'

Murdoch: 'I can't explain how my DNA got on Ms Lees' shirt.'

Wild: 'How do you explain there's a match with your DNA on the gear stick of the Kombi?'

Murdoch: 'I cannot explain how my DNA or a match with my DNA got onto . . .'

Wild: 'How do you explain how a match with your DNA is on the inside of the cable tie?'

Murdoch: 'Same as the last answer.'

Wild: 'Mr Murdoch, I put to you that what happened on July 14 is that you murdered Peter Falconio and you disposed of his body.'

Murdoch: 'No, I did not.'

The Crown prosecutor was about to conclude his case. But it would be nearly a fortnight before the jury retired to consider their verdict. Outside, the so-called build-up, when soaring temperatures and high humidity envelop this part of northern Australia before the monsoonal rains arrive, cloaked Darwin like a damp electric blanket. As if the build-up to the verdict wasn't enough, the weather over the next few weeks would be equally unbearable for the Britons who had flown halfway around the world in the hope of seeing justice done.

CHAPTER 36

....

A LIFE CLOSED DOWN

Tuesday, 13 December 2005 dawned with a heavy gloom hanging over Darwin as thick black clouds and rain rolled in from the Arafura Sea.

The weather might have added to the sense of foreboding Bradley John Murdoch must have felt as he made the journey from Berrimah Prison to the Northern Territory Supreme Court.

The judge, who was about to conclude his summing-up, had already indicated he would send the jury out at lunchtime.

Over the previous eight weeks and two days they had heard from 85 witnesses, seen 350 exhibits and sifted through thousands of pages of evidence.

Outside court six Jan Pittman, Murdoch's girlfriend, paced the first-floor gallery, admitting, 'He's preparing himself for the worst.'

Pittman, a big, warm-hearted woman, had stood by her man throughout the trial. In the early days they'd even talked of what they'd do together when he was found not guilty. Perhaps they'd hire a van and tour Australia, they thought. The irony might have escaped them.

Before Chief Justice Martin ended his summing-up, he reminded the jury of the importance of the DNA evidence, particularly the blood on the back of the T-shirt which matched the defendant's profile. If they were satisfied that the blood came from the accused, the only conclusion — as the prosecution suggested — was that it was deposited by Murdoch while he was attacking Joanne at Barrow Creek, he said.

'If that is your view, if you are satisfied the Crown's submission is correct and you are satisfied the man who attacked Ms Lees killed Peter Falconio, then the Crown would have proved its case of murder,' he stated.

The jury retired to deliberate at 12.51 p.m. Apart from a request for clarification from the judge over whether they could find for murder without a body, they remained behind closed doors for the rest of the afternoon and much of the evening.

At 6.30 p.m. they were given pizza for dinner. Downstairs in the cells, Murdoch was so relaxed about the verdict that he apparently fell asleep. In the media room, journalists played Scrabble, agreeing to award extra points for words connected to the trial.

When the moment came it took everybody by surprise. Shortly before 9 p.m. the judge recalled the jury, intending to ask them if they wanted to retire for the evening or continue their deliberations.

Suddenly, a court usher appeared in front of the judge and handed him a piece of paper. The jury had reached their verdict.

The tension was palpable. In the dock Murdoch slouched impassively in his chair. It seemed he'd given up all hope.

There was standing room only in the back of the court as reporters jostled with the simply curious for the best vantage point. In the public gallery Joanne Lees and the Falconio family fixed their eyes on the foreman.

Guilty on all charges!

Joanne placed a hand across her mouth as if to prevent herself from whooping with joy. Then she slumped on Paul Falconio's shoulder as he put a supporting arm around her.

In front of her, Joan, Luciano and Nick Falconio turned round to the second row where Joanne was sitting, and clasped her hand.

After four years and five months the young woman at the centre of one of the Northern Territory's greatest mysteries had been vindicated. Her account of what happened at Barrow Creek that night had been accepted by the jury and the man responsible for her terrifying ordeal was about to be jailed for life.

The judge clearly approved. 'For what it's worth, in respect to your verdict, can I say I entirely agree,' he said.

Turning to Murdoch, whose countenance showed no sign of shock or anger, Chief Justice Martin told him simply: 'There is only one penalty prescribed under Northern Territory law and that is life.'

Half an hour later Joanne and the Falconios emerged from the Supreme Court building to a phalanx of reporters and an explosion of camera flash guns.

Reading from a prepared statement she said, 'The past four years have been very traumatic for myself and the Falconio family and to see justice done today eases a great burden for us all.'

She thanked all those who had helped and supported her, particularly Vince Millar and Rodney Adams, the truckies who 'took me to safety on that night'.

'Today marks the conclusion of an intensive period of distress for myself and the Falconio family — this will enable us to take another step in the grieving process for Pete,' she added.

Joanne made it clear that there would be no closure until her boyfriend's body was found and she appealed to the killer 'to seriously consider telling me, Joan, Luciano and Pete's brothers what he has done with Pete'.

The Falconios reinforced her plea. 'The most important thing for my family now is to find Pete's body,' Paul said.

So where is Peter? It's a question that has remained frustratingly unanswered since 14 July 2001.

Was he buried in a spoon drain or thrown down a disused mine shaft? Or did something else happen that we may never know about?

Nick and Paul Falconio are certain he is dead. During late-night conversations in Darwin's pubs, they told me they never had any doubt that he was murdered and that Murdoch was responsible.

Pete's fate has brought a degree of pain and sadness to their family that they will never completely get over. For Joan and Luciano it is the unbearable loss of a treasured son. For the brothers, the senseless killing of their closest mate.

And Joanne? Although she gave two earlier media interviews and spoke in the witness box, it was not until 15 December 2005, when Bradley John Murdoch was sentenced to a non-parole period of 28 years, that the world was able to fully appreciate the effect the crime had had on her life.

In a victim impact statement tendered to the court, she revealed how she thought she was going to be murdered on the night the couple was attacked.

'I was terrified and extremely distressed when I was hiding, as I thought I would never see my family again and no one would know what happened to Pete and me,' she explained. 'I have suffered the loss of the one person who knew me best and loved me the most.

'Pete was in the prime of his life — the crime ended our dreams of travel, marriage, children, a future. I never imagined not being with him and not sharing my life with him.'

Joanne said her life had been 'closed down' since the crime took place in July 2001. 'I have had to delay my university studies . . . and I have been able only to take on employment which did not involve dealing with the public, as people's curiosity has made my life very difficult.

'Some aspects of the investigation process were hurtful and insensitive, as well as causing me considerable anxiety at a time when I had been through an experience that can only be described as horrific.

'The massive intrusion of the media into my life has also had devastating effects. I have had to move house eight times. I have experienced being in the train and seeing pictures of my face on the front page of people's newspapers. I have been watched and followed. My mother was very distressed with all the media coverage and the impact it had on her.

'People have to be wary of becoming friends with me because they might find themselves in the paper. This makes forming new friendships and maintaining existing ones a continuing challenge.

'I have visible scars from the physical injuries I received on that night. They are fading ... the emotional scars, however, remain.

'I am sceptical, untrusting, fearful and heartbroken. It is lonely being me.'

Joanne left the court shortly afterwards and said no more.

Nick and Paul Falconio believe she has been sorely misunderstood. They've known her for the best part of 10 years and probably understand her better than most.

'At heart she's fairly shy and perhaps a bit naive,' Paul told me. 'She really has to steel herself to face the media when she arrives at court each morning.'

And Nick, who in spite of all that has happened confided to me that he has grown so attached to Darwin he would even consider living there, added that anybody who had been in Joanne's position would appreciate how she behaved. 'You've just got to put yourself in Joanne's shoes. She's a really lovely person.'

So did those who questioned Joanne's story get it wrong?

Throughout this case I have endeavoured to keep an open mind. The jury might have reached their verdict, but, for others, doubts will inevitably remain about Murdoch's guilt or innocence.

Joanne was the only witness and even she didn't see the murder of her boyfriend. Apart from the DNA much of the evidence was circumstantial, and the body, which would provide incontrovertible proof of Peter's death, has not been found.

Until his remains are located, Joanne Lees, and all those who have been transfixed by the many twists and turns of this most extraordinary of cases, will continue to ask: 'Where's Peter?'

ACKNOWLEDGMENTS

....

I would like to offer my thanks to the following for their help and co-operation in my research:

Chris Tangey, who supplied me with video footage of the Luminol test on the VW Kombi.

Professor Barry Boettcher, who gave me the benefit of his expert knowledge in the field of forensic biology.

Phil Mills, assistant editor of the *Brighton Argus*, who arranged for me to access his newspaper library.

Likewise Steve Carter, library chief of the *Huddersfield Daily Examiner*, who was so helpful.

Narelle Hine, formerly of the *Broome Advertiser*, who was generous enough to share with me previous stories she had written about some of the key players in this drama and provide crucial background.

My wife, Vivienne, who accompanied me on many of my research trips and who provided an invaluable sounding board for the many and varied theories that emerged on an almost-daily basis.

My agent, Margaret Gee, who did so much to persuade me to write this book.

And Patrick Mangan, my editor, whose patience, advice and diligence during the writing process was much appreciated.